BEYOND THE BASICS

The
Management
Guide
for Library
and
Information
Professionals

G. EDWARD EVANS AND PATRICIA LAYZELL WARD

NEAL-SCHUMAN PUBLISHERS, INC.

NEW YORK   LONDON

Published by Neal-Schuman Publishers, Inc.
100 William Street, Suite 2004
New York, NY 10038

Printed and bound in the United States of America.

The paper used in this publication meets the minimum requirements of American National Standard for Information Sciences—Permanence of Paper for Printed Library Materials, ANSI Z39.48-1992 ♾

LIBRARY OF CONGRESS CATALOGING-IN-PUBLICATION DATA

Evans, G. Edward, 1937–
    Beyond the basics: the management guide for library and information professionals / G. Edward Evans and Patricia Layzell Ward.
        p. cm.
    Includes bibliographical references
    ISBN 1-55570-476-X (alk. paper)
        1. Library administration. 2. Information services—Management. 3. Library science—Vocational guidance. 4. Middle managers. I. Ward, Patricia Layzell. II. Title.

Z678.E89 2003
025.1–dc21
                                                                2003059900

TABLE OF CONTENTS

Part II: Understanding the Responsibilities

Part III: Understanding the People Factors

PREFACE

Good management leaves people with almost no sense that they are, in fact, "being managed." How do successful department heads, directors, and others in positions of responsibility perform this sleight-of-hand? By mastering an array of skills; by learning how to supervise, direct, connect, and lead.

The authors of this book coauthored *Management Basics for Information Professionals* (Neal-Schuman, 2000), used as a basic text for library and information studies programs. That book focused on the basics of management for information professional-archivist, information manager, knowledge manager, librarian, and records manager-at the start of his or her career. This new book, *Beyond the Basics: The Management Guide for Library and Information Professionals*, emphasizes the organizational responsibilities and people skills that supervisors, department heads, assistant directors, and directors acknowledge when they say "I wish they had taught me that in library school." We have drawn on our own management experiences to provide practical advice rooted in research.

Organization
Part I: "Understanding The Context"

Understanding the context in which services operate is vital. With that basic understanding in place, successful managers then realize that it is *changes* in the operating environment that have the greatest influence on the future direction of services. Understanding the operational context is a necessary prerequisite for planning.

Chapter 1, "Exploring The External Operating Environment," starts by reviewing the shifts that occurred in management thinking in the second half of the twentieth century, as well as current thinking at the start of the twenty-first century. It moves on to consider societal, economic, political, and technological changes and how these affect the way information services are provided.

Chapter 2 reviews the action to be taken when "Settling into a New Management Post." This chapter covers "nitty-gritty" topics not covered in the required administration class in LIS curricula. Moving into a management role brings challenges and opportunities. Some ways to make a smoother transition are noted.

Chapter 3, "Analyzing the Internal Operating Environment," focuses on factors that affect the internal organizational climate. Ways to assess the possibilities for change, to isolate and overcome potential barriers, and to recognize values (both historic and new) are also covered.

Part II: "Understanding The Responsibilities"

Chapter 4, "Managing the Organizational Responsibilities," covers creating and managing change, project management, and most importantly-time management. If managers don't first learn how to manage themselves, their colleagues, and those they supervise, will be frustrated which could limit career progression.

Chapter 5, "Mastering the Communication Responsibilities," looks at the need to hone communication skills, particularly those used to communicate beyond the immediate work team. Good managers must be able to communicate effectively with other departments, users, and the external community. The latter group includes those working at all levels in the "parent" organization (company, academic institution, or city, for example) and stakeholders in the community at large. Conflict resolution and negotiation are keys to success in working both inside and outside of the service. And this has to be achieved with due regard to ethical behavior.

"Assuming Control Responsibilities" is the topic of Chapter 6. Controlling fiscal matters and allocating funds has always been essential, but increasingly questions about performance, quality control, assessment, and effectiveness are being asked by the senior management of information services and the parent organization. Being prepared for and responding to those questions is crucial to success.

Part III: "Understanding the People Factors"

Earlier chapters have touched on people issues but have emphasized managerial skills. Part III places greater focus on individuals and how to carry through our management philosophy of working with and through people.

Chapter 7 considers "Managing Diversity" in terms of culture, race, and gender. The chapter commences by defining diversity-emphasizing its importance in strategic planning as well as the need to prepare organizational policies and practices concerning diversity. Finally, we look at the issues that should be reviewed when supervising a diverse staff and working with diverse groups of users.

"Providing Effective Service to User Communities" is becoming more complex as people change the manner in which they seek, access, and use information. Chapter 8 considers the issues and challenges associated with providing appropriate user services. First, the ways and means of assessing user communities are explored, together with the methods for analyzing data and developing effective service plans. The growing numbers of barriers to use are reviewed. Having a good service plan is fine but the service must be marketed and promoted services so some of the basic techniques for doing so are covered in the final section of the chapter.

Developing skills in "Working with Colleagues" is essential; Chapter 9 covers this important area. Motivation and team building is critical. In many services, paid and volunteer staff may work side by side or in teams, and this requires a set of specific skills to ensure that they work together effectively. Today society is emphasizing the need to address the problems of balancing work and home life, and handling stress and the associated tensions.

Chapter 10, the final chapter, focuses on "Preparing to Move Ahead" and considers the next steps for those who want to tackle new management challenges.

REFERENCES

Readers will notice that each chapter includes examples and readings drawn from all the sectors within the information profession; however a majority of the references are from the library literature. This is simply because more has been written about the management of the library sector than about managing archives, information agencies, knowledge and records services. However, our experience working across all these sectors has demonstrated that the management issues are common to all of them.

The authors' Web site will update the references. Originally set up to update *Management Basics for Information Professionals*, this site also features an annual review of the management literature. It is available at: www.lib.lmu.edu/mbif or www.neal-schuman.com/managementbasics.html.

OUR APPROACH TO MANAGEMENT AND TERMINOLOGY

We believe that managers are made, not born. "Made" in the sense of having both the motivation to learn and develop knowledge and skill sets, and in the sense of being given (by those who manage them) the opportunity and support to grow.

We chose the term *information professionals* to denote those who are mediators between information in a range of formats and the communities that they serve, in both the private and the public sectors. While there are some distinct differences between the information professions, they generally share similar approaches to management, face similar challenges-and, in this virtual age, increasingly work together.

Users has been chosen as the all-embracing term rather than clients, customers, or patrons. The generic term *service* includes archives, information, knowledge, library and records management services.

We wrote *Beyond the Basics: The Management Guide for Library and Information Professionals* to help those who manage library and information services achieve success in their careers. We hope our readers will discover that higher-level management can be satisfying as it challenging.

ACKNOWLEDGMENTS

We owe thanks to the many people who have influenced our ideas – colleagues, bosses and students with whom we have worked over the years in the United States, Iceland, Mexico, Australia, the UK, and the various countries where consultancies have been carried out.

Special thanks are due to Maurice Line who not only stimulated our ideas but also gave permission for some of his maxims that head up the chapters. More can be found in *Library Management* (1999:20, (1): 10-11.)

Pat Schuman, Charles Harmon, and Michael Kelley and the staff of Neal-Schuman provided friendly and professional support.

PART I: UNDERSTANDING THE CONTEXT

1: EXPLORING THE EXTERNAL OPERATING ENVIRONMENT

"An opportunity is a threat seen by an optimist."

IN THIS CHAPTER YOU'LL DISCOVER:

- why managers track changes in the external operating environment
- how the external operating environment influences the internal management of services
- how approaches to management have changed since the 1960s
- why management has changed: social, economic, political and technological influences from 1960 to 2002
- why there is increasing interest in collaboration, competition and accountability
- possible future directions for management and for information services

Archivists, information managers, knowledge managers, librarians, and records managers find as they move up the management ladder, in the private or the public sector, that they need to be increasingly aware of what is happening outside their service. So we start by taking a look at the influence the external operating environment has on the decisions they make. The higher up the ladder managers move, the greater the influence of external factors on their thoughts, decisions, and actions. They need an understanding of why, where, and how these influences operate and inform planning and decision-making at every level—from the bottom to the top of the organization.

No organization exists in a vacuum. That is a statement of the obvious. Information professionals provide a service and work in the reality of meeting users' needs and handling day-to-day matters that can easily blind managers to external forces. These forces present opportunities and challenges, so in order to make decisions managers have to be clear about the here and now...and look to see what is coming down the track. This is a basic requirement—recognizing what might be possible develops the vision that helps to set goals.

Another reality is that nothing is constant. Change is continual and no sooner have we adapted to one change—then another comes along. Sometimes it can be anticipated—for example, new developments in technology; or unexpected—a natural disaster or international conflict. It can have a global impact—a downturn in the world economy; or it may be local—a change of government. Managers continually scan the environment to anticipate changes that could impact their work.

Today that outward-looking approach is essential. Services have to be viewed as part of a total information industry, whether they are based in the private or the public sector. Managers must view archives, information, knowledge, library and records services, and the vendors and suppliers as forming one information industry, bringing together a powerful coalition. And there are two important words to describe the industry—it has always been *dynamic*, but now it is *competitive*.

CHANGING VIEWS ABOUT MANAGEMENT

All organizations, whether they are large or small, are influenced by management theory and practice. At a macro level, it affects the policies prepared by governing bodies. At a micro level, it informs the way managers and employees expect departments to operate. But like everything else, approaches to management change. A well-informed middle manager needs to have an awareness of past trends in order to understand how and why today's approaches have emerged.

A number of writers have charted the development of management thought and practices. One good example provides a critical review of what happened in the twentieth century. It emphasizes the successes and shortcomings of the concepts that preceded and shaped each new approach, setting it in the context of the period when it emerged (Crainer, 2000).

But keep in mind that management is still a relatively young profession. It only emerged from business administration in the early part of the twentieth century with the growth of business and management schools, such as those at Harvard and Stanford in the U.S., the Manchester and London Business Schools in the U.K., INSEAD in France, and the Australian Graduate School of Management.

> ### WORTH CHECKING OUT
>
> Management gurus
>
> Want to get an overview of the ideas of over 40 influential management thinkers? Try: Kennedy, Caroline. 2002. *Guide to the Management Gurus.* London: Random House.

These centers of learning graduated considerable numbers of managers who moved into the expanding private and public sectors, some of whom became consultants. The schools also produced management gurus who wrote the books and papers that have become essential reading for well-informed managers. People such as Peter Drucker (2001), Warren Bennis (1998), and Henry Mintzberg (1989) have had a lasting influence, while others have faded away.

Why did some fade away? As with other aspects of society, there are fads and fashions. These come and go while the fundamental structure remains unchanged. Managerial fads have been defined as "transitory collective beliefs that certain management techniques are at the forefront of management progress." (Abrahamson, 1996: 254) This suggests that many of the fashions may not have a track record for successfully improving organizational performance .

Lubans (2000) has identified some of the major fad formulas and philosophies. We have labeled his points "Lubans's List" and arranged them in a roughly chronological order in the box below.

LUBANS'S LIST

"Fad" Formulas
- Bureaucracy
- Scientific Management (Taylorism)
- Total Systems Analysis
- Zero Base Budgeting (ZBB)
- Management by Objectives (MBO)
- Strategic Planning
- One-Minute Managing
- Situational Leadership
- Teamwork, Participatory Management, Empowerment, and Coaching
- Future Search
- Continuous Improvement (CI)
- Total Quality Management (TQM)
- Reengineering
- Pay for Performance
- Scenario Planning

"Fad" Philosophies
- Ranganathanism
- Theories X and Y
- Zero Defects (ZD)
- The Pursuit of Excellence
- The S-shaped Curve
- Customer Service
- Lean and Mean or Fat and Mean
- Downsizing or Rightsizing
- Core Values
- Dilbertism
- Self-organizing Systems

His article concludes with the following comment: "few are ever totally discredited or fade away. Most stage a comeback, sometimes in disguise. Others merge or fade away, their paraphernalia relegated to the quick-sale counters in office supply stores" (Lubans, 2000: 131). The list is far from definitive and was not intended to be, but it provides a broad cross-section of the management fashions and fads of the twentieth century.

The transitory nature of fads became a field of study in business schools as researchers examined the dynamics of their rise and fall. One study indicated that there was some statistical support for the idea that management fashions/fads have a symmetrical life cycle of slow buildup followed by a rapid rise in interest in the popular press. After some research studies are published on the concept, there is a steady decline in interest, at least as reflected in the form of published articles (Spell, 1999: 344).

Ideas in fashion reflect changes in the operating environment. During the emergence of information and communication technologies in the 1980s, an emphasis was placed on the cost savings that could result from more efficient operations, so that fewer staff would be needed. As a result of social and demographic change producing a falling birthrate in western countries, there is now a shortage of skilled staff. This has resulted in an emphasis on intellectual capital and a return to the "softer" side of human resources management—people have moved back to the center.

More recently, concerns regarding the accounting and auditing of public companies has focused attention on corporate governance and ethics. It has raised major questions of accountability.

Our experience indicates that some fads lack a proven track record, but a number have a sound basis.

PUTTING IT INTO PRACTICE

Before trying to implement an approach or technique that seems to be promising, take time to go back to study the original paper and the context in which it was implemented.

Taking the idea from secondary or later sources may not reveal a critical element that could cause a problem in a different setting.

One example is the effect of culture; for example, what is acceptable in the workplace in a North American setting may not sit comfortably in other cultures—and vice versa.

What this suggests is that even the most experienced manager, not just the newcomer, should carefully consider if, when, and how to introduce the latest management fashion/concept that is receiving heavy press coverage. Examine the evidence to see that there have been demonstrated effectiveness/productivity benefits in organizations that are at least somewhat similar in character to the one in which you are working. Jumping on the bandwagon just because others are doing so can have very negative consequences.

However, we are not suggesting that the literature and what is happening elsewhere should be ignored, just that it is better to give careful thought to implementing something new. Do it only after thoughtful deliberation and consultation. Using something that has a track record can be a useful part of maintaining an effective and responsive organization. As Abrahamson noted, "management techniques that become fashionable have massive, sometimes helpful, but sometimes devastating, effects on a large number organizations and their employees....It follows from these observations that study of management fashion is a very serious matter indeed" (Abrahamson, 1996: 280).

Management Process and Style

Managers need to be able to distinguish between management *process* and management *style*. Looking at "Lubans's List," situational leadership or core values would represent a *style* while TQM and continuous improvement are *processes*.

> TRY THIS
>
> Label each of the terms in Lubans's List as a process or a style.
>
> Then try to think of at least two other styles and two processes.

Too rapid adoption or implementation of a new style or process can cause harm.

Keeping Up-to-Date with Management

Specialized workshops sponsored by national or regional professional associations are among the best places to learn about new styles and processes that have a track record of success. One example of a source for U.S. librarians is the Association of Research Libraries' Office of Leadership and Management Services (OLMS). They offer both in-person and Web-based programs. These range from the basics for new managers (Library Management Skills Institute I—The Manager) that address topics such as leadership, decision-making, and problem solving, to specialized areas like project management and assessment activities.

A word of warning—be aware that the specialized programs dealing with new concepts can generate excitement, particularly in a group setting. It should not override the need to think about how the ideas would work back at base.

Reading the *Harvard Business Review* is an enjoyable way to keep up with trends. The articles deal with the reality of management in the workplace; it is well edited and has cartoons for light relief. Professional journals cover management issues and a number focus on subareas, e.g. *Journal of Library Administration*, *Library Administration and Management*, and *Library Management*. In the fields of archives and records management, professional journals cover a spectrum of topics, including articles on management issues.

THE CONTEXT OF CHANGE 1960–

The post-1960 period spans the working life of the people employed in the organization—from those close to retirement to the youngest newcomers. A broad overview of the four decades illustrates the extent of change that can be experienced in the course of a career. It also sets the scene for an overview of the major social, political, economic, and technological developments that brought about changes in the delivery of services.

The period commenced with economic growth, a period of expansion, and a time of hope and opportunity in the western economies. However, the expansion resulted in a shortage of skilled staff and professional workers in every sector of the labor market. Many found themselves bosses at an early age with budgets that they might find difficult to spend.

Libraries took action by spending the book fund, resulting in piles of books accumulating in cataloguing departments. Funds could not be moved to other budget headings to pay for staff to process them. Result: frustrated users and staff, and no decrease in the following year's book fund. Underspending was not seen to be good management. Materials were acquired, but new items would remain unprocessed for a long time. This was also not good management.

To meet the challenges of rapid expansion and to reflect emerging trends in society, participative management emerged. This involved staff in decision-making through meetings and discussion.

Organizational development consultants came to the fore in the 1970s. This was partly a reaction to the organization and methods approach used in the late 1950s and 1960s to measure what workers were doing and how—a testing of the efficiency of the work design. Organizational development worked *with* people as a way to assist organizations in reshaping to meet the challenge of change as democracy entered the workplace. The emphasis on the human aspects of management reflected changing attitudes in society. An affluent society was recognizing the social issues that affected the disadvantaged in society. One outcome was the provision of new services in the public sector, notably outreach services by public libraries. They have done an admirable job of maintaining these services even during the economic downturns that have occurred during the intervening years.

FOR FURTHER THOUGHT

Funding authorities often forget, or do not realize, that public libraries are one of the very few community/municipal services that actually return money to the local economy. For example, the public library frequently hires students on a part-time basis to work as pages/shelvers. It also assists small business owners in improving operations and income by acting as a useful source of business information.

Think of some other ways in which the public library helps improve the local economy.

Concerns for the disadvantaged continued into the 1970s, but the economy of the western world began to slow down and new issues emerged. A perception that there was an overproduction of professional workers in general raised debate and provoked studies into the labor market for qualified staff. It cast shadows on other academic departments that produced comparatively few graduates, and caused stress for many in the information sector.

Mission statements replaced standards of service that had been based on quantitative counts. The publication of mission statements was followed by goals, objectives, and performance measures. These presented challenges for managers in the public sector—how can you measure the value of archives or library services? Incremental budgeting was out and zero-based budgeting was introduced.

In 1978, California voters passed Proposition 13, which reduced property tax by 57 percent. As a result, many legislatures thought seriously about the level of taxation they had imposed on the community, and how good this was for their reelection prospects. Public services were cut, and this had an impact beyond the U.S.

Even tighter economic conditions emerged in the 1980s, fueled by high rates of inflation. Reaganism in California was characterized by a right-wing approach to budget cuts. Concurrently, rapid developments in information and communications technologies had a major impact on organizations by changing the way in which work could be carried out. The growing information explosion caused the private sector to realize that information could be used in decision-making to enhance profits.

New universities were formed from institutes of technology and polytechnics. Private universities faced problems as enrollments fell due to changing demographics. TQM and quality issues became a focus of attention.

The 1990s saw a continued interest in quality, performance, and marketing. Diversity's definition broadened beyond race and gender. In the last two decades, new state universities were established in California, e.g. the Monterey Bay and San Marcos campuses of the California State University.

Making optimum use of facilities became important to the senior management of organizations in the private and public sectors. This resulted, for example, in schools teaching on Saturdays. Joint use services emerged in a number of countries to make the best use of facilities in rural communities and proved to be successful. This was extended to urban areas, including an increase in combined library facilities (e.g., combined school/public and combined public/university libraries). Some services in the public sector also increased hours of access with, for example, many public libraries opening on Sundays and universities extending hours of operation. Computing and library services in academic institutions also merged.

The theme of making better use of resources extended to staff as large organizations, assisted by the introduction of computing, delayered their hierarchies and cut out levels of management. Staff seeking promotion made moves between organizations, whereas in the past they might have expected to move up the hierarchy in their own organization.

Fundraising for archives, libraries, and museums became vital since the number of potential donors was—and still is—finite. While it is possible to coordinate fundraising activities within a "parent organization" (city, county, university), there is often competition between services from different organizations for donations from a single donor. The need to seek such funding continues to increase.

Records management services expanded and became more sophisticated in response to legal problems encountered by major companies. Public archives and record offices attracted greater attention due to an increased interest in family history and genealogy. There was a growing recognition that there are branches of information professions that share a variety of basic concepts, principles, and practices.

Competition increased and large organizations found it difficult to realign with changing market conditions. Japanese management practices, once held up as a model, received less attention as the Japanese economy faltered. Governments encouraged the privatization of services that had been publicly funded in the past. One response was to introduce the outsourcing of activities such as IT management, document supply, storage, and conservation.

At the start of the twenty-first century, current interests in management theory lie in organizational behavior, knowledge management, learning organizations, and culture and diversity. In terms of management practice, there is a return to focusing on people; for example, how to effectively manage a diverse community, recognizing the validity of the ways of other cultures. Collaboration and globalization pervade all occupations.

Governments are holding down spending in the public sector. The gap in salaries between the private and public sectors, and between the highest and lowest paid, has widened. Politics has an ever-increasing influence on management in the public sector. Mintzberg (1997) has described "managing on the edges," in which conflicting parties do battle with each other. In a study of the management of a national park, he describes the conflicts between politics and administration and between administration and operations, as well as between external pressures and internal processes. Managers in the public sector will recognize the description of the outcomes and his thoughts about managing on the edges. The idealism of the 1960s and early 1970s has vanished.

The operation of the private sector is under examination as economic conditions have changed. A bear stock market has reduced the value of all companies, not just the dot-coms. Stockholders have forced companies to become more accountable and reduce overheads as a way to produce profits. The service industries have suffered—law firms, accountants, and others have downsized.

We hope that this overview provides an important message for middle managers in their task of working with people. It illustrates the nature of the changes that can happen during a lifetime of working. Remember that there is likely to be a wide range of ages in any work team. The long-standing staff in any organization will have experienced major changes, to which they have adapted—from the good times, to possibly the not so good; from limited use of technology—perhaps even using punched cards and knitting needles as an aid to information retrieval in special libraries—to today's emerging digital services. If they had been unable to adapt, they would likely not be working in the organization. Those who have survived the changes may well have valuable experience to offer to less-experienced managers.

Social Change

Changes in management thought and practice reflect changes taking place in society at large. So some understanding of social, economic, political, and technological change is helpful. We have reviewed these changes in a linear way, but clearly their effects are intertwined.

Intergenerational life experiences are receiving more attention in the management literature because they influence changing attitudes to work.

Research has identified four cohorts born since the 1930s, which have been labeled the "veterans," the "baby boomers," "Gen X," and "Gen Y" (Zemke, Raines, and Filipczak, 2000).

The veterans were born before 1946, so that today many are retired and form part of the volunteer workforce commonly found in the public and voluntary sectors. Their life experiences often include the economic depression of the 1930s and a period of privation during the Second World War. They are the survivors; they are used to hardship, are loyal, and make commitments to their work, albeit work that is often unpaid. They see it as a way to return some of the benefits they have received, including receiving a better education than their parents. They are practical, dedicated, respectful, used to working in a hierarchy, and willing to make personal sacrifices

People born after the Second World War up to the mid-1960s are the baby boomers. During this period, the birthrate rose due to good economic times. Education facilities improved, resulting in more people attending universities. On graduation, they entered the workforce at a time of expansion in their chosen occupations. Many received rapid promotion to high positions. Baby boomers are optimistic, believe in consensus and personal gratification, and have a driven work ethic and a love/hate view of authority. During their careers they will have experienced considerable shifts in the way their work is performed. They will have worked through the introduction of computers and the Internet and changes in approaches to management.

A growing number of this cohort is now retiring, resulting in a new shortage of professional staff, which is causing concern. There is competition in the labor market for all qualified staff, and professional associations are working to attract people to their field. In turn, specialist education providers in the information sector are examining their curricula and marketing their programs to attract the best graduates from this shrinking pool.

The cohort born between 1966 and 1976 are labeled the Gen Xers. They grew up in the information society, experienced tough economic times, and entered the labor market when major changes were taking place in the workplace (Urgo, 2000). One impact of social change was that divorce became easier, and single-parent households were more common. This conditioned the attitudes of the Gen Xers, since they saw the preceding generation as having an easy time with opportunities that were now closed down to them. They are skeptical, have a balanced work ethic, are unimpressed by authority, prefer competence-based leadership, and are reluctant to commit.

The baby boomers were not always sympathetic to Gen X, seeing them as inarticulate and whining, and Gen Xers sometimes felt that the baby boomers hadn't moved beyond the '60s. Despite this negative view, Gen Xers are the first generation to experience the globalization of culture and business; they are information-savvy as the result of having computing skills and many exhibit a desire to learn and to be innovative and independent.

Various labels have been applied to the next generation, those born from about 1977 and on—Gen Yers, Nexters or the N-Geners. The changes emerging in Gen X became even more visible in the cohort that followed. It was the first to have real use of interactive and distributed communications technology and the capability to direct its own learning. Gen Yers are fiercely independent, have emotional and intellectual openness, hold strong views, and are optimistic, confident, assertive, ambitious, passionate, committed, and empowered (Tapscott, 1998). At the same time that Gen Yers entered the workforce, developments in technology, allied with changes in approaches to management, have led to the application of knowledge management within organizations.

At the time of this writing, a label has yet to emerge for a new cohort who are more aware of the fragile nature of society, who are experiencing difficult and changing economic conditions and the threat of terrorism, and are seizing opportunities for managing their own lives. They are likely to want to take a break from their work to travel and extend their experiences.

An older group in society has recently been identified—the sandwich generation—which consists of those in their mid-forties to late fifties. They feel they are sandwiched between the rising costs of sending their offspring to college while having to care for elderly parents who live longer and may need expensive care.

The effect of economic change has produced a different approach to careers. In the past, the veterans, and some of the baby boomers, tended to make few job changes. If they worked in a large organization with a hierarchical structure, they could expect to move up a ladder of promotion, perhaps to senior management level. But as organizations took on a flatter structure, opportunities for internal promotion changed.

With changing economic conditions, more jobs are offered on a short-term or contract basis. This has opened up the portfolio career and encouraged changes in career directions. No longer do employees enter the workforce expecting to stay with one employer for a long period of time; rather, they look for opportunities to gain advancement or extend skills.

Given the transferable skills acquired by information professionals, many have found that these can be applied in other roles—for example, in management beyond the information center in both the private and the public sectors.

Since career changes are becoming the norm throughout society, and it has become difficult to recruit staff, one of the consequences for managers is the need to organize induction and other training programs and workplace learning, and consider succession planning among team members.

Beyond the challenges for information services, other important social changes are taking place. Around the world there is the challenge of an aging population and, in the developed world, a falling birthrate. In the population at large there may be more people over the age of 60 than under the age of 16. In the U.S., the age of compulsory retirement has risen, and this option is being examined elsewhere as older people remain healthy longer. This has the benefit of reducing demands on social security and holding down taxation on the working population and businesses.

The participation rate of women in the labor force has risen dramatically since the 1960s. This brings the need to provide childcare and family-friendly work practices to minimize stress on employees so that they remain productive at the workplace.

One effect of the aging population is the pressure it has produced for some workers to take early retirement to care for elderly family members. In western societies, geographic mobility and smaller families may mean that there is not an extended family living close by. This is placing increasing pressures on working parents and children of the elderly.

As a result of increasing migration around the globe, governments are adopting social inclusion policies to promote diversity and encourage the assimilation of growing numbers of immigrants into the community. To enable the workforce to adapt to change, these policies place an increasing emphasis on education and lifelong learning.

DIG DEEPER

Extending your knowledge of theory in any relevant topic pays dividends for managers. Understanding social theory is important in studying organizations and people. One text among many is:

Turner, Bryan S., ed. 1996. *The Blackwell Companion to Social Theory*. Malden, Mass.: Blackwell.

Economic Change

Economic conditions are cyclical and history indicates that over a working lifetime there will be highs and lows. We all have hope that our standards of living and conditions of work will continue to rise. However, the start of the twenty-first century has demonstrated that this is not always so. National economies are just about maintaining growth in the western world, and the stock markets have shown considerable swings in recent years.

The area of new technology has seen considerable ups and downs in recent years. The promises of the dot-com revolution have yet to be met; yet we know that all new industries are enthusiastically promoted to attract investment. They mushroom and then the weaker companies fall by the wayside. Consider the development of the computer and the railroad, and, closer to home, online database services.

What produces the cycles? This is a complex topic, but some general points can be made. When the stock markets fall, it not only affects the value of individual companies, but, in turn, influences government fiscal policies, and also the individual. Most people have some investments in savings, retirement plans, and real estate in the form of their house or apartment.

Political factors in the world at large clearly have a major influence on the stock markets. In general, at times of conflict there is uncertainty and confidence falls. When there is no conflict, the markets are likely to move higher.

Governments have a major influence. In shaping macroeconomic policy, they determine levels of public spending and taxation, which, in turn, influence the level of demand in the economy with the aim of balancing unemployment and inflation. The decisions governments make affect activity and investment in business, industry, and the public sector. This can also have an adverse affect on services in the information sector that depend to some extent on endowment income. Keeping down costs in the public and private sector is one reason that outsourcing has grown in recent years.

Outside the U.S., not all the developing countries have benefited from growth in their economies, although international companies are increasingly transferring manufacturing to countries where production costs are lower. This leads the developed countries to depend more and more on the service industries to keep their economies buoyant. For some countries, a major economic issue is that of exchange rates. Since many overseas information services are dependent on U.S. suppliers, for example, for online databases, the purchasing power of their budgets can change. Globalization has resulted in major conglomerates providing services for the information industry, and most of them are based in the U.S.

Information is now recognized as a business asset and is valued by the corporate sector. Hence there has been an increasing investment in information, knowledge, and records management services, recognizing that this can increase productivity and profits.

Keeping a close eye on the national economy is essential. National newspapers and other media provide good coverage, as does *The Economist*. The language of economics may not figure in professional courses, so extend your knowledge.

DIG DEEPER

Getting familiar with the basics of economics will pay dividends in a career—and also help in managing personal finances. There are a number of textbooks, but one of the best is: Bishop, Matthew. 2002. *Pocket Economist: The Essentials of Economics From A-Z*. London: Economist and Profile Books.

The authors have worked through the economic good times and the bad, through growth and retrenchment. The real impacts fall on people. When finances are tight and staff may have to be laid off, the situation is stressful for everyone involved. This produces a considerable challenge, and probably some stress, for middle managers who are sandwiched between the bosses making hard decisions and the staff who experience the impacts; at the same time, service must not be disrupted and must continue to be offered with a smile.

Political Change

Political influences operate at a number of levels that affect the decisions that managers make—from those beyond national boundaries, to those in the workplace.

The number of regional political groupings is increasing. The groupings cross national boundaries and result in the introduction of a common currency in many Western European countries and alliances between different countries. In Europe, the European Union has brought services in the information sector to work together and share experience by offering funding for joint development projects

In general, national politics are currently characterized by stronger central control. Government policies and regulations affect both the private and public sectors, for instance, in employment practices by enacting legislation on aspects of diversity or by encouraging family-friendly policies.

The greater central control by governments has been coupled with shifts in politics to the center or the right. This affects publicly funded services, particularly when it is government policy to hold down public expenditure on recurrent and capital costs. It could produce voter resistance as public services deteriorate, and encourage a return to the politicized workplace.

However, benefits for users may well emerge as one outcome of greater government direction. Governments are demonstrating that they are more prepared to invest if the outcome is closer cooperation between related services to provide the community with increased access to learning and knowledge acquisition. In the U.S., the Institute of Museum and Library Services is a federal grant-making agency that promotes leadership, innovation, and a lifetime of learning by supporting U.S. museums and libraries. A similar government agency in the U.K. is Resource: The Council for Museums, Archives and Libraries. It provides strategic leadership, advocacy, and advice to enable museums, archives, and libraries to touch people's lives and inspire their imagination, learning, and creativity.

Professional associations in the information sector have linked together to form regional groupings, particularly in Europe and Southeast Asia, seeing this as a means to set up collaborative projects, exchange experience, and draw on funding from regional governments. In the U.K., the Institute of Information Scientists and the Library Association came together in one organization as CILIP—the Chartered Institute of Library and Information Professionals. Such linkages strengthen the advocacy role for the information professions.

Within organizations politics also operate, probably to an increasing degree. Managers, in competition with other departments, have to make strong cases for funding and other resources for their services. To support their request, they rely on a strong argument and an ability to make their case in writing or to make a lucid verbal presentation. And they ensure that the people working in their department are fully briefed as to what is needed and what approach is being taken to obtain the resources. Managers may choose to work on their own in seeking resources or may form alliances or coalitions with other managers to support their submissions. No department within an organization can be an island today. Managers must develop the skills to move effectively beyond their offices to seed their ideas among their staff and the wider community.

As services of all types face competition for resources and the challenges of legislation that might limit access to information, so information professionals are extending their political skills. They need to understand the politics of the organization to which they are responsible, who the decision-makers are, how to gain and hold their attention, and how to evaluate the outcomes. They need to look outside the organization to track changes in political matters that are happening in the wider world. Political awareness may not be in the curriculum, but it must be acquired.

Technological Change

Trying to foresee radical new developments in ICT (information and communications technologies) is not easy. Arpanet, developed by the U.S. Department of Defense as a communications network, preceded the Internet by twenty years, but its use within the information sector was confined to researchers for some years. An early form of fax machine was in use in the British Museum Library in the 1890s. Sometimes it may take a while for potential uses of technology to be recognized. Also, the information profession may not always recognize its achievements and influences. For example, work by Henrietta Avram at the Library of Congress in the post-war period demonstrated the benefits of using computers to build large-scale databases and the need for authority control.

What can be predicted is that technologies will change and new ones will emerge. In addition, experience indicates that on introduction new technologies will be very expensive in terms of acquisition and running costs, but the costs will fall comparatively quickly. Nevertheless, overall spending on technology does not decrease, for new technologies continue to emerge, as, for example, in the case of mobile phones and the rapid changes in their sophistication and capabilities.

Today, overall spending on computing and telecommunications is rising, along with associated costs. One reason is the emergence of digital archives and the digital library together with the resulting legal issues, such as copyright and licensing. This has become more contentious since information has become a tradable commodity.

In some countries, the use of ICT depends on national telecommunications policy and whether there is untimed or free local access. Broadband or wireless access is not universally available. There remains a growing information divide, although public libraries have helped their communities by providing access to the Internet.

The Internet has enabled the globalization of information services; the ability to span time zones can provide access 24/7 to Web sites and to people who can provide information. However, there is one major area of concern—the potential impact of international conflict on access to information and the emerging questions of imperialism and colonialism.

DIG DEEPER

Mathew Simon wrote a fine article about the challenges to, and value of, public libraries in today's technological world. Simon, Mathew. 2002. "Will the Library Survive the Internet? What Patrons Value in Public Libraries." *Public Libraries* 41 (2): 104-106.

The growth of the Internet also presents strategic challenges, and few could have accurately predicted the extent of expansion in the late 1980s. We know that different groups of people use computers for different reasons and, as a result, achieve very different outcomes while employing the same technology. It is apparent that information services around the world face similar challenges.

Until the early 1990s, computerization was seen primarily in terms of "automation" and connectivity to a utility, such as OCLC. Now there is the ever-growing influence of technological developments that are outside the control of the information service, but have profound impacts on the services it provides or how it carries out certain activities. Even when users access the Internet/Web through computers in, say, archives or a library, they seldom think of "the archives or library" as providing access to information, or even in providing assistance in using the Web. In this sense, the Internet is a competitor, for many people believe that *any* information they need is available for free on the Web.

The "free" aspect is diminishing, since more Web sites require some form of payment for full access. Readers may remember the relatively short life span of the free Web access to the *Encyclopedia Britannica* or Northern Light. The trend to charge started in 2001 and is increasing as more Web sites require annual membership fees.

One reason for the charge is that fewer companies are willing to pay substantial amounts of money to have banner ads appear on the Web pages. The April 10, 2002 issue of the *Wall Street Journal* reported that Yahoo! is relying less and less on banner ads and more and more on classifieds, listings, and referrals, all of which had been free in the past but now have associated fees (Eisinger, 2002: C1). Although the individual fees do not seem high (one U.S. dollar per month, for example) the cumulative total can be significant.

This trend is likely to continue to place greater pressure on libraries to increase the number of their public access computers and to pay some institutional membership fee. If more and more sites charge membership fees, staff will need to truly become digital collection managers to ensure that the service is using limited funds to provide access to the best-quality Web sites.

Nevertheless, the "competition" will, or should, force managers to ask some questions related to strategically positioning the service vis-à-vis competitors. One question is, what is the proper mix of services, collections, technology, and physical facility(ies) for remaining responsive to end-user wants and needs?

Global Digital Divide

The global digital divide raises a number of concerns. First, there is the issue of those countries that neither have a telecommunications infrastructure to support wider Internet access nor the per capita income to enable citizens to have access to a personal computer. But even in developed economies there are substantial numbers of people who cannot afford a personal computer. Free access in public libraries is one of the ways to address their needs.

Second, there is a divide between the U.S. and the rest of the world. For example, in the library environment the U.S. market needs and interests tend to drive both commercial and nonprofit developments for the field. In the nonprofit area, for instance, OCLC is steadily becoming the bibliographic utility for the world. As a result, it influences, if not dictates, how some library operations are carried out. Even the name given to the OCLC bibliographic database—"WorldCat"—reflects this influence. Another example is found in the May/June 2001 issue of the *OCLC Newsletter*—"During the next three years, OCLC and libraries will build on the framework of WorldCat as part of OCLC's *global* strategy" (emphasis added, p. 32).

Colin Steele, librarian of the Australian National University, confirms this point in terms of the commercial sector: "As long as U.S. libraries provide a relatively steady market for local content, profit-seeking publishers will continue to churn it out. U.S. standards and influences are applied instead of international standards" (Steele, 2000: 46). He raises a number of critical issues; perhaps the key issue, for which he does not have an easy answer, is how or by what mechanism the field can develop to internationalize developments. For, as he suggests, the U.S. research library community, even if it acted as a single force, probably does not have the economic ability to force multinational publishing/media conglomerates to change their ways in terms of pricing and packaging.

The third divide is institutional in character. It is becoming apparent in the U.S., and elsewhere, that in academia there is a digital divide as serious, if not more so, than there is at the individual level. Winston's research (2000) demonstrated that well-financed institutions spent four times the amount on technology per student than did the poorest schools. Such imbalances at the college/university level, combined with the strong statistical relationship, at least in the U.S., between family income and academic achievement, just further perpetuate economic and educational inequalities found at the elementary and secondary school levels.

Some other obvious trends are wireless network access, which has implications for facility design and layout, as well as cost considerations. While this is generally considered in terms of end-user access, there are possibilities in terms of library staff (see Ginzburg, 2001). The idea of delivery of digital information in all its forms (text, sound, and graphics/video) means a demand for ever-greater bandwidth and more "high end" technology. Those, in turn, usually require more people power to handle the "care and funding" of the technology. While one gets more speed and memory for monies spent, the frequency of that expenditure will continue to accelerate. Where to find the funds will be an ever-increasing challenge for managers at all levels.

What this means is that middle managers everywhere need to remain aware of developments in the U.S. library scene. Perhaps more importantly, it means that U.S. librarians need to become less isolationist in their professional reading and interests. While U.S. library staff are becoming more and more culturally diverse, just as is the library's service population, U.S. librarians tend to know very little about what their colleagues in other countries are doing and what their concerns are.

It has only been possible to outline some of the changes—social, economic, political, and technological—that are bringing about different approaches to service delivery. And since change is taking pace at an ever-increasing rate, more approaches will have emerged by the time this text appears in print.

UPDATE

Take each factor—social, economic, political, and technological—and update the broad review with two points that reflect current and local issues.

COLLABORATION

Collaboration comes naturally to anyone working in the information industry. Services in the information sector have always worked cooperatively to enhance access for their users, and they have worked closely with vendors and suppliers to create and develop the products needed. In the past, cooperation focused on joint acquisition programs and services such as interlibrary loans. Many of these services continue to operate using the mail or van service for sending books and journals between services in the same locality. However, the Internet and the advent of resources in electronic formats has enabled international working to provide even more enhanced services to users. We need to be ready to meet the challenge that at some point the visible and invisible costs will be examined by those who fund the service. Considerable benefits have emerged, such as the listing of resources held in archives and libraries, which has reduced duplication of holdings. Major digitization projects, training programs, and joint use services in rural areas are other examples of collaboration.

The national professional bodies have established international associations such as the International Council on Archives that organize conferences and set up working groups and committees that assist collaboration across national boundaries.

Earlier, the encouragement of governments was noted in drawing together activities across the information sector in agencies such as the Institute for Museum and Library Services. There are examples of museum and public library collaboration. According to one article, "Library and museum collaborations are the wave of the future. Sharing resources and expertise can help institutions save money, build new audiences and expand programming capabilities" (Diamant-Cohen and Sherman, 2003: 102).

DIG DEEPER

A recent book edited by Tomas A. Lipinski provides an excellent overview of the growing recognition of the fact that there are many similarities between archives, libraries, and museums, as well as the fact that they need to collaborate more with one another.

Lipinski, Tomas. 2002. *Libraries, Museums and Archives: Legal Issues and Ethical Challenges in the New Information Era.* Lanham, Md.: Scarecrow Press.

The title somewhat hides the fact that the content is broader than just legal and ethical issues.

Greater collaboration is also evident in approaches to managing organizations and working with people. There is wide consensus is that the "Lone Ranger is Dead," meaning that there has been a steady decline in the effectiveness of the sole individual at the top managing everything (if in fact that ever really worked for any length of time). Most management writers indicate the increasing use of "collaborative management" through the use of teams.

This trend started some years ago, when economics were forcing organizations to become "leaner." The trimming of the fat often was achieved through reengineering (staff reductions and/or reassignments), "flattening" the organization (reducing the number of middle managers), and employing more teams in order to bring needed skills together.

In 1999, Byrne wrote about the "leaderless corporation" in a special theme issue of *Business Week* looking at what the twenty-first century might hold for management: "Already, many companies are adopting work groups with no designated leader. In 1987, 28% of the largest 1,000 public corporations boasted at least some self-directed groups. By 1996, 78% had some....The trend will only intensify as a generation of team-oriented managers climb higher" (Byrne, 1999: 90).

Later, the question of work teams will be addressed, as well as the reduction of the traditional bureaucratic hierarchical structure that was so typical of services in the past. But here the point is made that, as teams become increasingly common, there will be a critical need to find an effective and appropriate way to address the fundamental issue of accountability when there is no designated leader.

As this text was being written, the U.S. was struggling with the issue of accountability in the Enron/Arthur Andersen case. Is an entire organization accountable for the actions of a unit or individuals? Certainly that case went far beyond a work team, but it highlights the fact that at the end of the day there must be accountability. Where and how to place that accountability is, and will be, a critical issue in a team environment.

Lubans makes a case for learning more about work teams. He notes that: "There is a growing emphasis on teamwork (within or apart from the traditional structure) in many organizations, including libraries. Library leaders need to know what a team is and why teams do and do not work. We need to know this in order to do well what is required of us organizationally, and for personal and professional satisfaction" (Lubans, 1998: 12).

Using teams can be an effective method for improving staff morale if, as it should, it provides:

- a variety of activity;
- authority to make decisions and mistakes;
- new learning opportunities; and
- staff to share their expertise.

A starting point for learning more about work teams is Katzenbach and Smith's "The Discipline of Teams" in the *Harvard Business Review* (Katzenbach and Smith, 1993). Bazirjian and Stanley (2001) have written another useful article that describes the assessment of team structures and discusses the actual use of teams in a library.

Besides teamwork within the service, the greatest change will be the need to collaborate with other organizations to face the challenges of providing the requisite information and technological resources and services to meet their service communities' changing and growing demands. Economically, we know we can never come close to addressing these needs if we attempt to do it alone.

One example of an approach to collaborative activities is reflected in the "Keystone Principles." Eighty academic library directors engaged in a series of discussions about strategic issues facing libraries at a Keystone, Colorado, resort in September 1999. From their discussions emerged the three Keystone Principles and identification of a number of action steps for libraries to take to address the principles.

We feel that there is a global application, both in terms of principles and action steps.

The three principles are:

- Access to information is a public good. Scholarly and government information is a "public good" and must be available free of marketing bias, commercial motives, and cost to the individual user.
- There is a need for bias-free systems and for libraries to create these new systems. Libraries are responsible for creating

innovative information systems for the dissemination and preservation of information and new knowledge regardless of format.

- A new knowledge commons will emerge—a cooperative coordinated enterprise of traditional library services and new electronic ones.

The concept comes into play in that the group recognized that only through joint or collaborative efforts could there be any hope of realizing the principles, and further, that this would be an ongoing process. While the wording of the action items is focused on academic libraries, it is easy to see how with minor changes they can be applied to any type of archive or library.

KEYSTONE PRINCIPLE ACTION ITEMS

Principle One—Libraries will direct resources and establish coalitions to create local, state, and national legislation consistent with Principle One.

Principle Two—Libraries will partner with faculty, other libraries, and/or other entities to quickly identify, create, manage, and disseminate new digital content critical to learning and research programs of their institutions.

Principle Three—Libraries will direct resources and create partnerships that ensure 24/7 availability of expertise in support of student and faculty research needs.

Putting it in practice

Now consider how the Keystone Principles could be modified to reflect the type of service in which you are working.

One of the factors driving the trends of more work teams and collaborative efforts is technology—especially the Web. Even a cursory review of the professional literature shows an increasing number of articles about how teams are enhanced through the use of technology, and even the introduction of virtual teams. Likewise, there is a growing body of literature about how technology is forcing libraries to collaborate with one another. The Keystone Principles' action items are full of references to technology and digital information. ("The Keystone Principles", 1999)

COMPETITION

One effect of the changed political environment has been an increase in competition, in the belief that this will reduce costs. In the information sector, a growing number of commercial services and vendors can supply cataloguing data, select stock, provide extramural storage, or recruit staff, creating competition for certain groups of staff on the payroll. The sophisticated online information products available in fields such as law now enable lawyers to have tailor-made information services provided at their desks and updated several times a day. This potential competition can be beneficial; if the outsourced service is cost-effective, funds can be released for other activities. Outsourcing has weaknesses, but also possible benefits.

Many users have greater choice in the services they can use to access the information they need—much more so than they had in the past. The upside for the information professional is that they can now be more entrepreneurial than in the past. They may spot a gap in the information market and move to fill it.

The advertising, marketing, and promotion of services need to be done just as vigorously and effectively as the competition. A publicly funded service can gain benefits by promoting itself as an ally/partner with other public agencies.

By their nature, services generally need not only to provide a reflective place, but also an atmosphere that will attract both regular users and non-users. The approach will be different in the various sectors. What will work in an archives service might not be as effective in a knowledge management center.

> ### FOR FURTHER THOUGHT
>
> What factors would best create the atmosphere that would attract people to your service?
>
> (To start you thinking...consider the differences between some public libraries and the bookshops that offer sofas and coffee bars...)

ACCOUNTABILITY

All services, whether in the private or public sector, are required to be accountable to their parent organization. In the public sector, government may impose performance measures with penalties imposed for failing to reach government-determined standards. In the private sector, outsourcing services may be an alternative to an internally provided service that is not seen as meeting the needs of the organization at an acceptable cost. This places considerable pressure on managers and their teams to meet standards set for their service, and there can be a very fine line between "success" and "failure."

The questions of accountability that arose in the Enron/Andersen situation noted above have made all organizations consider their standards of record keeping, accounting, auditing, and reporting to stakeholders. This applies equally in the public sector, where a close scrutiny is maintained of the use of all resources.

FUTURES

Information Services

Some issues can be identified as vital to the future of information services. For instance, information literacy, the effective use of information, is as important for archivists and knowledge managers as it is for librarians. Other emerging issues include the governance and the cost of globalization, national versus international interests, how the community will access services, and, perhaps more importantly, how we might meet their expectations.

Now, as in the future, there is the imperative to communicate effectively with and meet the needs of users, especially the remote users.

It will be essential to ensure that the information workforce stays ahead of the game in terms of outlook, education, training, workplace learning, and ingenuity. Cost-effectiveness is an important keyword.

The shape of the physical service will alter as more people will have easier access as an outcome of digitization. So the size, shape, and design of the physical building will change—and this is a challenge to both architects and service managers.

DIGGING DEEPER

Donald Sager reported on interviews with Kay Runge and William Ptacek, who were Public Library Association presidential candidates for 2001-2002. Both candidates provided interesting insights about the public library in the twenty-first century. The topics they cover are very similar to those covered above.

Sager, Donald. 1999. "Looking Through the Glass: Leadership Views the Future." *Public Libraries* 38 (2): 89-92.

NORDINFO (an institution under the Nordic Council of Ministers that facilitates cooperation between organizations in the library and information sector in the five Nordic countries) brought together a number of writers to give their forecasts of Global Issues in 21st Century Research Librarianship (Hannesdóttir, 2002). The topics they identified will affect every information service. They include:

- changes in the educational landscape, including distance learning, technology, and global trade policies
- evolution—leading change, marketing, performance measurement, information literacy, and outsourcing
- digital libraries
- staff development and new competencies
- collection development and preservation
- legal and copyright issues
- global cooperatives

Hickerson (2000), in his presidential address to the Society of American Archivists, presented ten challenges for the archival profession at the beginning of the twenty-first century.

- managing the identification, appraisal, retention, preservation, and provision of support for the use of documents generated in electronic form
- devoting greater resources to non-textual holdings
- recognizing that records are global
- devising new methods for describing and providing user access to the ever-expanding volume of contemporary records in all formats
- making our holdings accessible and useable by our core constituencies and to broaden use by expanded audiences
- expanding the scope of our collection development policies
- generating more basic and applied research on aspects of information management
- strengthening our national archival organization
- augmenting the range of skills, knowledge, and resources engaged in the archival enterprise
- maintaining the credibility of our role as respected evidentiary authorities and as trusted guarantors of society's interests, today and in the future

There are echoes in the two lists.

Management Challenges

Now the big question is—how will change affect management? Hofstede, who focuses on global management issues, asked the following questions:

- Do management processes change over time?
- Will there be anything new about management in the twenty-first century?

His answers to these questions are very similar to our views regarding the longevity of basic management activities: "Management processes basically have changed little over time, and will remain so. They differ less from period to period than from part of the world to part of the world, and even from country to country" (Hofstede, 1999: 34).

On the other hand, Todaro suggested that the twenty-first century will hold ten areas that library managers must confront as they strive to maintain effective service programs and be responsive to changing needs.

• Develop a social context. • Survey organizational culture. • Lead and follow. • Know the customer. • Assess.	• Emphasize teamwork • Create a flexible management style • Plan strategically • Communicate • Create centers of and for learning (Todaro, 2001: 176-178)

There is little conflict between the two authors' positions. The list above contains nothing totally new but rather suggests the need for extra attention to these areas over the coming years. In fact, the above list is reflective of sections throughout this book, with some additional topics such as diversity and project management.

WORTH CHECKING OUT

A prospective view of management theory and practice

"Views of 21st Century Management," in Chowdhury, Subir, ed. 2000. *Management 21C: Someday We'll All Manage This Way.* London: Financial Times Prentice-Hall.

Middle Managers

Although some of the challenges that lie ahead of today's middle managers have been noted above, many are yet to be discovered. We have selected ten areas that are clearly visible and related to the trends and issues identified in this chapter.

FORESEEABLE ISSUES

- collaboration pressures
- strategic and marketing issues
- staff development for team/collaborative work
- assessment, quality control, and accountability

- communication/negotiation/conflict resolution
- fiscal control
- work team usage planning
- diversity of staff and users
- ethics
- outsourcing

Management will clearly become more complex. Managers will need to value their team; be adaptable, good communicators and change agents; and have a vision for the future, with techniques in their toolkit to realize the vision. Above all, they will need to believe in themselves and stay ahead of the pack.

The point to stress is that changes will happen. Some can be antici-pated—but there will always be the unexpected. Staying well informed about developments within the profession—and in the wider world—will help to see what is coming down the track, and, perhaps more impor-tantly—how fast it is approaching.

THINK ABOUT

Your view of the world in five, ten, and fifteen years...

What will be the impact on services?

Which area is easiest to predict?

....and which is the most difficult?

AFTER READING THIS CHAPTER YOU SHOULD BE AWARE:

• that no service operates in a vacuum;

• that external factors affect management planning and decision-making, most of which are outside the influence of managers;

• that services are working more closely together both inter- and cross-sectorally for mutual benefit; and of directions man-agement and services may take.

REFERENCES

Abrahamson, Eric. 1996. "Management Fashion." *Academy of Management Review* 20 (1): 254-284.

Bazirjian, Rosann, and Nancy M. Stanley. 2001. "Assessing the Effectiveness of Team-Based Structures in Libraries." *Library Collections, Acquisitions, and Technical Services* 25 (2): 131-157.

Bennis, Warren. 1998. *Managing People Is Like Herding Cats*. London: Kogan Page.

Bishop, Matthew. 2002. *Pocket Economist: The Essentials of Economics from A-Z*. London: Economist and Profile Books.

Byrne, John A. 1999. "The Global Corporation Becomes the Leaderless Corporation." *Business Week* 20 (30 August): 88-90.

Chowdhury, Subir, ed. 2000. *Management 21C: Someday We'll All Manage This Way*. London: Financial Times: Prentice-Hall.

Crainer, Stuart. 2000. *The Management Century: A Critical Review of 20th Century Thought and Practice*. San Francisco: Jossey-Bass.

Diamant-Cohen, Betsy, and Dina Sherman. 2003. "Hand in Hand: Museums and Libraries Working Together." *Public Libraries* 42 (2): 103-105.

Drucker, Peter. 2001. *The Essential Drucker: Selections from the Management Works of Peter F. Drucker*. New York: HarperBusiness.

Eisinger, Jesse. 2002. "Ahead of the Tape." *Wall Street Journal* 239 (70): C1.

Ginzburg, Barbara. 2001. "Goin' Mobile: Using a Wireless." *Computers in Libraries* 21 (March): 40-44.

Hannesdóttir, Sigrún Klara. 2002. *Global Issues in 21st Century Research Librarianship: NORDINFO's 25th Anniversary Publication*. Helsinki: NORDINFO.

Hickerson, H. Thomas. 2001. "Ten Challenges for the Archival Profession." *American Archivist* 64 (1): 6-16.

Hofstede, Geert. 1999. "The Universal and the Specific in 21st Century Global Management." *Organization Dynamics* 28 (1): 34-44.

Katzenbach, Jon R., and Douglas K. Smith. 1993. "The Discipline of Teams." *Harvard Business Review* 71 (March-April): 111-120.

Kennedy, Caroline. 2002. *Guide to the Management Gurus*. London: Random House.

"The Keystone Principles." (Accessed August 12, 2003). Available: http://www.arl.org/training/keystone.html.

Lipinski, Tomas. 2002. *Libraries, Museums, and Archives: Legal Issues and Ethical Challenges in the New Information Era*. Lanham, Md.: Scarecrow Press.

Lubans, John. 1998. "How Can Something That Sounds So Good Make Me Feel So Bad?" *Library Administration and Management* 12 (1): 7-14.

Lubans, John. 2000. "I Borrowed the Shoes, But the Holes Are Mine: Management Fads, Trends, and What's Next." *Library Administration and Management* 14 (1): 131-134.

Mintzberg, Henry. 1989. *Mintzberg on Management: Inside Our Strange World of Organizations*. New York: The Free Press.

Mintzberg, Henry. 1997. "Managing on the Edges." *International Journal of Public Sector Management* 10 (3): 131-153.

Sager, Donald. 1999. "Looking Through the Glass: Leadership Views the Future." *Public Libraries* 38 (2): 89-92.

Simon, Mathew. 2002. "Will the Library Survive the Internet? What Patrons Value in Public Libraries." *Public Libraries* 41 (2): 104-106.

Spell, Chester. 1999. "Where Do Management Fashions Come From and How Long Do They Stay?" *Journal of Management History* 5 (6): 334-348.

Steele, Colin. 2000. "Forging Global Information Equity." *Library Journal* 125 (12): 46-47.

Tapscott, Don. 1998. *Growing Up Digital: The Rise of the Net Generation*. New York: McGraw-Hill.

Todaro, Julie Beth. 2001. "The Effective Organization in the Twenty-First Century." *Library Administration and Management* 15 (3): 176-178.

Turner, Bryan S., ed. 1996. *The Blackwell Companion to Social Theory*. Malden, Mass.: Blackwell.

Urgo, Marisa. 2000. *Developing Information Leaders: Harnessing the Talents of Generation X*. London: Bowker-Saur.

Winston, Gordon C. 2000. "The Positional Arms Race in Higher Education." Discussion paper, Williams Project on the Economics of Higher Education Finance.

Zemke, Ron, Claire Raines, and Bob Filipczak. 2000. *Generations at Work: Managing the Clash of Veterans, Boomers, Xers, and Nexters in Your Workplace.* New York: AMACOM.

Launching Pad

Bryan, Robin. 2001. "Circulating E-book Readers: The Charlotte-Mecklenburg Experience." *Public Libraries* 40 (5) supplement: 21-26.

Curtis, Susan, Barbara Mann, and the Cooperative Reference Services Committee. 2002. "Cooperative Reference: Is There a Consortium Model?" *Reference and User Services Quarterly* 41 (4): 344-349.

Drucker, Peter. 2002. *Managing in the Next Society.* Oxford: Butterworth-Heinemann.

Ellis, Judith, ed. 1993. *Keeping Archives.* 2d ed. Port Melbourne: Thorpe, in association with the Australian Society of Archivists.

Evans, G. Edward. 2002. "Management Issues of Cooperative Ventures and Consortia in the USA." Parts 1 and 2. *Library Management* 23 (4/5): 213-226; (6/7): 275-286.

Evans, G. Edward, Patricia Layzell Ward, and Bendik Rugaas. 2000. *Management Basics for Information Professionals.* New York: Neal-Schuman.

Fishburn, Dudley. 2002. "The World in 2003." London: *The Economist.*

Friend, Fred. J. 2002. "Library Consortia in the Electronic Age." *Alexandria* 14 (1): 17-24.

Gilbert, Gail R. 2000. "Courting Athletics, Creating Partnerships." *Library Administration and Management* 14 (1): 35-38.

Hitt, Michael A. 2000. "The New Frontier: Transformation of Management for the New Millennium." *Organizational Dynamics* 28 (3): 7-17.

Kranich, Nancy, ed. 2001. *Libraries and Democracy: The Cornerstones of Liberty.* Chicago: American Library Association.

Lippincott, Joan K. 2002. "Developing Collaborative Relationships." *College and Research Libraries News* 63 (3): 190-192.

Lubans, John. 2001. "To Save the Time of the User." *Library Administration and Management* 15 (3): 179-182.

Marsden, Christopher. 2001. "Sectors and Domains: Some Reflections on Co-operation and Integration." *Journal of the Society of Archivists* 22 (1): 17-23.

Miller, Danny, and Jon Hartwick. 2002. "Spotting Management Fads." *Harvard Business Review* 80 (10): 26-27.

Ogbonna, Emmanuel, and Lloyd C. Harris. 2002. "The Performance Implications of Management Fads and Fashions: An Empirical Study." *Journal of Strategic Marketing* 10 (1): 47-66.

Pilling, Stella, and Stephanie Kenna, eds. 2002. *Cooperation in Action: Collaborative Initiatives in the World of Information.* London: Facet Publishing.

Pugh, Derek S., and David J. Hickson. 1997. *Writers on Organizations.* 5th ed. London: Penguin Books.

"Required Reading for Library Administrators: An Annotated Bibliography of Influential Authors and Their Works." 2002. *Library Administration and Management* 16 (3): 126-136.

Riggs, Donald E. 2002. "New Libraries Remain an Excellent Investment." *College and Research Libraries* 63 (2): 108-109.

Shoaf, Eric. C. 2001. "Fifteen Months in the Trenches." *Library Administration and Management* 15 (1): 4-13.

Sinclair, Niall. 2002. "'Back to the Future': Electronic Records Management in the Twenty-First Century." *Records Management Journal* 12 (3): 103-107.

Srkantaiah, T. Kanti, and Michael Koenig. 2000. *Knowledge Management for the Information Professional.* Medford, N.J.: Information Today.

Todaro, Julie Beth. 1999. "A Vision of the Past for the Future." *Library Administration and Management* 13 (2): 78-80.

Wilding, Tom. 2002. "External Partnerships and Academic Libraries." *Library Management* 23 (4/5): 199-202.

2: SETTLING INTO A NEW MANAGEMENT POST

"Set high standards, give full support."

IN THIS CHAPTER YOU'LL DISCOVER:

- how middle management experience shapes career development
- the role of the middle manager
- how to prepare for the new responsibilities
- ways to give the right impression on the first day
- natural reactions to the new post and how to handle them
- the pressure points
- how to succeed as a middle manager

STARTING FROM THE TOP

There are two questions that management texts often don't address, and which are generally taken for granted:

- Do you know what you need to know?
- What should you do on the first day in a new post?

Let's start right away by focusing on how to prepare to take up the post and settle into the new job. Later we'll move on to consider other vital factors—but the first important point is that what happens at middle management level can have a profound influence on your career development. So make the most of a great opportunity—you can achieve so much.

A KEY CAREER STEP

Moving into a middle management post is the key step in a career. At this level you gain valuable skills, experience, and understanding that helps you immediately and determines your future career direction. Much can come from reading, but living through the realities of management—having successes and probably a few "I can do that better next time" experiences—fills in the gaps and molds the individual.

The experience shapes the goals you set for your career development, and leads you to consider the many options that are open to you. Some people set their sights on moving up the ladder within a large organization. This provides the experience of being a small fish in a large pool, moving between specialist posts and extending skills while moving upwards. Working in a small organization gives the opportunity to be a big fish in a small pool. A shift to a different type of information agency may be attractive, but make it part of a plan—the longer you stay in one sector, the more difficult it is to move to another. And there is also the option of pursuing the career in the broader field of management, for management with the addition of information skills are transferable.

The time spent as a middle manager provides the opportunity to look upward and outward to see how your talents might best be used. Just taking up a new post presents challenges: assuming a management role adds different challenges since people responsibilities are added to the job description, and political skills are honed.

THE ROLE OF THE MIDDLE MANAGER

The stereotype of the middle manager has changed. At one time they were seen as being sandwiched between the "tops" and the "bottoms." The middle manager was someone who was a defender of the status quo, a dinosaur heading to extinction who didn't like change. In many organizations, the level of middle management was swept away as new information technologies, coupled with economic restraint, resulted in cutbacks that effectively delayered the former hierarchies.

Today middle managers have emerged with new and exciting roles. They live in the challenging space of an organization, where they are seen as being entrepreneurs, communicators, therapists, tight-rope artists, enablers, facilitators—and, most importantly of all, change agents (Huy, 2001).

This is an exciting role in the information organization as the community at large becomes more information-literate, an increasing emphasis is placed on lifelong learning, and business sees access to timely, accurate, and relevant information as yielding a competitive advantage. All of this is driven by the promise of the digital age. As information organizations restructure to meet changing circumstances, the middle manager has the pivotal role in achieving change.

Organizations can fall apart in the complex world of the information organization without middle managers, for they are the vital link between the users and senior management.

Middle managers face a challenge, for they are generally appointed for their technical competence gained at entry-level positions. They haven't yet had the opportunity to demonstrate management skills, and so need to understand how their responsibilities and work will change at the new level. And there is another significant change in their role. Up to now it was all about personal achievement, but at this level success comes from enabling others to achieve and in building a high-performing team. So becoming a middle manager offers challenges for personal and professional development and develops the essential conceptual, political, and human skills.

WORTH CHECKING OUT

Good advice for new managers

Hill, Linda H. 2003. *Becoming a Manager: Mastery of a New Identity*. Boston: Harvard Business School Press.

Watkins, Michael. 2003. *Take Charge: Success Strategies for New Leaders*. Boston: Harvard Business School Press.

Myths of Management

Until you have worked in the day to day reality of managing, it is not easy to see what the job consists of beyond the pages of a textbook and the magic acronym POSDCoRD. This acronym represents Planning, Organizing, Staffing, Directing, Coordinating, Reporting, and Directing, which for many years underpinned the foundation of management courses (Gulick and Urwick, 1937). We form ideas about what a manager should do—and then they are modified as a result of experience. Being a manager is more complicated than the acronym indicates.

Six myths of management are worth remembering:

Myth 1: You must call all the shots.
Myth 2: You can't trust anyone.
Myth 3: You must remain objective at all times.
Myth 4: You must defend your staff.
Myth 5: You cannot back down.
Myth 6: You're the best teacher. (Stettner, 2000)

We would add an important rider to number 4—defend your staff in public, but if they have done something wrong, talk with them in private. And there is another myth that all information professionals forget at their peril:

Myth 7: Information organizations operate for the benefit of staff, rather than for users.

The last point is vital to remember. Much of what appears explicitly in this text refers to the organization of services. But the services are provided for users, and users are at the core of the work of the information professional. Never forget that vital point—without users, the services would not exist.

The middle manager's first priority is to focus on maximizing the efficiency and effectiveness of the service so that it meets the real needs of users. This role becomes more challenging as users increasingly need, and expect, a rapid response delivered 24 hours a day and 7 days a week, providing relevant and accurate information in their preferred format when they want it.

The middle manager makes this happen by having a continuing dialogue with users to assess changing needs, with front line staff in close contact with users, and with back room staff who provide the support. The manager, in a liason function, continues the dialogue with the boss. At the same time, middle managers stay ahead of new developments, train their team, monitor the quality of the service provided, and stay within budget.

NEVER FORGET

Services are organized for the benefit of users, not staff.

Users needs are paramount—needs change and services adapt to meet expectations.

If this doesn't happen, users will turn to other sources. They have the choice—services have competition.

PREPARING FOR THE NEW ROLE

Know Yourself

Laying the foundation for success starts before taking up a post. People always remember the *first* time they met someone. Time invested in preparation before that vital first day sets the tone for the way in which you can operate as a middle manager within the organization.

How well do you know yourself? Checking out your self-awareness will help you develop strategies for working with people. One of the key phrases in the management literature is "emotional intelligence."

DEFINITION

"Emotional intelligence is the ability to be able to perceive one's own feelings and those of others" (Goleman, 1995: 43)

People who have the ability to recognize their emotions and the effect these can have on their own performance and that of their colleagues are credited with having a high EQ or Emotional Quotient. Knowing their key strengths and weaknesses makes them self-assured about their capabilities. They are aware of how their past—the culture they came from, the influence of their education and their family—has shaped their reactions today. Tomorrow's leaders are those who can empathize, collaborate, and influence.

Debate has centered on whether EQ is a part of a personality that can't be changed or if, with the right kind of training, it can be developed. Research suggests that emotional intelligence can be split into three categories:

- the enablers (sensitivity, influences, and self-awareness);
- the drivers (motivation and decisiveness); and
- the constrainers (emotional resilience, conscientiousness, and integrity).

It is argued that the drivers and constrainers form enduring elem an individual's personality and are therefore more difficult to (However, the enablers can be developed—for example, self-awareness can emerge through interpersonal skills training. The drivers and constrainers are best handled with coping strategies; for example, those with low emotional resilience should avoid highly stressful situations (Dulewicz and Higgs, 1999).

Creating self-awareness is the first step. Reading can help, and coaching or a training program will develop recognition of personal strengths and how they contribute to a high EQ.

Men and women have been found to have significantly different profiles when tested for EQ. Women generally have much stronger interpersonal skills than their male colleagues, while males demonstrate a significantly higher sense of self and independence.

WARTS AND ALL—HOW DO YOU RATE?

Take a sheet of paper; draw a line down the middle and horizontally across the middle of the page. Title the two columns "Key Strengths" and "Weaknesses."

Write down your own view of your attributes and shortcomings in the columns on the top half of the sheet, fold it in two, and title the columns "Key Strengths" and "Weaknesses" on the lower half.

Ask someone who knows you well, and will not pull punches, to write down their view…then compare the two lists. Are they the same? If not, and they probably will be different, talk through the outcomes with the person who knows you well and whom you trust.

Take any criticism they offer as a means to get to better know yourself.

Another way to gain self-awareness and better understand colleagues is to take one of the tests that have been developed to identify personality types. Keirsey (1998) developed a temperament sorter that provides questions to help determine your personality type, and the Keirsey Temperament Sorter II can be taken online. Feedback is provided without charge, and there is the option of purchasing a more detailed analysis.

WORTH CHECKING OUT

Your personality type

Visit the Keirsey Temperament Sorter II, available at www.keirsey.com.

Keirsey's approach is based on the Myers-Briggs Type Inventory. It identifies four types that are labeled Artisans, Guardians, Idealists, and Rationals, and each type can be further analyzed into four subgroups.

Artisans are perceptive, adaptable, athletic, cheerful, realistic, impulsive, and easily bored; they seek adventure and an adrenaline buzz, love impact, have a mechanical aptitude, and pride themselves on finesse or skill. They work best in stimulating varied environments and need the freedom to act.

Idealists are enthusiastic, humane, subjective, imaginative, crusading, and up in the clouds; they seek identity, love integrity, pride themselves on empathy, and value friendship. They work best in expressive personal environments and need an appreciation of their uniqueness.

Guardians are dependable, factual, thorough, routinized, and painstaking; they seek security, love obedience, pride themselves on dependability, value regulations, and insist on others following rules. They work best in organized secure environments and need responsibility and a place.

Rationals are thinking, abstract, exacting, intellectual, logical, inventive, and terse; they appear arrogant, seek insight, love justice, pride themselves on competence, and value technology. They work best in innovative intellectual environments and need competence and success.

Keirsey applies the description of each temperament to leading, parenting, and mating, and then indicates how each temperament will probably get along with each of the others. It is an interesting test to take, and you may find the results are surprising. But remember that while personality tests are helpful, they can reflect the mood of a person at the time when the test was taken. And don't cheat—be honest with yourself. When you have taken the test check the results with the person who assisted with the "Warts and All" test above.

Take a Break between Posts

Take time for preparation. There is benefit to be gained from "thinking" yourself into the new role. You are taking a major step forward.

Often there is unused leave to take when quitting a post, and if you have the opportunity to take a break before moving to the new post, then grab it. It will provide an opportunity to gather useful information; review information gathered before the post was accepted, fill any gaps, and think about the situation you are about to enter. In retrospect, most people wish they had taken more time to prepare for their next post.

There will be a pile of documents to deal with. Check through and organize them so that the following information can be easily retrieved:

- the job description and materials describing the department and parent organization;
- notes you made during the interview process about the parts of the organization you saw and who you met;
- any additional material provided to help you make up your mind before accepting the post;
- your impressions about the image of the organization and the service, based on printed publications and relevant Web sites;

- the benefits and conditions of employment;
- provisions made for induction both to the organization and the department;
- the opportunities for training and professional development in the post and the specialist field, and for attending professional meetings and conferences;
- the location of the service in relation to the user community and whether the premises are user-friendly and attractive to work in; and most importantly,
- a profile of the likely users.

Here's a checklist of some additional sources of information that you may be able to access:

- the Web site of the organization and the subdepartment where you will be based;
- recent annual reports;
- accreditation, quality, or similar reports in the public domain;
- information leaflets provided for users;
- an unobtrusive visit to the site if it is open to the public;
- the professional grapevine;
- the professional press;
- local media; and possibly
- the previous holder of the post.

ADD TO THE LIST

Take the checklist and customize it to fit the organization you are joining.

Take this information and build up your first impressions of the service, the parent organization, and the department where you will be based. Can you identify its strengths and weaknesses? Make a note of these impressions and return to them at a later date.

This exercise is worth doing even if you have been promoted internally within the organization. In some organizations it is the generally accepted practice to promote internally, and so moving up the ladder brings with it an understanding of how the service operates. But in other organizations, it may be less easy to be promoted internally than to be a newcomer. Making your mark through internal promotion can be difficult. Colleagues will know your strengths and weaknesses, and the grapevine is very powerful. You will need to exert a degree of authority that may not have been necessary in your earlier role. Just make yourself look more formal. And check through the list of useful information with a fresh eye; don't assume you know all the details.

If you are a newcomer, people will expect you to ask more questions, and you can be more objective. On the other hand, you may feel isolated in the early days before you have been able to build a network and have people to share ideas with. And everyone is watching you...

Remember that people take baggage with them when moving jobs. What worked in one organization or department might not work in another. Listening skills are important, and the professional grapevine works in two directions.

MAKING A GOOD IMPRESSION

The message you need to give out is that you are relaxed, a good listener, open to new ideas, and looking forward to the new job. Looking confident helps to make a good first impression on colleagues and bosses, especially when that impression is based on information and awareness.

Feeling comfortable will help to give a relaxed aura, so plan ahead. When you were interviewed and met the new colleagues at their desks, what clues did you get about the dress code? If in any doubt, choose clothes with care and be conservative on the first day.

Take with you basic office supplies such as pens, pencils, small stapler, legal notepad, Post-it notes, and a small notebook in your brief case. They should be provided for you...but you never know.

Getting there in good time also helps you be relaxed. Check out the length of the journey at the time of day when you will be expected, where to park if driving, and which entrance to use if it is a large organization. Aim to arrive ten minutes early—much better than being five minutes late and looking harassed before you have started. Before leaving home, read a morning newspaper or catch up with the news—it can help with small talk.

Different organizations have their own practices concerning new members of staff. Some have a formal process involving the human resources department; others suggest you go straight to the area in which you will be working. Hopefully someone will be there to welcome you and handle formalities such as signing papers to participate in benefits, a staff club, etc. You can be overwhelmed in meeting colleagues across the organization; there will be a lot of information to absorb, so strong listening skills will be an asset.

Expect that someone from senior management will talk with you about your role—the responsibilities and expectations. Sometimes these are not quite the same as those portrayed during the interview, and you need to know how they will judge whether you have met their expectations. If you are lucky, your boss will give you the history of the post; certainly they will discuss the upside, but they may overlook the downside. An early discussion about expectations should be good practice in any organization, but we have had the experience of being thrown in at the deep end, asking about "induction," and finding it didn't exist and that no one had thought about it— with no senior managers in sight. It can happen, and if it does, start making telephone calls...

Yes, you are doing a lot of listening, and no one can take in that much new information at once and remember all of it. That small notebook you took with you is a very useful place in which to jot down names or points that might be forgotten when a great deal of new information is given to you in a short space of time. We suggest this rather than a personal digital assistant (PDA), for technology can fail at the wrong time. Meet colleagues and write down their names and roles.

Along with the listening skills, body language is important—both your own and that of the people you are meeting. Walking tall makes a good impression—even if you are 5'2". Body language indicates the mood of the workplace, the relationships between people, whether they are welcoming you. Having good emotional skills or a high EQ assists in understanding and interpreting body language and learning how to read postures, gestures, and facial expressions.

Given the pressures of the first day, those listening skills are very important. The essence of the messages can be missed, particularly if local jargon, terminology, and acronyms are used.

Check out the rituals by observing and asking questions. It can be a major sin to miss the Friday afternoon sundowner with the boss…and if you don't know about it…

Have a firm handshake, smile, make eye contact, listen rather than talk, and be interested in everyone. Notice how staff are addressed—is it formal or informal? Remember that the janitors know everything!

There is an analogy that describes how to make a good impression, become familiar with the surroundings, and take charge. It uses the metaphor of moving house. Meet the townspeople (colleagues) by walking around, making introductions (to department heads), learning the local lore (politics), and seeing what resources are available (equipment and expertise in the system) (Thompson, 1999).

FROM OUR EXPERIENCE

Be thrilled about the job, but don't see it through rose-colored glasses. Be keen, but be objective.

NATURAL REACTIONS

Taking on a new role is a bit like riding on a roller coaster—it is all up and down. Not everything will run smoothly. Seven transition stages for new managers of volunteers equally relate to the experiences of middle managers.

1. *First stage: Immobilization.* The new supervisor feels overwhelmed by the changes. This may be typified by the thought: "This job is a lot bigger than I thought. Everyone is making demands. How can I possibly do everything?"
2. *Second stage: Denial of change.* This phase allows the individual time to regroup and fully comprehend the change. "This job is not so different from my other job. Let's see, first I'll take care of this and then I'll begin to work on that."

3. *Third stage: Depression.* Awareness sets in regarding the magnitude of the changes that must be made in one's habits, customs, relationships, etc. "Why did I ever leave my other job? I wish I could afford to quit. I hate my job!"

4. *Fourth stage: Acceptance of reality.* Feelings of optimism return and the person is ready to let go of the past. "Maybe this isn't so bad. Forget about that old job. I'm doing fine."

5. *Fifth stage: Testing.* This is a time of trying out new behaviors and ways of coping with the new situation. "If I meet with staff every Thursday and try this schedule, I think I can manage."

6. *Sixth stage: Search for meanings.* Concern shifts to trying to understand both how and why things are different now. "Now I feel comfortable in this job. It is different but not really that bad."

7. *Seventh stage: Internalization.* In this final stage, the new supervisor incorporates the new meanings into behavior. "I like my job and I'm good at what I do." (Baldwin, Wilkinson, and Barkley, 2000: 25–26)

Strategies to Get You from Stage 1 to 7

IMMOBILIZATION

When you feel overwhelmed, the best antidote is to take action.

1. Remember you have information at hand that will be useful in making sense of the department, the organization, and your responsibilities. Use it, but remember that reading it is not a substitute for action.

2. Think about the different expectations people will have. In general, there are two schools of thought about new managers. On one hand, they are expected to make an early impact; on the other, they need to take a longer-term view to plan strategies with their team. One way to meet both expectations is to look for small gains from speedy and effective action, and start thinking about the strategy which will make you better informed when you work with your staff. Treat the early days like a honeymoon and get to know the organization and the people in it. And remember all parties will be on their very best behavior.

3. Talk with your manager about the ways that they prefer to work with their team. Talk with them about their expectations, get copies of any vital planning documents, and find out their vision for your department and the service. What do they see as its strengths and weaknesses? Ask questions and be proactive without being too eager.

4. Bring the people you are managing together for a short meeting and briefly introduce yourself. Indicate you will be seeing them for one-on-one meetings. Make some general remarks about your role—but don't tie yourself down with promises. Getting to know your team quickly as individuals is vital, and you may or may not have access to their personal files. If you do, then the last set of performance appraisals will provide some background information—but you will need to make your own judgment

at a later date. You need to know what makes each member of the team tick, so make appointments for those one-on-one interviews. Fifteen minutes for each should be sufficient. Keep the discussion general—it is really a way to start to get to know individuals, and for them to meet you. Do this as soon as possible.

5. Have a second general meeting of the whole team when the individual sessions have taken place. Set down your broad objectives, expectations, and preferred ways of working. There will need to be adjustments on both sides, and the sooner this is done, the better.

CHECKLIST FOR A FIRST GENERAL MEETING

- Determine the best time for the majority of the team, and set start and finish times. Thirty minutes should be long enough.
- Schedule more than one meeting if necessary. If shifts are worked, treat each group equally.
- Set your objective for the meeting—what messages/feedback should be conveyed at this stage?
- Have only two or three points on the agenda to allow for feedback.
- Check the room.
- Have a flipchart and marker to hand in case you need it.
- Appoint a minute-taker before the meeting.
- Chair with friendly confidence (even if you are not feeling so confident).
- Manage the time to get through the points and allow for questions.
- Review the outcome of each point to help the minute-taker.
- Get the minutes out quickly via an Intranet if all members of the team have access, or on paper if they do not.

---

6. If a formal induction program to the organization is offered, seize it. Getting to know other newcomers helps to develop a network that can stretch across the organization. It is time well spent.

7. Remember the following advice, which we can endorse from our experience:
   1. You supervise the people in your unit. You don't own them.
   2. Everyone in your unit will be better at something than you are.
   3. Don't confuse your goals with the process of attaining them.
   4. Remember that procedures exist to help people be effective.
   5. Invert the table of organization: act as if employees are bosses.
   6. Act as if bosses are employees.
   7. Not every problem needs to be solved—at least not right away.

8. Sometimes doing the supervisor's job well just means not doing it badly.
9. Doing your job well is not enough—you must also appear to do it well.
10. Save your supervisor from being surprised especially when the news is bad.
11. Don't be a snitch.
12. Never put anything in writing that you couldn't live with if you found it tacked on your office door.
12. Don't take your good employees for granted

(Sowards, 1999)

DENIAL OF CHANGE

Now you need to get organized—and move further down the track.

1. After the first general meeting, schedule time to check through files relating to the department about financial matters, when the next accreditation or performance review is due, etc. In earlier times, paper files indicated the contacts a manager had. Today they are often replaced by phone calls and e-mails, and vital information may be lost. Hopefully you will have been able to talk with your predecessor about vital contacts that may not have been documented.

2. Talk with users—you have enough information at hand to be able to do so with a degree of confidence. It pays dividends to make contact with them in the early days to get a sense of how they are feeling about the service. The front line staff will be able to identify regular users and introduce you. Talking with them will illuminate the data that the system collects about users. Getting personal reactions in the form of, hopefully, a warm smile, tells so much more. Many services have "comments books," suggestion boxes, complaint forms, or other ways to collect feedback. Check these out to identify the problems users have found.

3. Start networking with other managers in the immediate department and in related departments. Depending on the type of organization, you may need to set a time to meet them in their offices, or there may be a place where everyone in the organization has coffee or lunch and an informal chat is possible. And there is also the water cooler! Building working relationships across the organization provides essential political information and allies.

Research indicates that people with strong personal networks are more satisfied in their jobs and stay longer at their organizations than employees with weak networks. Research also indicates that most of the real work in most organizations is done informally, and managing the networks can present problems. The researchers suggest that social network analysis can be used to map out relationships, and they describe four roles that can be identified to help to turn ineffective informal networks into productive ones.

- The first person to stand out in a network will be the *central connector,* the person everyone talks to the most.
- The *boundary spanner* is like a roving ambassador who serves as the eyes and ears of the group.
- The *information broker* connects the various sub networks in the organization.
- The *peripheral specialist* is an outsider who has specific kinds of information or technical skills that are passed on to other members of the group as needed. (Cross and Prusak, 2002)

4. Check the filing system and the records management policies and procedures and follow them from the start. Regularly file and weed out electronic documents that do not need to be retained.

DEPRESSION

You have to get out of the trough quickly—for the benefit of your team and yourself. It is make or break time.

1. Don't procrastinate—the easiest way out at this stage. The job that gets put off seems so simple when it has actually been completed! Procrastination, or "it needs just a little more thought," quickly transforms a job into an impossible task.
2. Make sure that you, and your team, have a win. Every new manager generally has a honeymoon period in which reasonable requests may be granted by senior management. Some possibilities will emerge from the interviews that will benefit the team as a whole.
3. Sit back and check out your new office. Are you feeling comfortable? What might have suited the former position holder might not suit you. Check the ergonomics—the height of the desk, size of the chair, position of the keyboards and monitor, wrist rests, etc. How is the desk positioned? It should face the door, so that you can see people coming toward you. Having your back to people can mean that they won't want to interrupt you, and you won't see them coming. If it can't be avoided, use a mirror. If you are in an open plan office, having a desk that faces someone else is distracting—plants can make a natural barrier.
4. Keep clutter off the desk surface and only retain the items you use every day—pens, notepad, etc. Have an in and an out tray. Pending trays grow full and items stay pending. If you want to personalize the desk have just one photograph, an object, or a picture on the wall. Personalization can also come with your choice of a theme and screensaver on your personal computer.
5. Extend your network—both within and outside the organization. Go to a professional meeting.
6. Keep your depression to yourself—and don't make public comparisons with your last job.

Acceptance of Reality

This is the stage where you really start to move.

1. Continue to look at how you have organized your work as the workload increases. There are ways to help to reduce it. Work out your best time, when energy levels are high, and use this for the more complex tasks, and use other times for less-demanding tasks. Break up large tasks into smaller ones, setting a timetable for completion for the whole task—and keep to it.
2. Check the in tray and e-mail twice a day—at the start of the day and after midafternoon so that urgent matters can be attended to. Keep phone calls short and publicize times when you are happy for people to drop by. Sometimes you'll need not to be disturbed, so get an amusing card to hang on the door to give this message.
3. Use of a diary or planner can be very important, especially since you may not have support from a secretary or personal assistant at this level. You have a choice of systems:

   - automatic alert using your personal computer
   - PDA (personal digital assistant)
   - conventional desk diary that fits into a briefcase
   - Filofax, Day Runner, or similar system

   Choose the system that works for you—and use it!

4. Keep a hardback legal-size notebook as a handy and permanent way of making notes at a meeting. It acts as a reminder of what you need to do. And sometimes minutes of meetings may not be accurate. Watch how TV reporters and public servants use them as a record. They can be very useful at a later date.
5. Check that the e-mail system is set up so that you can access it at home. Put passwords in the diary that travels with you for external databases that you may need to access remotely.
6. Continue networking. It is easy to become too involved with matters in the immediate work group.
7. See what's happening across the organization. Join committees, go to work-related social events, and become visible in the local community.

Testing

Now you need to extend your people skills.

1. Learn to delegate. The tasks will begin to mount up, but you should have a clear idea of their priorities, so identify what can be delegated and to whom. Give clear instructions, ensure they have been understood, set a deadline or reporting system, and keep a friendly eye on progress. Don't accept tasks that others should be doing.
2. Practice "management by walkabout." This provides a way to keep an unobtrusive eye on delegated staff, see whether the team is working well, and keep in touch with users.

3. Set up regular meetings—with the team and your manager. Make the meetings short but productive. Information organizations generally work shifts, so meetings become important as a way for people to know what is happening across the department and in the wider organization—that might affect them. If a separate meeting is not organized for those not on duty when the meeting is held, they must be informed of what will be discussed and the outcomes so that they can offer their thoughts via a third party. You also need feedback on emerging problems or concerns—from both your team and management—and on achievements.

4. Handling difficult people is the downside of moving into a management role, and is probably something you would prefer not to have to deal with. When a new boss appears, sometimes a member of the team tries to challenge them—test their patience and knowledge, hide information, and behave in a way that may be disruptive.

Before taking action, stop to consider:

- What damage can the behavior cause?
- Why might it be happening? Consider the dynamics of the team. Might there be personal reasons?
- Can you get information in confidence from a trusted person outside the team? This can indicate whether this is a long-standing or new problem.
- What are the options for handling the situation?

Talk to the difficult person in an informal way and try to understand the reasons for their behavior. Don't get to the point of being annoyed. Set a time when you know you are at your best. Be a good listener and ask questions. Gather facts, be objective, and set a time for a review of the situation. If matters are not resolved on review, then it may be necessary to invoke the organization's disciplinary procedure—but this will involve other people and might escalate the problem. Whatever action you choose to take, don't let the disruptive behavior continue, especially if it is a challenge to you as a manager. Don't overreact. Take a long walk to release tension. Remember that members of the team and your boss will observe the way you are handling the problem—be fair, be friendly, and don't get upset.

SEARCH FOR MEANINGS

At this stage, you should be learning to trust your judgment and developing an understanding of the organizational and professional politics.

1. *Use your creativity and intuition.* Taking decisive action can be scary in the early days. But work on two attributes you have—creativity and intuition—and remember that making decisions and taking action do not only depend on having numbers in front of you. The numbers can help, but can be augmented through the use of creativity and intuition.

2. *Be open to new ideas.* At first it is easy to be concerned about making mistakes, looking foolish, breaking with tradition, taking a risk, stepping out

of line, or being criticized. But these can be barriers to thinking creatively about a problem, about planning, or about change. To counter the negative views, be open to new ideas, ask why, become more curious, believe that it can be accomplished, stretch your mind, and, above all, make time to think.

3. *Trust your judgment.* This is an intuitive inner process that we find difficult to explain, for it is the action of the brain analyzing information faster than we understand. For that reason, intuition can be undervalued and we can be wary of using it—rather like our feelings about creativity.

4. *Think before putting creativity and intuition into action.* Make sure the idea isn't stupid. An effective use of intuition and creativity requires self-awareness, confidence, and experience before it becomes thinking out of the box.

5. *Develop your political skills.* Political skills enable managers to negotiate, obtain resources, tolerate ambiguity, be sensitive to people and situations, be flexible, and be restrained. They can help you gain some power in the wider organization, have control over some resources, become indispensable, and influence decisions. Your goals are more easily achieved through the assistance of allies and friends.

6. *Analyze the power structure.* Every organization has its own politics. There will be a power base—and sometimes it does not reside at the top. Rivalry may exist between departments or sections. Take an anthropological approach and identify the "fiefdoms" and "the tribes" and learn their languages, customs, and practices.

7. *Identify the external political forces.* Who are the movers and shakers out in the user community and in the funding agencies? What role does the local branch of the professional body play in the development of local services? How far does the local professional body get involved with regional, national, and even international professional politics?

8. The political tactics that win arguments and hence resources are:

- using objective criteria in formulating arguments;
- building alliances;
- bringing in people who could be affected by decisions, but who might not otherwise be in the loop;
- involving outside experts;
- learning the skills of conflict resolution; and
- marketing the service to users—they are the key allies.

But don't step outside your tested level of political competence. Learn about the organizational agenda, who pulls the strings, and how to work cooperatively. Go slowly, and remember—Machiavelli was a librarian, but it takes a little time to develop political skills!

INTERNALIZATION

In this final stage there is recognition that the job is good, and you are doing fine! But there are some points to watch.

1. *Strike a balance between work and home life.* Living in an age of increasing pressures can make this a challenge. In the early days, it is all too easy to forget that there is another side to life and feel that "just another couple of hours will get this out of the way," and the briefcase and laptop go home. From painful experience we can safely say that this is not a good idea. Getting away helps to refresh the mind and is likely to promote creative thinking. Meeting other people promotes the social skills.

   - Don't linger in the office or work late—get away.
   - Do something else in the evenings to help you relax.
   - Don't go in to the office on scheduled days off—unless there is a real emergency.
   - Take all your annual leave and plan a holiday—it is something to look forward to.
   - Don't work all the time at conferences—do the social program and see something of the town.

2. *Identify stress and work to relieve it.* Managers experience pressure points. Research has identified those that should be acted upon in order to survive and thrive in today's pressurized work environment. In general, it was found that managers enjoy their work and feel challenged, but do not always have the resources they need to do their jobs, and frequently take the strain upon themselves. The highest pressures come from:
   - constant interruptions
   - time pressures and interruptions
   - poor internal communications
   - lack of support
   - poor senior management
   - too many internal meetings
   - office politics
   - handling change
   - securing the right information
   - keeping up with e-mails (Wheatley, 2000)

RECOGNIZE SIGNS OF ROADBLOCKS

We all meet roadblocks in handling new responsibilities. We have high hopes of what we can achieve, and know that others hold those expectations too—especially new colleagues. There are signs that need to be recognized, and actions that need to be taken. Watch out for the following signs.

Feeling insecure—It can be difficult to ask for help when you feel overwhelmed, unloved, and unsure if you are up to the job. If nothing is done, stress builds up, trust breaks down, it spreads to the team, and the service suffers. Remember that you are still new to the management game and still learning. You can't master all the new skills at once—it takes time. Don't be scared to share a problem, and do it with a smile on your face!

Failing to delegate effectively—New managers find it hard to delegate for fear of loosing face, don't yet know staff well enough to trust their skills and judgment, and feel they shouldn't overload the team. New managers need to build trust in their staff, help others achieve, and delegate so they don't work themselves into the ground. If they fail to do so, the service will slowly grind to a halt—and users will suffer.

Focusing too much on the nitty-gritty and losing the big picture—you have to make time to think ahead, plan, and implement. Effective delegation frees time for those tasks only the manager should be doing.

Failing to address problems that affect the performance of the service—The needs of the users are paramount. Don't wait too long to take action, but allow just enough time for others to take effective action.

Needing to check with the boss—You must maintain a dialogue. Bosses are always busy, but you must make them schedule time to pass on to you the information that floats in the ether of the organization. You need to know what your role is, what they expect, in which directions they want to move their department, and, more importantly, in what directions your own thoughts are moving. Hopefully your immediate boss will be working at the same site; but if not, make time to go and visit them, or invite them to your department. In the latter situation, it is easy for communication to falter—don't let this happen.

ENSURE THAT YOU

- understand the way your role has changed—it's not only about personal achievement, but also helping others to achieve;
- have clarification from your boss of his or her expectations;
- know your responsibilities and accountability—where they begin and end;
- recognize if insecurity or stress is creeping up on you—this makes it difficult to ask for help or advice;
- delegate;
- focus on the big picture and the longer term rather than placing total concentration on the immediate tasks;
- act quickly if something or someone is not performing up to scratch;
- communicate effectively up and down and sideways in the organization;
- maintain visibility;
- listen to advice;
- allocate time for reading and thinking; and
- have an outside interest

OUR CHECKLIST FOR SUCCESS

- Never, never forget that the user is the only reason the service exists.

- Be enthusiastic.
- Accept change as the norm.
- Be aware of how little you know about the job in the early days.
- Look after yourself.
- Make yourself feel good.
- Nurture your sense of humor—a smile and a laugh is always welcome when the going gets tough.
- Have a shared vision and establish ways to achieve it.
- Develop explicit values for the service.
- Motivate your team.
- Demonstrate trust in the team.
- Set high standards for the team and help others to develop.
- Remember that older or longer-standing members of the team may have useful experience to offer.
- Be aware that mistakes and failures will happen; demonstrate that you learn from the experience.
- Hold to high ethical standards.
- Never stop learning.
- Give and receive information.
- Establish a good working relationship with your boss.
- Accept advice and tips from more senior colleagues.
- Build networks across the organization, the user community, and the profession.
- Remember that management by walkabout pays dividends.
- Know when to move on.

We end with a quote from Steven Covey, author of *The Seven Habits of Highly Effective People*:

"Managers need to genuinely listen to people, seek to understand them and mentor them. They need to demonstrate respect, and communicate people's worth and potential so clearly that they come to see it in themselves—which is the true essence of leadership."

AFTER READING THIS CHAPTER YOU SHOULD BE AWARE:

- that you will gain experience and skills that shape your career development.
- that there are many challenges and opportunities offered to middle managers today.
- that careful preparation is a sound investment.
- that it is important to know yourself—both your strengths and weaknesses.
- that you need to make a good first impression.
- that being organized is important.
- that there are potential pressure points.
- that there are specific roadblocks you may hit.

REFERENCES

Baldwin, David A., Frances C. Wilkinson, and Daniel C. Barkley. 2000. *Effective Management of Student Employment.* Englewood, Colo.: Libraries Unlimited..

Covey, Stephen. 2001. "Principles Hold Key to Leadership Success." *Professional Manager* 11 (5): 42.

Cross, Rob, and Laurence Prusak. 2002. "The People Who Make Organizations Go—Or Stop." *Harvard Business Review* 80 (6): 104-112.

Dulewicz, Vic, and Malcolm Higgs. 2002. *Making Sense of Emotional Intelligence.* London: NFER-Nelson.

Goleman, Daniel. 1995. *Emotional Intelligence.* New York: Bantam Books.

Gulick, Luther H., and Lyndall F. Urwick, eds. 1937. *Papers on the Science of Administration.* New York: Institute of Public Administration, Columbia University.

Hill, Linda H. 2003. *Becoming a Manager: Mastery of a New Identity.* Boston: Harvard Business School Press.

Huy, Quy Nguyen. 2001. "In Praise of Middle Managers." *Harvard Business Review* 79 (1): 73-79.

Keirsey, David. 1998. *Please Understand Me II.* Del Mar, Calif.: Prometheus Nemesis Book Company.

Sowards, Steven W. 1999. "Observations of a First-year Middle Manager: Thirteen Tips That Can Save You." *College and Research Libraries News* 60 (7), 523-525, 541.

Stettner, Morey. 2000. *Skills for New Managers.* New York: McGraw-Hill

Thompson, Susan. 1999. "Riding Into Uncharted Territory: The New Systems Librarian." *Computers in Libraries* 19 (3): 14-16.

Watkins, Michael. 2003. *Take Charge: Success Strategies for New Leaders.* Boston: Harvard Business School Press.

Wheatley, Ruth. 2000. *Taking the Strain: A Survey of Managers and Workplace Stress.* London: Institute of Management.

Launching Pad

Ashkanasy, Neal M., and Catherine S. Daus. 2002. "Emotion in the Workplace: The New Challenge for Managers." *The Academy of Management Executive* 16 (1): 76-86.

Bluh, Pamela. 1997. "Tips for the Aspiring Author." *Library Administration and Management* 11 (1): 9-10.

Cross, Rob, and Lawrence Prusak. 2002. "The People Who Make Organizations Go—Or Stop." *Harvard Business Review* 80 (6): 105-112.

Di Vecchio, Jerry. 1998. "Transforming an Oral Presentation for Publication." *Library Administration and Management* 12 (3): 138-141.

Giesecke, Joan. 1998. "Preparing Research for Publication." *Library Administration and Management* 12 (3): 134-137.

Goleman, Daniel, Richard Boyatzis, and Annie McKee. 2002. *Primal Leadership: Realizing the Power of Emotional Intelligence.* Boston: Harvard Business School Press.

Golian, Linda M., and Rebecca Donlan. 2001. "The ACRL/Harvard Leadership Institute." *College and Research Libraries News* 62 (11): 1069-1072.

Jay, Ros. 2001. *Fast Thinking: Flying Start.* London: Pearson Education.

Kamp, Di. 1999. *The 21st Century Manager: Future-Focused Skills for the Next Millennium.* Dover, N.H.: Kogan Page.

Quy, Nguyen. 2002. "Emotional Balancing or Organizational Continuity and Radical Change: The Contribution of Middle Managers." *Administrative Science Quarterly* 47 (1): 31-69.

Todaro, Julie. 2001. "The Truth Is Out There: What's a New Manager to Do?" *Library Administration and Management* 15 (4): 249-251.

Walker, Carol. 2002. "Saving Your Rookie Managers." *Harvard Business Review* 80 (4): 97-102.

3: ANALYZING THE INTERNAL OPERATING ENVIRONMENT

"People do not mind being in a rocking boat so much if they know where it is going and it is somewhere they want to go."

IN THIS CHAPTER YOU'LL DISCOVER:

- how to understand the organizational culture
- the characteristics of the organizational culture in which information professionals work
- how to diagnose the organizational climate
- that local practices exist
- about the process of change and how to manage it
- the success factors for change projects
- that creating a vision is vital
- that values, morals, and ethics are of increasing importance

ORGANIZATIONAL CULTURE

One factor in achieving initial success for any new manager is to understand the organizational culture in which they have to operate. They must do this as quickly as possible. Each organization, in every sector, has its own unique ways of doing things.

This is one of the trickiest issues that we all face when moving between organizations, or even different departments in the same organization. But gaining this understanding is important, because:

- understanding the culture increases managerial effectiveness
- creating an appropriate organizational culture is a key to organizational effectiveness
- changing a culture is hard—but it has to change over time

Every organization strives to increase its effectiveness, which in turn helps it to be become more competitive. This holds for both the private and the public sector. All organizations, particularly those in the fast-moving information professions, have to be able to adapt to change as quickly and painlessly as possible.

> **REMEMBER**
>
> The examples of change outlined in chapter 1.

The organizational culture, sometimes labeled the corporate culture, determines the way in which management operates at the macro level (for example, by choosing to collaborate with other services) or at the micro level (for example, by introducing flexible working policies to enable staff achieve a work/life balance).

> **DEFINITION**
>
> **Organizational culture**
>
> "A complex set of values, assumptions and beliefs that defines the ways in which a firm conducts its business" (Pettigrew, 1990).

The problem that a newcomer faces can be seen in the definition above—culture is implicit, rather than explicit. It is generally conveyed by word of mouth and actions. Trying to come to grips with it quickly is not easy. Two other writers expand Pettigrew's definition and indicate why the challenge arises.

Hofstede writes extensively on the subject of culture and describes it metaphorically as "the software of the mind;" culture is "the collective programming of the mind which distinguishes the members of one group or category of people from another" (Hofstede, 1997: 5). Based on our experience, we find it is a good description.

This concept can be extended by looking back at the writings of Schein, who was one of the first of the management gurus to write about organizational culture. He indicates that culture has three dimensions (Schein, 1985).

1. The first dimension consists of the assumptions—the ingrained subconscious views of human nature and social relationships.

   - What is the relationship between staff in different work groups and at different levels in the organization—how do they address each other? Is it formal or informal? Is it by first name, given name, or title?
   - Is team working the norm at all levels of the organization?
   - Does tradition rule—or is change a normal way of working?

2. The second dimension consists of the values—the preferred alternative outcomes, as well as how to achieve them.

   - Which people are involved in decision-making?
   - Are support staff fully involved in the decisions that affect their role and work?
   - Are the professional staffs involved with senior management in decision-making? And is it real involvement, or is it lip service?

- Is independent thought encouraged?
- Does the organization believe in competition or cooperation?

3. The third dimension consists of the artifacts—the rituals, slogans, traditions, and myths.

- What is the dress code?
- Are birthdays celebrated?
- Are there personal possessions on desks, e.g. family photographs?
- Are social events organized which draw in families of staff members?

The organizational culture has four purposes—it:

- gives members of the organization identity;
- provides a collective commitment to the organization;
- builds social stability, which is the extent to which the work environment is perceived to be positive and reinforcing; and
- allows people to make sense of the organization. (Sannwald, 2000)

Identifying the Organizational Culture

Many organizations provide explicit evidence about their culture in the style in which they write their strategic plans.

These documents set out mission and vision statements, objectives, operational plans, and levels of performance which the service is expected to achieve. Strategic plans emerged in the 1960s when Chandler (1962) put forward the idea of applying strategy to business management. It was originally seen as a responsibility of senior management, but today it is understood that strategic planning should involve input from all levels of the organization, so that everyone can "sign on" to the plan.

Central to the plan is the vision statement, which sets out a clear mental picture of the service and how the vision is to be achieved. The mission statement indicates what business the organization is in. A values statement indicates the core values or guiding principles of the organization.

The clues that strategic plans provide about the culture of an organization include evidence that all members of staff have been involved in the process, which can often be seen in the level of detail of the document. The writing and style give other clues, particularly if it appears to have a public relations element which does not always relate to the strategic objectives of the organization or if it goes over the top in making promises to stakeholders. It can be a fascinating exercise to look at the strategic plan in the light of the evidence you have collected about the organization

In the information sector, there are good examples of meaningful statements, and the strategic directions statement given below is one of them. You can almost hear the discussion that took place among the members of staff when it was being prepared. It clearly states NARA's role and how staff operate to meet expectations. At the heart of its mission are the users of its services.

EXAMPLE

The U.S. National Archives and Records Administration

Our Vision, Mission and Values

Vision

The National Archives is not a dusty hoard of ancient history. It is a public trust on which our democracy depends. It enables people to inspect for themselves the record of what government has done. It enables officials and agencies to review their actions and helps citizens hold them accountable. It ensures continuing access to essential evidence that documents:

- the rights of American citizens
- the actions of federal officials
- the national experience

To be effective, we at NARA must do the following:

- determine what evidence is essential for such documentation
- ensure that government creates such evidence
- make it easy for users to access that evidence regardless of where it is, where they are, for as long as needed
- find technologies, techniques, and partners worldwide that can help improve service and hold down cost
- help staff members continuously expand their capability to make the changes necessary to realize the vision.

Mission

NARA ensures, for the citizen and the public servant, for the President and for the Congress and the Courts, ready access to essential evidence.

Values

To succeed in our mission, all of us within NARA need to value the following:

Risk-taking: experiment, take chances, try new ways, learn from mistakes, and be open to change.

Communication: propose ideas, dialogue with others, develop trust, and act openly, honestly, and with integrity.

Commitment: be responsible, accountable, and always willing to learn.

Loyalty: support the mission, help fellow workers, proceed as a team, and recognize that our government and our people truly need our service.

(www.archives.gov/about_us/vision_mission_values.html)

Other documents may provide clues to the culture; for example, annual reports prepared by many services or leaflets prepared for users may be available from the organization's Web site.

Identifying the Nature of the Culture in the Absence of Documentary Evidence

Although most organizations have strategic plans or publish an annual report that yields evidence, some do not, and so other sources have to be considered.

Being interviewed for a new position provides some of the clues. It is easy to forget in the heat of an interview that although you want to give a good account of yourself, the prospective employer is also on trial. A post that seems attractive may not be the right choice if you find out enough about the organizational culture to make you feel that it is not your type of organization.

A BIG MISTAKE

One of the authors heard through the grapevine of a vacancy for a senior appointment that had been a dream for many years. A considerable distance was traveled with enthusiasm for an interview. Less than a day was allocated to talk with the staff, visit a multisite campus, and be interviewed. The post was offered after the interview and the organization requested an early answer, as the search had been in place for some months without success. The salary, benefits, and level of position were appropriate and the post held new challenges. So the offer was accepted. But on taking up the post it was clear that the organizational culture was at the furthest end of the spectrum from that of the previous post. It was a mistake for both parties and the stay was short. Make sure you have all the information required to make a decision, take time, tap into the professional grapevine, and remember that organizations change over time. The organization may not be the one you thought you knew.

We have expanded Mintzberg's (1979) four factors that help to identify the characteristics of an organizational culture:

1. The older the organization, the more formalized its behavior.
   - How long has the service been established? How was the interview conducted—was there a panel sitting behind a desk, or was everyone sitting in comfortable chairs in a circle?
2. The larger the organization, the more formalized its behavior.
   - This may be indicated by the way in which the selection process operates; for example, the role of a human

resource management team acting as an interface between prospective employees and the service or department itself.

3.   The larger the organization, the more elaborate the structure.
- In large organizations, a number of specialists—some of them external—may be drawn into the selection process.

4.   The atmosphere reflects the age of the industry.
- This is clear in newer organizations. The pace is fast; the emphasis is on entrepreneurship, and the atmosphere less formal.

There is another characteristic to look out for—how much the organization takes diversity issues into account. For example, there is a growing literature on the question of the masculinity of organizations—but curiously none on the femininity of organizations. If you are a woman, you may enjoy the challenge of working in an organization where all, or most, of the senior management is male—much depends on their approach at the time of the interview. And conversely, a man might feel uncomfortable working for senior management that is formed mostly of women. Other minority groups should consider this point. Does the organization appear to have selection practices that encourage diversity?

A picture will gradually emerge as a result of your own careful study, the information made available about the parent institution and the service and the comparison of this with what can be gathered from other sources, e.g. the professional press, the organization's Web site, etc.. Some traits will take time to surface, e.g. the way in which decision-making takes place, the myths, folk tales, symbols, language, and staff attitudes, though the professional grapevine may offer some of the myths and folk tales.

Over the years, we have found that it takes a little time to come to grips with the culture when moving between organizations, particularly when there is no strategic planning process in place, and there is limited evidence readily available. There are still very traditional organizations that have yet to move even into the twentieth century. In such a situation, understanding can only develop over a longer period of time through observation, listening to senior management at committee meetings, and discrete conversation with other middle managers. To assume that such an organization operates in the same way as another, even though it may exist in a sector offering similar products and services to others, is to make a serious error of judgment.

Aside from the trait of being able to work effectively within the organization—in gaining resources for their team, for example—middle managers are key drivers in the process of change. Change is never easy to manage, because the organizational culture develops over time. A greater attention is being focused on the relationship between organizational culture and change in the information sector as services join together in collaborative projects. Change is an important factor in achieving success, and becomes of greater importance with the merger of two services. An understanding of the culture of each service and realizing their similarities and differences can help managers to work together more closely.

AN EXAMPLE

There is increasing pressure on services funded by local government to seek ways to make efficient use of resources.

One area in which this has happened is in the merging of a public and a school library to create a community library. To the local authority, it can be seen to make good sense for a building, stock, and staff can be shared—but at the operational level some barriers have to be overcome.

CULTURAL DIFFERENCES

School library	Public library
Focus on learning and information	Focus on recreation and information
Materials selected for young people	Very limited or no censorship
Primary staff qualification in field of education	Primary staff qualification in librarianship
Clearly identified group of users	Users have wide age range and interests
Salaries and conditions aligned with teachers	Salaries and conditions aligned with local government

WORTH CHECKING OUT

Organizational culture

Shepherd, Murray, Virginia Gillham, and Mike Ridley. 1999. "The Truth is in the Details, Lessons in Inter-University Library Collaboration." (*Library Management* 20 (6): 332-337.)

The authors describe successful collaboration between three Canadian university libraries. Management recognized cultural differences between the three systems.

Not All Organizations Are Perfect

Although we always hope to work in a well-managed organization, it doesn't always happen, so we can use clues to identify problem situations. Research has identified four common types of corporate neurosis that are linked to personality problems in chief executives and can sow the seeds of failure. Our experience indicates that these problems can equally be found in the private and the public sectors.

There is the *paranoid organization*, where there is a lack of trust among the managers, power is concentrated in the hands of a few, and people are risk-averse. The compulsive organization, in common with the paranoid, lives by ritual, so that every move is carefully planned and it is difficult to push through new ideas or change.

In *dramatic organizations* there is hyperactivity, impulsiveness, and a dangerously uninhibited personality. Managers live with gambling and avoid facts and details. Power is centralized in one leader who takes bold decisions—and risks.

Depressive organizations are passive and purposeless and operate on boredom, resisting change.

The *schizoid organization* is akin to the depressive. There is apathy at the top and senior managers avoid consultation. Junior managers live by gossip and infighting for recognition and favors that might take them up the ladder. This strategy reflects the political ambitions of people protecting their patches. (Kets de Vries, 1984).

Some similar observations from the information sector have been made by Line (1999). He discusses different types of organizational cultures by using analogues in the animal world, suggesting that the lion, chimpanzee, bonobo, gorilla, hyena, wolf, dog, sheep, cow, and elephant cultures are more desirable than the cat culture. This operates on the principle that cats cannot be made to do anything they do not wish to do. On the other hand, in the sheep culture the head is usually a powerful ram that sees off rival rams in no uncertain manner. But the ram himself has no idea of where his flock is going, and is easily managed by a more or less remote shepherd.

Subcultures

To compound the challenge of understanding the organizational culture, there are a number of subcultures. They can be departmentally based; for example, the cataloguing department within a library. They can also be comprised of specialists who work across departmental boundaries; for example, records managers. Other subcultures revolve around groups emerging from within the organization, which meet together socially; for example, the Music Club. Some staff members may belong to a number of subcultures. A typology for forms of subculture identifies three types:

1. Enhancing—an organizational enclave where the core values of members are more fervent than those held by the dominant culture
2. Orthogonal—an enclave that basically accepts the dominant values of the organization while simultaneously espousing its own occupational values
3. Counter—an enclave that espouses values which directly challenge those of the dominant culture (Martin and Siehel, 1983)

The orthogonal subculture is the one most likely to exist where information professionals work, since they will have a strong allegiance to the values of their professional group, as well as to those of their employer.

One way to look at an organization and its subcultures is to consider it as a series of tribes. Each has its own language (jargon), beliefs (values), history (when and how it started), and experiences (achievements), etc. Taken together they shape the way the members of the "tribe" behave in their daily work and how they react to situations.

> FOR FURTHER THOUGHT
>
> Think about any organization in which you have worked and list the differences that you can identify between the culture in one department and another.
>
> For example, consider the culture of the "front line" staff as compared with the "back room" staff, e.g. those on the enquiry or reception desk with the conservators or cataloguers.

Sometimes communication is not as effective as it should be across the subcultures. They become silos characterized by boundaries that are difficult to cross and inhibit communication. In this situation, information can flow up and down the silo, but not across silos. This results from each of the subcultures, or work teams, having their own jargon, working practices, and social habits. Clues about the existence of silos and the effect that they can have on socialization are found in places such as the staff room and cross-departmental meetings

> REMEMBER
>
> In any large organization there will be a number of subcultures that are departmentally based. Three dimensions are likely to reflect different local assumptions, values, and artifacts. Moving between departments, or working with staff from different departments, involves a steep learning curve about the local culture. Assumptions may not be portable across departmental boundaries.

The Organizational Culture in Which Information Professionals Work

Some generalizations can be made about the organizational culture in which most information professionals work, whether they are based in archives or information, knowledge, or records management services or libraries.

1. It will be service-oriented:

- There will be a user community. Some may come to the physical location of the service, some may use another branch in person, some may access the service virtually, and most probably there will be a mix.

2. It generally operates on behalf, or is part, of a larger organization.

- Even the most senior managers of the service may not make the final decisions about all operational issues, for example the size of the budget.

3. There is a political imperative that it must align with the mission and strategic planning process of the parent organization.

- It cannot exist as a separate entity. It needs the support of the parent organization if it is to survive and flourish. Furthermore, it needs strong representation at the time when strategy is being formulated, plans are being developed, and budgets allocated by the parent organization.

4. Employees are organized into groups that have different levels of staff. Each person in the group has a vital part to play in meeting the needs of every member of the user community.

- Increasingly services introduce specialist posts, e.g. Webmasters. Specialists and support staff work together to provide a seamless service to users.

5. Staff and users work under time and quality pressures that continually increase.

- In the public sector there is increasing pressure to provide quality services at the lowest possible cost to the taxpayer, and these may be subjected to inspection to ensure they meet prescribed standards. In the private sector, pressure increases as information is used as a tool to increase productivity and profit margins.
- As services become more expensive to provide due to the increasing sophistication of technology and the need for highly trained staff, so their staff are required to work more efficiently and effectively.

6. Services are subject to continual change resulting from shifting environmental influences, the changing needs of the parent organization, and emerging technologies.

- Governments exert a major influence beyond the public sector. The private sector is affected through the introduction of policies resulting from, for example, the growth of e-business and e-commerce. Globalization is a major pressure.
- These factors can, and often do, change the direction of the parent organization and how it is going to achieve its goals, driven by new technologies and economic conditions.

ORGANIZATIONAL CLIMATE

The organizational climate is less stable than the organizational culture. It changes more frequently and reflects the ways in which an organization handles its environment and people, for example the decision-making procedures. It emerges from the internal factors that are primarily under the influence of the managers. There is clearly a close relationship between culture and climate, but the difference is that the climate consists essentially of shared perceptions, whereas the culture is made up of shared assumptions (Ashforth, 1985).

DEFINITION

Organizational climate

"is strongly linked to corporate culture in creating the general feeling, and atmosphere of an organization. The climate…can affect aspects such as productivity, creativity and customer focus, and each particular organization needs to create a climate that will facilitate organizational success."

("Corporate Climate," www.economist.com/encyclopedia/)

Identifying six dimensions of climate can expand the definition:

- leadership facilitation and support
- work group cooperation, friendliness, and warmth
- conflict and ambiguity
- professional and organizational esprit
- job challenges, importance, and variety
- mutual trust (Jones and James, 1979)

Clues about the climate will be more visible than clues concerning the culture.

Look for answers to these questions:

1. How easy is it for users to access the service?

- Where is it physically based—at the center of the community?
- Is it physically or virtually accessible to a range of users?
- In serving a virtual community—how clearly is it signposted and accessed from the parent organization's home page on the Internet/Intranet?
- How do the hours of service relate to the potential needs of users?

2. What image does it present?

- Is the layout of the physical service and Web site clear?
- Does it have good signage and directions?
- Is the design attractive and suited to the culture of the organization?

- Are the staffs approachable and friendly—do they smile, have a warm voice, or send e-mails that focus on the receiver?

3. What are the rites and rituals?

- Rites of welcome—how are new users introduced to the service? Is there a follow-up? How are new colleagues initiated into the team?
- Rites of passage—are there leaving parties?
- Rites of renewal—are there "away-days"?
- Rites of integration—are there coffee breaks and plotting?
- Rites of creation—is there major organizational change?

Some management consultants have found that rituals can be a substitute for management, and suggest that there needs to be substance rather than spin.

4. Are the senior members of staff accessible to users and employees?

- Does a helpful receptionist staff an area where their offices are located?
- Are they available by e-mail, and are their addresses publicized?
- Do they respond promptly to phone messages and e-mails?
- Is there a suggestions or complaints mechanism that is simple to use and provides efficient and effective feedback to users?

For newcomers to the staff there are other clues—and one important clue is how decisions are made. Is decision-making participative, consultative and decentralized, or centralized?

Sometimes the clues are evident from the first day when you step across the threshold. You can see the smiles that the staff give, or don't give; the look of the place; how easy it is to identify where you want to get to.

Now try an exercise before continuing.

TRY THIS

Think back to the first time you entered the building in which you work.

- What first springs to mind?
- Who did you first speak with?
- What was it about?
- Were they helpful?
- Did you get lost on the way to your destination?
- What was the "feel" of the place?

Now—how would you sum up that experience—good or bad?

Could anything be done to improve it?

LOCAL PRACTICES

Diagnosing the organizational climate starts to uncover the local ways of doing things—when practices may be not quite "followed by the book." They happen in many workplaces, and the manager has to know how and why they deviate. Does a policy need updating? Were members of staff not consulted when a new practice was introduced? Local practices may be found at the levels of the parent organization, the service as an entity, or a subdepartment, e.g. acquisitions.

The point has been made that the subcultures develop their own rituals and practices over time, and generally have their own "language." This language is based on the technical terminology of the specialists working in the subculture. When this is abbreviated in daily use or when local acronyms emerge, it becomes difficult for newcomers to understand, especially those whose first language is not that spoken in the workplace. Learning this "local language" is vital for survival, but is not always easy, since it clearly won't be written down.

Local rituals and customs can be a tiger trap. Some have already been identified, but here are some other examples:

- During the first few minutes of the working day or shift—is there general conversation, for how long, and what are the usual topics?
- How are newcomers introduced to the team—is it to everyone, and which form of their name is used?
- Are special events celebrated—and who buys the cake or drinks?
- Is there a sundowner, or social gathering, at the end of the week when everyone gets together and reviews events, etc.?
- How much personal news and gossip is exchanged, and with whom?

Each tribe develops its rituals over time, and the longer they have been established, the less easy it is to change them. One of the authors recalls suggesting that the layout of chairs in a crowded staff room be changed to create more openness and space—and meeting great disfavor. The tribe can become inward looking and defensive of change—even if the change is merely the introduction of new members. How the tribe operates can vary between national cultures.

Comparing documents prepared by the parent organization, e.g. a university, and the department identifies the existence of local approaches to management. Do the plans prepared by the department dovetail with the aims of the parent body? Is there reference to the organization's plan, or is the department planning in isolation? Is it inward or outward looking?

Probably the most informative documents to check out are the organizational manuals. Look at the parent organization's human resource management manual; are the procedures that have been set down followed in the department or subdepartment? For example—do the hiring practices reflect the organization's policies on diversity issues? Are staff appraisal procedures followed systematically and correctly?

The departmental staff manual also provides clues. Is it made available to all members of staff? Are the procedures followed as they were set down? Have they been amended, but changes not documented? Are there local practices that are not documented in the staff manual? And the key is—when was each section last reviewed, and how are staff notified of changes?

Discovering any differences between the explicit and the implicit is one of the reasons that the advice offered to new managers, at any level, is to wait a period of time, some say 100 days, before introducing changes. It is better for the incoming manager to find some wins in the shorter term that benefit everyone in the department, and celebrate this success. Read back into the history of the department through minutes of meetings at local and organizational levels. Develop a network that will make the implicit visible—and use eyes and ears.

CONSIDER

The rituals and characteristics of the team in which you are currently working.

EXAMINE

A staff manual and note which procedures are being followed "by the book," and if any are not. Why might this be happening?

IMPROVING THE ORGANIZATIONAL CULTURE AND CLIMATE

As a new manager you want to make an impact, but you should wait a while and learn about some of the contextual issues that affect the culture and climate, which will be helpful in thinking about change.

Managerial Philosophy

Since the organizational climate is determined to a great extent by senior management, the amount and quality of the contact with staff will be important. And this is a two-way process, with the members of staff knowing the boss, and the boss knowing the staff. One of the hallmarks of a good manager is how well the boss knows each member of staff, at least having some idea of where they work and enough awareness to be able to talk with them comfortably.

One of the authors worked for a charismatic vice-chancellor of an Australian university with some 20,000 students and a very large staff. He went out of his way to get to know staff and many students by practicing "management by walkabout," to use an Australian phrase. Staff appreciated it, but it also provided him with information about the way that people were feeling and how the organization was performing. Remember the earlier point about a smiling face? This works both ways—staff who see a smiling, confident boss catch the feeling and they walk tall. All managers need to "go walkabout" or "show the colors" for at least part of their working week, and this includes middle managers.

Managers determine the level of openness of the service by ensuring that everyone working in their departments is aware of what is happening in the wider organization. Managers need to provide feedback from committee meetings, especially those that have been examining resource issues. Staff should be encouraged to join a committee, task force, or working party. This is a way to meet with colleagues in the wider working environment and gather information. And this should be happening at all levels of staff in an open organization. Management also makes decisions…and should be seen to be making decisions and implementing action.

Over the years we have seen how dress codes change in the work environment. This may relate to the age of the organization—or the image of the parent organization. It is the senior managers who set the tone for a formal, semi-formal or informal approach. Some U.S. organizations have "casual Fridays" to provide some balance in tone.

Decision-making and Organizational Politics

Working out how decisions are *really* made when you are a newcomer is not always easy. But you need to know how the system works if you are to gain any influence over it.

The first step is to observe what happens at committee or similar meetings. Meetings can be very revealing, particularly to a newcomer. Some points to look for:

- Who participates in decision-making—and how? Does participation occur in the meetings or in the background?
- Who attends staff and committee meetings? How are these people selected—are they elected by staff in a democratic way, or nominated, and if so, by whom?
- Who speaks at meetings, about what, and in what tone of voice? Does everyone have an opportunity to give his or her viewpoint?
- Who leads the discussion, and what is the body language around the table? Is there a committee "bully"? Are there any "sleepers"?
- Who prepares the agenda, and who can contribute to it? Can any member of the committee ask for matters to be raised, or is there a set agenda?

- Do minutes of meetings reflect the discussion and decisions? Are they accurate?
- Is information conveyed to the staff at large? Who conveys information and decisions, by what means, and how quickly? Is this by word of mouth, by circulation, or an Intranet?
- How frequent are the meetings? Is there a timetable and an agreed interval?

Our experience of consulting indicates that the situation is not always as clear-cut as it should be. Agendas can be "managed." People may attend and contribute to a meeting that they have no right to attend and influence the decisions made. Minutes may not accurately reflect discussion and decisions. Sometimes staff on lower grades may have their ideas and input muted by senior staff—although they are supposed to be working in a democratic situation. Observing meetings is very instructive.

While decisions should be arrived at in a democratic way, this does not always happen. One example is the frustration women have experienced when working at senior levels if discussion on resource issues has taken place in the men's room. In traditional organizations, social events may be a time when the most senior managers "decide" a course of action. As a middle manager you are probably not present at these "meetings," but you need to keep your ear to the ground if you suspect that this is happening. And it is easier to do this in a rural than an urban situation. Remember that most organizations have "leaks"—just find the right place—or person!

These are some ways in which politics can be played within an organization. Certain people gain power—and use it. Learning how the politics is played is very useful—but don't start playing until you have learned all of the rules!

THE PROCESS OF CHANGE

Every newly appointed manager can see things that they feel could be done better; every manager wants to be seen to be managing and to put their mark on the service. But introducing change needs investigation, careful thought, planning, preparation, and implementation.

Change is complex, time-consuming, risky, and can be frustrating, but it has to happen if a service is to move forward. Nothing can remain static: constant change is a way of life that challenges everyone in the workplace. It is a natural process that has existed since the planet was formed. Everyone experiences it throughout his or her personal and work life. Given that it is so common, why is it such an issue, especially for managers? Hundreds of books and articles exist and continue to be produced about how to handle changes in the workplace.

WORTH CHECKING OUT

Change and the Need to Change

In 1995, the *American Archivist* devoted an entire issue to change and the need to change. There is food for thought in the various articles for any information service that carries out archival activities. See: *American Archivist.* 1995. 58 (3).

There are a number of factors that account for this phenomenon, but there are key components that make change particularly challenging today—speed, connectedness, and control. The speed with which change takes place is constantly increasing, especially in the technological area. There is little time for understanding the implications of the change and developing a means of accommodation. At times the changes seem to be contradictory in character, so that there is no workable single accommodation that will address all the changes.

The trend toward globalization affects most aspects of society. The connectedness means that what might appear to be a small change can, in fact, have far-reaching consequences, rather like the ripple created by dropping a stone into a still body of water. Sometimes new managers forget this fact and fail to consult or consider the possible outcomes of "a small change" in their area. Often the results are far more significant in some other operating unit. The need for effective liaison activities is quickly apparent in such cases.

Speed and connectedness translate into a sense of loss of control. There is little or no control over the speed of change and the need to adjust. Connectedness requires one to consider the impact on others, and perhaps to modify the planned change—shared control at best. Sharing managerial control is often a challenge for the most experienced manager, let alone a newcomer. These factors clearly indicate the importance of managing change as effectively as possible. To be successful in bringing about change requires that the manager has:

- a clear vision of what success should look like;
- a commitment of the essential resources and budget;
- a clear and communicated plan of activities; and
- a way to validate the outcomes on completion of the process.

One approach to managing change is the use of organizational development (OD) techniques, which have been widely discussed in management literature for many years (Bennis, 1966; Blake and Mouton, 1968; Fordyce and Weil, 1971; Hanson and Lubin, 1988; French and Bell, 1990; Burke, 1994).

DEFINITION

Organizational development

"…is a planned effort to help people work and live together more effectively and productively over time, in their organization."

(Hanson and Lubin, 1995: 28)

It is a method for helping managers improve organizational performance in either a traditional or team setting, and often employs a consultant to facilitate the change process. The programs can involve team building, methods for handling change, conflict resolution, etc.—anything that will help people in the workplace become more effective. While the consultant assists in program development, may provide training, facilitate discussions, and act as something of a mediator, at the end of the day the consultant leaves and it is up to the people in the organization to make the plan work or fail. Many of the techniques OD employs can be of value in the process of change, without undertaking a full-blown OD project that takes time to develop and implement.

Because of the resources needed for an OD project, including consultants and facilitators, there has been a shift toward the concept of the Learning Organization. The Learning Organization emphasizes the idea that everyone in an organization needs to be involved in the "learning process."

DEFINITION

A Learning Organization

…is one in which "people continually expand their capacity to create the results they truly desire, where new and expansive patterns of thinking are nurtured, where collective aspiration is set free, and where people are continually learning how to learn together."

(Senge, 1990: 3)

One way to understand what a Learning Organization is about is to think about problem solving. Certainly it is essential to solve a problem, but what is most important in the long run is to learn the *process* of solving the problem. When that is combined with a focus on solving the issue or problem rather than placing blame, the manager has a powerful tool, as long as everyone understands the process. Again, this concept is just as useful in the traditional work environment as it is in team settings.

PUTTING IT INTO PRACTICE

Two Illinois public libraries carried out a project to provide staff training and development in using Senge's (1994) principles for a learning organization. Essentially, the principles assist an organization to be better able to handle growth and change. An interesting aspect of the joint effort was that the two service populations were almost complete opposites, especially in terms of population size and economic and educational levels. Des Plaines Public Library's community was primarily blue-collar with a modest income, while the Ela Area Public Library District in Lake Zurich served a relatively small, upper-income community. In spite of the many differences, both libraries faced similar issues of growth and change.

After a half-day workshop and overview of the principles that was attended by all the staff, twenty-one volunteers representing both libraries agreed to meet once a month for seven months for a one-day workshop. Volunteers represented both full and part-time staff and professional and support personnel, as well as a variety of years of library experiences and job categories. The focuses of the workshops were on four main topics—learning and teaching styles, change, empowerment, and risk-taking. Overall, the libraries saw the results as very useful, and the process could be a model for other information services interested in addressing growth, risk-taking, and change.

(Hayes and Baaske, 2000)

Many of the OD and related concepts often come in play when change is taking place. Significant or major changes call for special handling by managers—this applies to both growth as well as reduction situations. The introduction of a new way of handling a process is another example.

One such example from the past ten years is the growing use of OCLC's PromptCat service among academic libraries. (PromptCat is a service that provides almost or completely shelf-ready materials to libraries.) Because this service is offered for materials on order, some of what were the catalog departments' traditional activities are shifted to the acquisitions department. There are two major staff concerns when such a program is under investigation. On the acquisitions department side is the very real issue of additional work without any reduction in other duties/activities. (Generally, there is, in fact, some reduction in other work; because the service is highly dependent upon electronic transfers, there can be substantial reduction in keyboard time.) For cataloging staff the concern is, "Will I be out of a job?" While this is generally unlikely—most librarians have a host of cataloging activities for which there is not enough time or staff—there may be significant reassignments, since certain classes of materials will arrive cataloged and ready for the shelves. Hirshon and Winters (1996) have produced a good book about human factors in outsourcing.

> WORTH CHECKING OUT
>
> **Outsourcing**
>
> Hirshon, Arnold, and Barbara Winters. 1996. *Outsourcing Library Technical Services: A How-To-Do It Manual for Librarians.* New York: Neal-Schuman, in which they devote a chapter to "The Human Factor in Outsourcing."

MANAGING CHANGE

Managers must be able to handle two types of change—planned and imposed.

Planned change is something that the manager's unit or organization wants to happen.

Imposed change normally comes about as a result of external forces, such as government regulations, economic conditions, or technological developments.

Planned Change

Kotter (1999), a prolific writer on change, identified eight steps for handling planned change—urgency, coalition, vision, communication, empowerment, short-term wins, consolidation, and institutionalization. Let's look at a typical change in a library setting: the outsourcing of some of the cataloging activities at the Loyola Marymount University (LMU) using OCLC's PromptCat program, as well as converting an acquisitions approval plan to a blanket order program.

Creating a sense of urgency, or at least a very serious sense of need for change, is the first task. People generally prefer the status quo in the workplace, assuming that the environment is reasonably satisfactory. So it is necessary to get people thinking about and seeing the need to make a change.

For the LMU library technical service staff, there was the nice but problematic situation in which each year there was a double-digit increase in the materials budget. Increases of that type required staff to acquire more items than they had in the previous fiscal year—unspent funds would revert to the parent institution.

However, the increases in funding for materials did not bring with them any increase in staffing. After twelve years of growth at this level, the staff and technology could not keep up with the increases. The backlog of uncataloged materials was overflowing the available shelving and staff were re-boxing materials after they were checked in. Acquisitions personnel were handling and rehandling approval plan items and eventually returning a high percentage of items to the vendor.

Thus, with every passing year, both the acquisitions and cataloging department staff saw a growing problem in their area. In that environment, it was relatively easy to create a sense of urgency to do "something." What that "something" might be was not clear.

For change to take place, it is necessary to have a coalition of individuals who will "champion" the need for change and the plan that is developed. In this case, the coalition consisted of four individuals—the heads of acquisitions, cataloging, and collection development, and the associate university librarian. (Smaller organizations or units do not require large coalitions; two or three individuals usually are sufficient.)

This group explored a number of possibilities, including making a special plea for additional staffing which would basically allow things to remain unchanged in terms of work activities. That option was unworkable and they settled on OCLC's PromptCat as the most viable option. Their challenge then became one of developing a clear vision of what would be done and how this would work.

One of the first issues they had to work out among themselves was any apparent change in workload. For example, there were some activities that cataloging had done that other PromptCat users typically moved to the acquisitions unit. Essentially they realized that they would need to "sell" the change to their staff, making it necessary to identify some benefit for all the parties. They also needed to reassure cataloging department staff that there would be no loss of position; given the unit's workload, this was not a significant challenge.

Once they developed a definite vision of what they wanted to do, they had to spend a considerable amount of time communicating that vision to everyone in the library, not just staff in technical services. Clearly PromptCat would be a significant change, especially since the library would convert its approval plan into a blanket order plan.

The group employed a variety of methods to communicate their vision and sell the idea. Several issues of the staff newsletter contained discussions of the issues and potential benefits of the library outsourcing some of the cataloging of certain types of material. (For several months the staff meeting agenda listed PromptCat as a topic for discussion. It is important to note that this change also would have an impact on how faculty and librarians would or would not be involved in the selection of materials to be covered in the program.) Naturally there were meetings of the department staffs to talk about the pros and cons of the proposal. The major "sales pitch" was to arrange for anyone interested to visit two local libraries using PromptCat in order to see it in action and to ask questions.

Meetings, one-on-one discussions, site visits, and so forth, normally identify issues, challenges, barriers, etc. to implementing a change. Change leaders must empower individuals to remove barriers and/or address the concerns identified, or do so themselves.

The change leaders had two major issues/concerns to address: the quality of the outsourced cataloging and the perception that the acquisitions department was being asked to take on some of the cataloging department's responsibilities. In both cases, the leaders decided to let the staff explore the concerns and make recommendations. Both departments undertook a small study, which achieved results that satisfied the staff and allowed the project to move forward.

In the long run, the library hopes to outsource all its copy cataloging: however, starting with a full-blown program (approximately 11,000 items per year) could be very problematic. Rather, it started on a smaller scale, in hopes of some early short-term wins. The conversion of the approval plan to blanket order only involved 3,500 to 4,500 items. Once the profiles for the library's automation system, the approval vendors, and OCLC were successfully completed, the program moved ahead with significant staff satisfaction. Plans went forward in mid-2002 for the addition of standing orders to the program.

Essentially, the staff is in the process of consolidating the program. The entire library staff views the program as a success and is eager to see it expand. Faculty is still trying to understand how the program works, despite library efforts to communicate with department chairs and faculty library liaison representatives. These are busy people and it often is the case that the library must wait for the individual to need the information before it can be certain the person actually understands the situation/issue.

Over the next several years, the library and its end users will institutionalize the program when all the copy cataloging items are part of the program. The blanket order aspect is institutionalized for the staff, as they now talk about how much time and effort they save with the program and when they are going to add other items to the program.

The entire change process will have taken three plus years. That may seem like a long time, and, compared to many organizational change processes, it is; however, because Kotter's steps were followed, the change has been accepted. Staff members who were skeptical and/or worried about the program are now the advocates for expanding the program.

WORTH CHECKING OUT

Change and innovation

Clayton, Peter. 1997. *The Implementation of Organizational Innovation*. New York: Academic Press.

Holman, Peggy and Tom Devane, eds. 1999. *The Change Handbook: Group Methods for Shaping the Future*. San Francisco: Berrett-Kochlor.

Imposed change

Changes imposed from outside the unit or organization present a different set of challenges for the manager. Often the manager has no or little control over how or when the change will occur. Sometimes the outside change agent will follow the steps outlined above, but all too frequently it falls to the manager to determine how to institute the required change(s)— often with a very narrow timeline for implementation. No matter what the changes are, there will be some type of impact on the staff and concerns will be generated. Addressing the concerns requires some understanding of the psychological aspects of the change situation at hand.

Restructuring, downsizing, hiring freezes, and salary changes, as well as many other situations, normally create four psychological stages in the staff:

- disbelief and denial;
- anger, rage, and resentment;
- emotional bargaining—anger or depression; and finally
- acceptance. (Mirvis, 1985: 67)

During the first stage, there is often shock that changes might/will take place. It is also a time when there is a belief that the changes cannot, or will not, work, and when some staff may actively resist the changes. Having the staff involved and allowing them maximum input will help, as will providing honest and forthright explanations about what is involved in the study or proposed change(s). Indicating the benefits is also helpful. If there will be staff reductions, be forthright about it. Trying to hide such facts until later will cost the manager great credibility with the staff.

Stage two sees the denial/shock usually shifting to anger, especially if there are to be staff reductions that require layoffs rather than "normal attrition." That anger normally focuses on the immediate supervisor, rather than the actual person or factor making the changes necessary.

During the third stage, staff likely to be impacted by the change start thinking about their options. Some consider resigning, and occasionally do so, before there is any final decision—often these are the most qualified individuals who would be less likely to lose their positions. They find it easy to get other jobs. Others become depressed and the quality of their work and productivity declines.

Eventually there is an acceptance that what seemed unthinkable will in fact take place.

FOR FURTHER THOUGHT

What are some other types of changes that would generate the reactions discussed above?

It is easy to understand that some members of staff, and possibly users, will experience stress during the process of change. Twelve of the most common workplace "stressors" have been identified. The environment of rapid and frequent change in which information professionals are working today has the potential to cause all twelve factors to arise from time to time. They are:

- loss of identity as organizational size changes
- lack of information, poor/inconsistent communication
- fear of job loss or demotion

- possible transfer/relocation
- loss or reduced power, status, prestige
- disrupted/uncertain career path
- change in rules, regulations, procedures, reporting structure
- change in colleagues, supervisors, subordinates
- ambiguous reporting systems, roles, procedures
- devaluation of old skills and expertise
- personality/workplace culture clashes
- increased workload (Cartwright and Cooper, 1997: 34)

Some of the factors are more controllable than others; for example, work-load increases are often difficult to control, at least in the short term. Providing more information than might seem necessary can be very help-ful—"the word" does not always get out as much as you might assume. Keep the communication process open to feedback; make it clear that questions and expressions of concern are welcome. Be as specific as possible about the "whats, whys, whens, and wherefores" of events/projects that may be stress-ful situations. Work at developing a team approach, if not actual work teams. Involving staff in the processes as much as possible helps them have a sense of control over their destiny.

ASSESSING THE POSSIBILITIES FOR CHANGE

Many people do not enjoy change. Some hope that they will wake up the next day and change will go away. Experience tells us that there are many who are enthusiastic about the concept of change, but don't enjoy the reality of living through it. Some members of the team may have experienced many changes in the workplace, such as the introduction of information technolo-gies. In chapter 1 we indicated some of the changes that have taken place in approaches to management since the Baby Boomers entered the professions.

FOR FURTHER THOUGHT

Chapter 1 emphasized the importance of scanning the environ-ment for trends and signals for change. Sometimes useful infor-mation can be found in the speeches or publications of senior managers of the parent organization of the service. One example is the opportunity afforded to public librarians when Roger Kemp (1998), the author of a major text on municipal govern-ment management, examined trends affecting public libraries. His views carry substantial weight with municipal managers, and his list of trends includes many of the topics noted below. The primary difference between the lists is that his focused on trends that have significant financial implications for city managers.

Kemp, Roger. 1999. "A City Manager Looks at Trends Affecting Public Libraries." *Public Libraries* 38 (2): 116-119.

Remember that change happens through people, so assessing people, their experiences, and their attitudes to their work may reduce the risk-taking. It shouldn't stop the process of change, but rather, it should sensitize the manager to the issues that could emerge.

REMEMBER

The points made in chapter 2 about personality types

Here is a checklist for success—or potential failure.

THE ORGANIZATIONAL CULTURE.

- Check back at how the service has developed in recent years. Does change happen regularly, so that it is anticipated and taken for granted by the team?
- Does the parent institution have a record of change, encourage planned programs of change, and have procedures for planning change?
- Is there likely to be cooperation and collaboration with other departments or subdepartments that could assist with the process of change? Have any silos been identified?
- Where does the proposed change fit into the strategic plan for the department and the parent body?

CURRENT WORKLOADS.

- What other projects are on hand, and how much time and energy are required to bring them to successful completion?

THE USERS.

- Changes in the service will affect users and so must align with their needs. Would the change improve the quality of service they receive? Would it save their time? Is it likely to be acceptable?
- Are they comfortable with change through the nature of their own work culture?
- Are they working under such pressure that they won't want another matter to handle? Would it affect their productivity?
- Is the relationship between the users and the team open and friendly?
- In what ways can you communicate easily with all potential users? (For example, using an Intranet, the Internet, or notice boards.) Do you have access to a good graphic design team to create the material explaining the change to users?

- You will need their support and advice, so how much personal support and backing do you have from the next level in the management hierarchy? Then—how much backing do they have from the highest level of management?
- Has senior management indicated that some change is needed? This might have been raised during the recruitment process.
- Or, have you been recruited to bring about change?
- How far will senior management want to get involved in the process?
- What is the argument for change? What benefits will accrue? What are the visible and invisible costs, and how will the change be introduced? These are some of the questions that a report to senior management should answer.

Financial resources.

- Change generally requires expenditure, both visible and invisible; for example, the costs of other tasks not being carried out while new policies or procedures are being introduced. Estimates have to be prepared. What level of resources is likely to be needed?
- Is there adequate funding available that could be allocated to the project? Sometimes services have special funds—e.g. from endowments—or grants may be obtained from external agencies.
- Can a strong case be made to senior management or an external source for project funding?
- Or, can it realistically be implemented using existing resources, perhaps by trimming areas of the budget without detriment to the overall budget?
- What are the financial implications of not making the change? Often this can be calculated. An evaluation and worked examples of the costs of outsourcing and not outsourcing the cataloging of Slavic materials at the Ohio State University provides an example of how this can be done (El-Sherbini, 2002).

TECHNOLOGICAL CHANGE.

- Upgrading technology calls for a large investment that can be a tiger trap. Is the technology and vendor support available locally, particularly for software? What is the situation regarding hardware supply and telecommunications? What are the local costs?
- Do you have a good working relationship with the IT staff of the parent organization and the department?

- Do the senior management of the service and the parent organization have the knowledge and skills to be able to examine the proposal and provide an informed decision?

THE WORK TEAM.

- This is where the banana skin can appear, but if the project meets the guidelines above, you will feel confident, and this feeling will be passed to the team. Does the project pass the test?
- Does the team have a positive vision about its future?
- Which generations do the team members belong to? As people grow older it may be more difficult for them to adapt, as they may have strong organizational/job loyalty. Generally younger team members will welcome, encourage, and embrace change, but they may have lower levels of organizational/job loyalties. What are the reactions likely to be?
- Are there potential and acceptable mentors or change agents?
- Might key members of the team decide to quit?
- Have you considered separately the tenured, contract, and outsourced or telecommuting staff?
- Would the change affect current work practices?
- Will anyone lose responsibility or even his or her post?
- Could any displaced staff be offered another appropriate post?
- How is the labor/trade union or professional body likely to react?
- Is the team willing to discuss issues openly, and compromise when this is appropriate?
- Can time be allocated for staff development and the process of change?
- Do members of the team have a fear of failure?
- How many changes have been implemented in, say, the past two years, and what has been the success rate? Have there been any failures in implementing new policies or procedures? If so, why has this occurred?
- Has the proposed change been tried before and failed, and if so, why? Talk with the supervisor of the section, or look back through departmental reports. If the proposed change has failed in the past, find out why and devise a different approach to take to avoid the loss of trust.

YOURSELF.

- Have you had experience in carrying out successful change programs, and what have you learned from this?
- Have you been a team member when someone else has introduced and implemented a change program, and what did you learn—the good, the bad and the ugly?
- Do you have the skills and understanding needed for the proposed project?

- If you feel you need more training, can this be undertaken?
- Do you have a mentor who can advise you?
- Can you draw on a personal network, both inside and outside the service, to gain experience from others who have introduced similar changes and brought them to a satisfactory conclusion? This is the most effective way to learn about sensitive issues that can surface during the process of change.
- How can you rearrange your work schedules to make time available for managing the process?
- Do you have good working relationships with the team, users, and senior management?
- Do you have the judgment to understand what can be realized?
- Finally—do you have a good sense of humor and a balanced approach to life?

FOR FURTHER THOUGHT

Reflect on your work experience to date and add to the list of points above.

WHAT MIGHT THE TEAM SAY TO YOU?

- If it ain't broken, don't fix it.
- We need more time to investigate.
- The users aren't ready for this yet.
- We tried it a couple of years ago and it didn't work.
- But it means we will have to change everything!
- There's new technology on the horizon; why not wait till then?
- Just because it worked at X doesn't mean it will work here.
- I urge caution.
- It's a brave thought.
- We don't have the time.
- Doesn't this run counter to policy?
- And you could add to the list…but what would be your answers?

Rosbeth Moss Kanter (2001), writing of how to succeed in the digital age, identifies ten reasons why people may resist change.

- The loss of face—will dignity be undermined?
- A loss of control—will decisions be taken out of one's hands? Will there be a power shift?
- Excess uncertainty—not knowing what is coming next, which she likens to the sensation of walking off a cliff.
- Surprise, surprise!—no chance to prepare.

- The "difference effect"—rejecting change because it does not fit existing mental models and is unfamiliar.
- "Can I do it?"—concerns about future competencies; will I still be successful after the change?
- Ripple effects—annoyance at disruption to other activities and interference with unrelated tasks.
- More work—resistance to having additional tasks, new things to learn, and no time to do it all.
- Past resentments—memories of past hostilities or problems that were never resolved.
- Real threats—anger that it will inflict real pain and create clear losers.

Why Change Programs Fail

Now let's return to where we started to examine the process of change. Research indicates that some organizations have been able to adapt to shifting conditions and have a far better future. However, in many situations the outcomes have been disappointing and have resulted in wasted resources and frustrated staff. Observation has identified eight errors in handling change:

1. Allowing too much complacency.
2. Failing to create a sufficiently powerful guiding coalition.
3. Underestimating the power of vision.
4. Undercommunicating the vision by a factor of ten.
5. Permitting obstacles to block the new vision.
6. Failing to create short-term wins.
7. Declaring victory too soon.
8. Not anchoring change in the corporate culture. (Kotter, 1996)

CREATING THE VISION

The need to create a vision has been mentioned several time already—the question is, how to do it? In the past, writers describing the process of change have stressed the value of the participative style of leadership. But as technological and economic change takes place, questions have been raised as to whether this style is either appropriate or effective. What is now being emphasized is the development and communication of a vision by the leader.

This vision must impact on technical, strategic and financial capabilities, and gain the support of the stakeholders. It must create a sense of purpose, urgency, and separation from the past. Managers have to "walk the talk."

In creating the vision, the leader develops and sets down:

- a rationale
- the stakeholder benefits
- values
- performance objectives
- the impact on the organizational structure and processes
- the operating style

Building a vision

- Core ideology provides the glue that holds an organization together through time.
- Core values are an organization's essential tenets.
- Core purpose is a raison d'être, not a goal or business strategy.
- You discover core ideology by looking inside. It has to be authentic. You can't fake it.
- Organizations need an audacious long-term goal to progress toward an envisioned future.
- You must translate the vision from words to pictures with a vivid description of what it will be like to achieve your goal.
- There must be such a big commitment that when people see what the goal will take, there's almost an audible gulp.
- The basic dynamic of visionary organizations is preserving the core and stimulating progress. It is the vision that provides the context.

After Collins and Porras (1996).

Change that happens within the department requires the agreement of the next manager up the hierarchy, but the implementation will be the responsibility of the middle manager. It must take place within the vision and framework agreed by senior management. If all levels have been involved in the process, then it draws upon the thoughts that have emerged from the team to "color in" the departmental plan.

Remember

- No department is an island.
- The alternative to introducing change might be lurching from crisis to crisis and keeping fingers crossed that everything will be OK.
- Change is a constant activity—few, if any, changes would last forever and they need a regular scheduled review.

The management gurus stress the importance of communication and of managers proving that they have a commitment to change. We talk about this in more detail in the next chapter when reviewing organizational responsibilities.

VALUES, MORALS, AND ETHICS

> ### DEFINITIONS
>
> **Values** relate to principles and standards, are based on ethical codes and morals, and may be rooted in national cultures.
>
> **Morals** are concerned with what is right or wrong, and determine the way in which organizations and people behave and react to situations.
>
> **Ethics** consider the way in which moral questions are handled.

Values have become increasingly important as components of an organization's strategic plan. Moral and ethical questions, while always present in the daily work of any professional, assume greater importance depending on events in the external operating environment. While these issues are not always discussed in the professional press, they lie at the core of a professional's beliefs and influence the way they set about their daily work—and particularly the way that they manage. Values, morals, and ethical behavior underpin the work of the middle manager. However, some semantic problems emerge, as there is often a blurring of the differences between values, morals, and ethics. There is a clear relationship, but often it can be difficult to ascertain.

Values

In our discussion of strategic planning, we stressed that everyone should take part in the planning process, and that team involvement in developing the departmental plan is of significant value.

Given below is a sample set of values from the Library and Information Service of Western Australia. The fact that so many know and use the service indicates that the staff really have signed up to the values. They practice what they preach, which is remarkable, for although the service is based in Perth, the state capital, its members are spread across a huge landmass. In addition to a concentration of the population living in Perth and its suburbs, there are tiny diverse communities scattered across the state, some in very remote areas. Each small community has a library, which is supervised by a regional librarian; staff regularly travel to Perth for training and to refresh the book stock, and there is online access to central resources. Having a values statement helps the staff of the service, wherever they are located, to know what the management, funding agency, and users expect of them—and, importantly, what their colleagues expect.

EXAMPLE

Organizational values

Our Values

1. Our clients are the focus of our services, our planning and how we measure our success.
2. We strive for excellence and demonstrate innovation in our work and leadership in our fields.
3. We plan what we do and we do what we planned.
4. We communicate openly and widely with each other and the wider community. We share information fairly and responsibly.
5. We respect our colleagues and treat them with consideration. We listen to each other's point of view and encourage each other's creativity and initiative.
6. We work as teams—with common goals and rewards and with a cooperative responsibility for assessing and improving our services and skills continuously.
7. We make effective and efficient use of the resources we hold in trust in the public interest.

"Our Values." Library and Information Service of Western Australia. 1999-2003. (www.liswa.wa.gov.au/values.html)

Producing a values statement requires good leadership, discussion among everyone on the staff, and a clear understanding of what is involved in turning a set of values into operational policies and practices. The values need to be few in number, consistently applicable in word and deed, and enduring.

The preparation of values statements can sometimes meet difficulties. Experience indicates that conflicts may surface in the value systems of three groups:

- the parent institution
- the professional framework
- the service itself

The priorities that would be preferred by the professionals working within the service might not be shared by the parent organization. This is a situation that would be more likely to occur in the private sector, rather than the public. While information professionals place a high priority on access to information, there are likely to be limitations placed on who can access what in a private company where considerations of confidentiality are paramount. If special libraries are taking part in a cooperative program, there may be restrictions on providing documents or information to other members of the scheme. In some organizations, there may not be equal access to all potential users. Some middle managers may have to walk a fine line in deciding who receives service and the order of priority in which inquiries are handled.

A number of issues emerging in the library sector in recent years have created a renewed interest in professional values, such as the debate over children's access to the Internet and user fees in public libraries. The central or "core" values of libraries have been defined as:

- stewardship
- service
- intellectual freedom
- rationalism
- literacy and learning
- equity of access to recorded knowledge and information
- privacy
- democracy (Gorman, 2000)

Gorman's definition has been reinforced by research conducted by Dole, Hurych, and Koehler (2000), who explored the question of whether there are universal values for librarians. Their review of the literature indicated that authors cited some or all of the following as core professional values:

- intellectual freedom
- protecting library users' right to privacy/confidentiality
- intellectual property rights
- professional neutrality
- preservation of the cultural record
- equity of access

Their international survey indicates that there is a differentiation of values among countries, which they feel results from the need to respond to different social and economic conditions in the developed and developing countries. They report the findings in detail but, taking data from one table, this indicates that for all but students the first priority value of professionals from different sectors of librarianship was service to the user. Sixty two point five percent of the law librarians recorded the highest percentage among professional responders, and after the students came the library school faculty. Apart from service to users, the researchers found that the function of the professional determines the priorities and emphasis of their values. One example is that academic librarians and archivists place great emphasis on preservation records, whereas school librarians and information brokers emphasized information literacy.

The values held by the staff of the service are likely to have developed over time and to reflect the values held by the profession at large. They will probably focus on:

- providing a high level of service to users
- displaying high levels of professionalism
- working as a team
- being involved in decision-making
- having a commitment to making the service even better
- having respect for others
- demonstrating trust
- continuing professional development

However, there may be a divergence of opinion that could emerge from, for example, political or religious views.

In most situations, there is likely to be congruence between the professional and service values, but new managers should be aware that conflicts of opinion can arise, and they require sensitive handling.

Morals

Value statements developed within an organization guide the behavior of the manager by indicating what is seen to be "right" within the organization, for example, by indicating the need to respect colleagues.

But all managers should understand that morals guide their work by forming the basis of their perceptions of right or wrong. Managers must demonstrate that they live up to what is perceived to be correct behavior in the culture in which they are working. We make this comment because moral judgments are influenced by the belief system of an individual, which is culture-dependent. But all managers should act with integrity, impartiality, openness, and honesty, and be accountable for their actions.

These are sound principles, but in practice managers meet situations that challenge their moral viewpoints and standards of behavior. Some of these challenges might be:

- Knowing the dividing line when being offered hospitality or gifts by vendors. Going to a reception or party at a professional conference is acceptable. Allowing the vendor to accept the expenses for attendance at a conference is not acceptable, unless there is agreement from the employer.
- Considering giving benefits or preferment to a user or colleague from the same ethnic, social, or religious group without a sound reason discussed with the employer.
- Deciding what are, and are not, legitimate expense claims—recognizing the "padding" of expenses.
- Withholding vital information when decisions are being made; for example, the performance of a software package, selection of a document supplier, or reduction of staff.
- Telling a "white lie" to a colleague in a tricky situation.

We all believe that we act in an honest and upright way—but face many challenges.

A difficult moral question can arise if information comes to light that indicates that a senior manager, or the organization, has made a decision that results in improper conduct. Clearly, evidence should be gathered before deciding whether whistleblowing is appropriate and before contacting the CEO or going to the relevant professional body or media. The consequences will clearly have serious outcomes for the transgressor, the whistleblower, or both. Managers have been known to resign "on matters of principle"; it is a drastic step but may be required if the manager is uncomfortable in the situation.

Ethics

Most professional associations have prepared codes of conduct, which guide their members in making ethical judgments. Examples are those prepared by the Society of American Archivists (1992) and the American Library Association (1995). The ALA's code of ethics provides a framework to guide ethical decision-making and covers eight points: providing a high level of service; upholding the principles of intellectual freedom; protecting users' rights to privacy; respecting intellectual property rights; treating colleagues with respect; not advancing private interests at the expense of users, colleagues, or employers; distinguishing between personal convictions and professional duties; and striving for excellence. The ALA supports the code by providing additional information on its Web site (www.ala.org). One example is a question and answer page on librarian speech in the workplace. This explanatory statement by the ALA Council provides detailed information and references to external sources, including the codes of other organizations and reviews of legal cases.

WORTH CHECKING OUT

Professional ethics

Iacovino, Livio. 2002. "Ethical Principles and Information Professionals: Theory, Practice and Education." *Australian Academic and Research Libraries* 33 (2): 57-74.

Managers have to make careful judgments on a number of questions beyond the points covered by professional guidelines. For archivists and records managers, one major issue is that of what should be preserved and how records should be held—questions of custody and access. In the corporate sector, concerns have been raised by the case of Enron, where records that should have been retained were shredded. In South Africa, questions of remembering and forgetting under the apartheid system have been discussed (Harris, 2002).

One of the dilemmas that can emerge involves the reviewing of books: the issues of negative and fair reviews, superficial and biased reviews, and timeliness and promptness in providing reviews have been discussed in a special issue of *Journal of Information Ethics* (McCuen, 2002).

The health care sector must consider a number of ethical questions. One of the most serious concerns the death of a healthy volunteer in a drug trial. It might have been avoided if the supervising physician had known the potentially adverse effects. *PubMed*'s online database is only searchable back to 1966; if a more thorough search had been conducted, the death might have been prevented (Perkins, 2001). Patients' rights legislation and information made available on the Web are causes of debate—what information should be freely accessible, and how accurate is that information? (Taylor, 2001)

In services provided for the public at large, ethical questions generally surface as a result of policies and practices concerning the selection of documents, access to and censorship of materials, retention policies, and what questions a reference librarian should be expected to answer.

Ethical questions are likely to take up an increasing amount of the middle manager's time, for the issues continue to change. For example, the digital library has raised issues of user privacy (Sturges, Teng, and Iliffe, 2001). Other questions raised by information technology are reviewed in a special issue of *Library Trends* (Wengart, 2001.)

WORTH CHECKING OUT

The need to reevaluate codes of ethics

David Horn wrote an essay about the need to constantly reevaluate and revise codes of ethics—it is not a matter of doing them once and for all. His thoughts are as timely today as when they first appeared in 1989.

Horn, David E. 1989. "The Development of Ethics in Archival Practice." *American Archivist* 58 (winter): 64-71.

Ethics also influence other areas of the middle manager's responsibilities. Juznic et al. (2001) write about answering ethically disputed questions asked by users of public libraries, including how to commit suicide and necrophilia. They make the point that the reality was that the issue was one of quality, rather than of ethics. Hannabuss (2000) draws attention to the growing commercialization of the information marketplace and the fact that the issues of negligence and liability mean that information professionals must look to a mixture of ethics, law, and self-interest to ensure personal and professional effectiveness—and security.

AFTER READING THIS CHAPTER YOU SHOULD BE AWARE:

- that the organizational culture is implicit rather than explicit…it is shaped by the mission statement, aims, etc.
- that each organization has subcultures, and subcultures have their own language, rituals, etc.
- that the organizational climate is less stable than the organizational culture and reflects the way an organization handles its people, users, and operations.
- that change requires thought and preparation, and not everyone welcomes change.
- that values, morals, and ethics are of increasing importance.

REFERENCES

American Library Association. 1995. Code of Ethics of the American Library Association. Chicago: American Library Association. Available: http://www.ala.org/Content/NavigationMenu/Our_Association/Offices/I ntellectual_Freedom3/Statements_and_Policies/Code_of_Ethics/Code_o f_Ethics.htm.

American Archivist. 1995. 58 (3).

Ashforth, Blake E. 1985. "Climate Formation: Issues and Extensions." *Academy of Management Review* 8: 837-847.

Bennis, Warren. 1966. *Changing Operations.* New York: McGraw-Hill.

Blake, Robert R., and Jan S. Mouton. 1968. *Corporate Excellence Through Grid Organization Development.* Houston, Tex.: Gulf Publishing.

Burke, W. Warner. 1994. *Organizational Development: A Process of Learning and Changing.* 2d ed. Reading, Mass.: Addison-Wesley.

Cartwright, Susan, and Cary Cooper. 1997. *Managing Workplace Stress.* Thousand Oaks, Calif.: Sage Publications.

Chandler, Alfred D., Jr. 1962. *Strategy and Structure.* Cambridge: MIT Press.

Clayton, Peter. 1997. *The Implementation of Organizational Innovation.* New York: Academic Press.

Collins, James C., and Jerry I. Porras. 1996. "Building Your Company's Vision." *Harvard Business Review* 74 (5): 65-77.

Dole, Wanda, Jitka M. Hurych, and Wallace C. Koehler. 2000. "Values for Librarians in the Information Age: An Expanded Examination." *Library Management* 21 (6): 285-297.

El-Sherbini, Magda. 2002. "Outsourcing of Slavic Cataloguing at the Ohio State University Libraries: Evaluation and Cost Analysis." *Library Management* 23 (6 and 7): 325-329.

Fordyce, Jack K., and Raymond Weil. 1971. *Managing With People: A Manager's Handbook on Organization Development Methods.* Reading, Mass.: Addison-Wesley.

French, Wendell, and Cecil Bell. 1990. *Organizational Development: Behavioral Science Interventions for Organizational Improvement.* 4th ed. Englewood Cliffs, N.J.: Prentice-Hall.

Gorman, Michael. 2000. *Our Enduring Values: Librarianship in the 21st Century.* Chicago: American Library Association.

Hannabuss, Stuart. 2000. "Being Negligent and Liable: A Challenge for Information Professionals." *Library Management* 21 (6): 316-329.

Hanson, Philip, and Bernard Lubin. 1988. "Team Building as Group Development." In *Team Building: Blueprints for Productivity and Satisfaction,* edited by W. Brendan Reddy and Kaleel Jamison. San Diego: University Associates.

Hanson, Philip, and Bernard Lubin. 1995. *Answers to Questions Most Frequently Asked about Organizational Development.* Thousand Oaks, Calif.: Sage Publications.

Harris, Verne. 2002. "Contesting Remembering and Forgetting: The Archive of South Africa's Truth and Reconciliation Commission." *Innovation* 24: 1-8.

Hayes, Jan, and Ian Baaske. 2000. "Preparing Staff for the Library of the Future." *Public Libraries* 39 (5): 280-285.

Hirshon, Arnold, and Barbara Winters. 1996. *Outsourcing Library Technical Services: A How-To-Do-It Manual for Librarians.* New York: Neal-Schuman.

Hofstede, Geert. 1997. *Cultures and Organizations: Software of the Mind.* New York: McGraw-Hill.

Holman, Peggy, and Tom Devane, eds. 1999. *The Change Handbook: Group Methods for Shaping the Future.* San Francisco: Berrett-Kochlor.

Horn, David E. 1989. "The Development of Ethics in Archival Practice." *American Archivist* 58 (winter): 64-71.

Iacovino, Livio. 2002. "Ethical Principles and Information Professionals: Theory, Practice and Education." *Australian Academic and Research Libraries* 33 (2): 57-74.

Jones, Alan P., and Larry R. James. 1979. "Psychological Climate: Dimensions and Relationships of Individual and Aggregated Work Environment Perceptions." *Organizational Behavior and Human Performance* 23 (2): 201-250.

Juznic, Primoz, et al. 2001. "Excuse Me, How Do I Commit Suicide? Access to Ethically Disputed Items of Information in Public Libraries." *Library Management* 22 (1/2): 75-79.

Kanter, Rosabeth Moss. 2001. *Evolve! Succeeding in the Digital Culture of Tomorrow.* Boston: Harvard Business School Press.

Kemp, Roger. 1998. *Managing America's Cities: A Handbook for Local Government Productivity.* Jefferson, N.C.: McFarland & Company.

Kemp, Roger. 1999. "A City Manager Looks at Trends Affecting Public Libraries." *Public Libraries* 38 (2): 116-119.

Kets de Vries, Manfred. 1984. *The Neurotic Organization: Diagnosing and Changing Counterproductive Styles of Management.* San Francisco: Jossey-Bass.

Kotter, John P. 1996. *Leading Change.* Boston: Harvard Business School Press.

Kotter, John P. 1999. "Leading Change: The Eight Steps to Transformation." In *Leader's Change Handbook,* edited by Jay A. Conger, Gretchen M. Spreitzer, and Edward Lawler III. San Francisco: Jossey-Bass.

Line, Maurice. 1999. "Types of Organisational Culture." *Library Management* 20 (2): 73-75.

Martin, Joanne, and Caren Siehel. 1983. "Organizational Culture and Counter-Culture: an Uneasy Symbiosis." *Organizational Dynamics* 12 (2): 52-64.

McCuen, Richard H. 2002. "Professional Values and Ethics in Book Reviewing." *Journal of Information Ethics* 11 (1): 30-36.

Mintzberg, Henry. 1979. *The Structuring of Organizations: A Synthesis of Research.* Englewood Cliffs, N.J.: Prentice-Hall.

Mirvis, Philip H. 1985. "Negotiation after the Sale." *Journal of Occupational Behavior* 6 (1): 67.

Perkins, Eva. 2001. "Johns Hopkins' Tragedy: Could Librarians Have Prevented a Death?" *Information Today* 18 (8): 51, 54.

Pettigrew, Andrew M. 1990. "Is Corporate Culture Manageable?" in *Managing Organisations*, 2d ed., edited by David Wilson and Robert Rosenfeld. London: McGraw-Hill.

Sannwald, William. 2000. "Understanding Organizational Culture." *Library Administration and Management* 14 (1): 8-14.

Schein, Edgar H. 1985. *Organizational Culture and Leadership*. 2d ed. San Francisco: Jossey-Bass.

Senge, Peter M. 1990. *The Fifth Discipline: The Art and Practice of the Learning Organization*. New York: Doubleday.

Shepherd, Murray, Virginia Gillham, and Mike Ridley. 1999. "The Truth Is in the Details: Lessons in Inter-University Library Collaboration." *Library Management* 20 (6): 332-337.

Society of American Archivists. 1992. *A Code of Ethics for Archivists with Commentary*. Chicago: Society of American Archivists.

Sturges, Paul, Vincent Teng, and Ursula Iliffe. 2001. "User Privacy in the Digital Library Environment: A Matter for Concern for Information Professionals." *Library Management* 22 (8/9): 364-370.

Taylor, Mary K. 2001. "Patients' Rights on the World Wide Web." *Medical Reference Services Quarterly* 20 (2): 57-70.

Wengart, Robert, ed. "Ethical Issues in Information Technology." *Library Trends* 49 (3): 391-537.

Launching Pad

Barker, Richard A. 2002. "An Examination of Organizational Ethics." *Human Relations* 55 (9): 1097-1116.

Beer, Michael, and Nitin Nohria, eds. 2000. *Breaking the Code of Change*. Boston: Harvard Business School Press.

Bollinger, Audrey S., and Robert D. Smith. 2001. "Managing Organizational Knowledge as a Strategic Asset." *Journal of Knowledge Management* 5 (1): 8-18.

Fulmer, William E. 2000. *Shaping the Adaptive Organization: Landscapes, Learning, and Leadership in Volatile Times*. New York: AMACOM.

Holden, Philip. 2000. *Ethics for Managers*. Aldershot, England: Gower.

Jackall, Robert. 1989. *Moral Mazes: The World of Corporate Managers*. New York: Oxford University Press.

Lencioni, Patrick M. 2002. "Make Your Values Mean Something." *Harvard Business Review* 80 (1): 113-117.

Loadman, Jane. 2001. "Does the Position of Records Management Within the Organisation Influence the Records Management Process?" *Records Management Journal* 11 (1): 45-63.

Marco, Guy. 1996. "The Terminology of Planning." Parts 1 and 2. *Library Management* 17 (2): 17-23; (7): 17-24.

McNamara, Carter. 1999. "Managing Ethics in the Workplace." *Journal of Information Ethics* 8 (2): 5-8.

Morgan, Steve. 2001. "Change in Academic Libraries: Don't Forget the People." *Library Management* 22 (1/2): 58-60.

Palmer, Ian, and Richard Dunford. 2002. "Who Says Organizational Change Can Be Managed? Positions, Perspectives and Problematics." *Strategic Change* 11 (5): 243-251.

Patkus, Ronald, and Brendan A. Rapple. 2000. "Changing the Culture of Libraries: The Role of Core Values." *Library Administration and Management* 14 (4): 197-204.

Prowle, Malcolm. 2001. *The Changing Public Sector: A Practical Management Guide*. Aldershot, England: Gower.

Richards, Rob. 2000. "Stewardship, Partnership, Self-Understanding: An Exploration of Values in Acquisition Work." *Against the Grain* 12 (3): 87-90.

Shuler, John A. 2002. "Freedom of Public Information v. Right to Public Information: The Future Possibilities of Library Advocacy." *Journal of Academic Librarianship* 28 (3): 157-159.

Tam, Lawrence W. H. ,and Averil Robertson. 2002. "Managing Change: Libraries and Information Services in the Digital Age." *Library Management* (8/9): 369-377.

Van de Loo, Erik. 2000. "The Clinical Paradigm: Manfred Kets de Vries: Reflections on Organizational Therapy." *European Management Journal* 18 (1): 2-22.

Wallace, Joseph, James Hunt, and Christopher Richards. 1999. "The Relationship Between Organisational Culture, Organisational Climate and Managerial Values." *International Journal of Public Sector Management* 12 (7): 548-564.

PART II: UNDERSTANDING THE RESPONSIBILITIES

4: MANAGING THE ORGANIZATIONAL RESPONSIBILITIES

"There is always a best solution, even if it is not a good solution."

IN THIS CHAPTER YOU'LL DISCOVER:

- that managers have a number of distinct roles
- the nature of responsibilities, roles, accountability and trust
- the need to ensure that there is a collaborative working environment
- how to make teams work
- the basics of decision-making
- the fundamentals of planning
- that there are differences between leading and managing
- how to negotiate effectively
- the phases of project management
- why self-management is important

MANAGERIAL ROLES

There is a slang term in the U.S. about "hats" that one often hears—"I'm wearing such-and-such a hat"; "Oh, I need to change hats"; "What hat am I to wear now?" The speaker is referring to the various roles one has in the work world and life in general. One of this book's authors, Ed Evans, fills several roles during the work week at the university—senior administrator of the library, professor of anthropology, university archaeologist, liaison with the local indigenous people (Tongva-Gabrielino), university copyright officer, and senior administrator of the unit that supports instructional technology in the classroom. Within each of these roles, but especially the first and last ones mentioned, he also carries out different managerial roles.

Managers at all levels have a variety of roles that they must play at different times and situations. In our opinion, the person who has done the best job of both identifying the basic roles as well as studying their many variations is Henry Mintzberg. He identified three broad categories of roles for the manager—interpersonal, informational, and decisional (Mintzberg, 1973, 1975).

Within the interpersonal category he identifies three distinct roles—figurehead, leader, and liaison—which are addressed in this chapter. His informational category contains roles related to communications in some manner—nerve center, disseminator, and spokesperson—which are discussed in chapter 5. The last category, decisional, includes roles such as disturbance handler, resource handler, and negotiator, which are explored in chapter 6. Other writers, such as Giesecke (2001), use different labels for grouping roles, as well as identifying more or fewer roles than does Mintzberg. For example, Giesecke uses the labels facilitator, leader, and catalyst for her grouping.

As noted above, Mintzberg has three distinct roles in the interpersonal category. The manager is the individual most identified with her/his area of responsibility—he or she is the *figurehead*. That is, to some degree, the individual becomes the unit in the minds of others, including that person's subordinates. The *leadership* role is generally understood, but it is explored in more detail later in this chapter, as the trend toward greater collaborative/team-oriented work impacts this role. The *liaison* role becomes key in developing working relationships with units that need to interact with the manager's unit. Being an effective liaison requires the ability to relate to others' issues, to compromise, and to negotiate, which is covered later in this chapter.

Many new managers have difficulty with Mintzberg's informational role of *nerve center*. As a "front line" person one can, to a large degree, more or less structure the day's activities and have a reasonable degree of certainty that the day will go as planned. Becoming a manager reduces that expectation to the level of a hope. Rarely will a manager be able to plan her/his day's activity and actually be able to carry it out completely. Issues crop up that require immediate attention, which means that something else must be set aside. Often the new manager feels under siege, with too many things all requiring attention now. Learning to handle this role effectively is essential for the newcomer (this is explored later in this chapter under "Self-Management").

The *spokesperson* role is related to the figurehead role. Generally, only the unit manager has opportunities to speak officially with other unit managers and top management about the issues of concern to the unit. In such discussions, the effective manager is one who can balance her/his unit's issues with those of the overall organization. Equally important is the role of the *disseminator*—to communicate necessary information in a timely manner both within and without the unit. New managers often have trouble finding the correct balance between over- and under-communicating.

Decisional roles also present some challenges for the new manager. Very few individuals enjoy being the *disturbance handler*, especially when such events are people-based, as is usually the situation—often the reaction is "let them work it out among themselves." Certainly it is necessary to involve the individuals in the process of resolving the situation, but leaving it to the participants alone rarely leads to an acceptable resolution. A third party, in this case the manager, is usually critical in finding a satisfactory solution. (Chapter 5 provides suggestions for handling this role.) *Negotiator* is a related role, which has a special skill set explored in the same chapter.

Acting as the *resource handler* by handling and allocating resources is another role that few new managers have much, if any, experience with outside their personal life. While there is a tendency to think of resources in terms of money, the concept is much broader—staff, equipment, and even time are resources the manager must handle. One of the activities managers have recently had to address is resource reallocation. Resource reallocation frequently brings with it change. Sometimes the change is positive—for example, new staff, equipment, or funding. More often, at least in the recent past for publicly funded services, the change is negative—less staff, less money, or new service requirements without additional resources. No matter what the type of change, it is the change process itself that will be more or less difficult for a unit. How well the manager understands that process will determine how difficult it will be for the unit.

IN A NUTSHELL

Mintzberg's managerial roles

- Interpersonal—figurehead, leader, liaison.
- Informational—nerve center, disseminator, spokesperson.
- Decisional—disturbance handler, resource handler, negotiator.

Mintzberg 1973, 1975.

Whatever the labels and roles encountered, the fact remains that not everyone is good at or comfortable with fulfilling all roles. Nevertheless, managers will be called upon to perform each role; spending time thinking about how to handle them is well worth the effort.

SOME ROLE QUESTIONS TO PONDER

- How comfortable am I in being *the* person representing my unit?
- What leadership style will work for me?
- How will I find time to learn about other units in enough detail to become a good liaison between my unit and the others?
- How can I be an effective spokesperson for my unit while also taking into consideration the "big picture"?
- How well do I handle multitasking?
- Do I have the skills to quickly determine what information needs to go out and to whom it should go?

- Do I have the knowledge and skills to be effective in the area of conflict resolution?
- What types of information do I need to be effective at allocating resources?

ROLES, RESPONSIBILITY, ACCOUNTABILITY, AND TRUST

Keep in mind there is a difference between roles and responsibilities. A role is a type of behavioral activity, whereas a responsibility is essentially mental, in the sense that one agrees to do something. Upon accepting a middle management position, the appointee agrees to carry out a list of "duties and responsibilities." For example, the description may indicate that the manager "is responsible for the selection, training, and supervision of eight support staff." It is something that is agreed to and will result in behavioral activity, but it is not in itself a behavior. In essence, responsibility is what the manager must *do*, roles are how one carries it out, and accountability is being answerable for the results.

In the role of resource allocator, the manager makes judgments about how to organize the work activities. One element is delegating certain duties to subunits or individuals. Using the above example of staff selection, a manager might delegate to a committee the responsibility of interviewing candidates for a vacant or new position in the unit and making a recommendation of who to hire. The committee has the responsibility to conduct the interviews and make a recommendation. What new managers sometimes forget is that delegating the responsibility for something does not mean that they are no longer responsible for the activity. They forget that responsibility has a dual character—it is almost always shared. Top management may delegate something to middle management, who in turn delegate it to the front-line staff. If the front-line staff fail to carry out the activity, both middle and top management bear some of the blame for the failure, not just the front-line staff.

Accountability is not shared in the same fashion. The front-line staff are completely accountable for what they did or did not do. The middle manager would be fully accountable for not making certain that the front-line staff were "on track" and doing the "right thing." Top management is fully accountable for monitoring all the activities within their organization; in this example, asking for updates from the middle manager about the situation. Our point is that delegating responsibility actually increases the responsibility of the person or group doing the delegating.

Because of the dual nature of responsibility and the retention of accountability, new managers often do one of two things. Either they do not delegate enough (try to do it all) or attempt to delegate but do not provide the authority/resources necessary to effectively carry out the assignment. Both approaches will result in problems for the unit, especially if teams or committees are used for carrying out the activity.

Developing trust or confidence in the staff is sometimes a challenge for a new manager. Lack of confidence or a fear that staff will be unable to do something "right" can result in trying to do it oneself, which will generally result in two outcomes. First, the staff will see the lack of trust and begin to have doubts about the new manager's capabilities. Second, the manager will not be able to do everything alone, at least not for very long (resulting in burnout), and some of the activities will not be done right. Finding the right balance between over- and under-delegation is critical to long-term success as a manager. Successful middle managers create units that have high levels of trust on both sides and a sense of being a "team," even if there is no formal team activity in a managerial sense.

THE COLLABORATIVE WORKING ENVIRONMENT

In chapter 1, we noted the increased emphasis on formal teams at all levels of the organization. Collaborative work can take a number of forms, and as a result has a variety of labels in management literature. "Collaboration'" generally refers to external work (with other units or organizations) and "team" usually relates to internal activities.

Most information professionals still work in traditionally structured organizations with "departments" or "units," performing activities such as acquisitions or handling inquiries. Some have shifted to a team-based approach; one example in the library sector is the University of Arizona, which started the shift in 1991. Several articles have appeared about the university's efforts in moving to a team-based structure, and Diaz and Pintozzi (1999) provide a good summary of the challenges and issues faced during the first eight years. Regardless of what the structure may be, fundamental management activities still take place. These fundamentals are handling change, decision-making, planning, delegating/organizing work, performing quality control, communicating, maintaining staff motivation, providing leadership, and overseeing staffing, fiscal control, technology, and facilities management. What changes in the team-based environment is the nature of the "control" a manager has. As the label suggests, the middle manager inhabits the position between the front-line staff and senior managers, which always results in pressure from both sides. In a team-based setting, these pressures can become much higher if the manager does not understand how his or her management skills should be adjusted for effective outcomes.

We expect that the team-based environment will become increasingly common. But keep in mind that from one perspective this is not a new idea; our expectation regarding the increase in team work arises from the trends outlined in chapter 1. The rate of increase is likely to vary with the type of service and the needs of the parent organization.

Every organization consists of one or more "work teams." No one working for an organization is totally independent from everyone else. Without interrelationships, there is no organization. This has been true throughout time; what has been taking place over the last half of the twentieth century and the start of the twenty-first is an ever-increasing involvement of the staff in planning and decision-making. Henri Fayol (1841-1925), after studying successful nineteenth- and early–twentieth-century organizations, developed a set of fourteen principles of management, one of which was esprit de corps (Fayol, 1967). For Fayol, this meant a sense of harmony and cohesion among the staff. Today, one hears/reads about the importance of teamwork; is this really different from what Fayol identified as important to organizational success nearly a century ago? The answer is yes and no.

Yes, in that it remains important for staff to have a sense of belonging and working together; no, in that staff is given increasing control of how and when work is done, and even, within limits, what is done. Much of the change arose from behavioral and employee motivation studies.

PROGRESS IN BEHAVIORAL AND EMPLOYEE MOTIVATION STUDIES

Hugo Munsterberg, 1913

Henri Fayol, 1916

Abraham Maslow, 1943

Fredrick Herzberg, 1959

Douglas McGregor, 1960

Chris Argyris, 1973

William Ouchi, 1981

W. Edwards Deming, 1986

Peter Scholtes, 1988

The list could go on for many pages but it makes the point that there has been a steady progression over the years to ever-greater staff involvement in the management of organizations. (Note that we are not suggesting that there is a straight-line connection between the writers mentioned.)

DEFINITION

A team

consists of "people who have some relatedness to each other or reason for working together as a function of doing their jobs or accomplishing a task. A team may be relatively permanent....Teams may be temporary and have a life together as long as it takes to accomplish a particular task."

(Hanson and Lubin, 1995: 19-20)

First-time managers of teams must understand that developing a smooth-functioning, effective team requires a considerable amount of time and effort. Teams require ongoing support, so the manager must continually ensure that the team has what it needs. A useful analogy to keep in mind is that of a professional sports team. There are the players who actually engage in the matches; a coach or coaches who guide and train the players; and a wide range of support/management staff who handle administrative and logistical issues. And, of course, there is an owner or group of financial backers. All of these groups are the "team," not just the players who engage in the matches.

Sports teams almost always have a "captain" who fills Mintzberg's roles of figurehead and spokesperson. The head coach also serves as a spokesperson, as well as filling a number of other roles, as do the other groups involved. All share some responsibility for the success or failure of players in the matches. However, it is in the area of accountability that there is no sharing. Players are only accountable for their individual performances. Coaches are accountable for how the players perform as a group. Top management may be well aware that there are problems with the skill levels or physical capabilities of some of the players, but when there is a consistent losing record it is usually the coaches that are dismissed, rather than the players as a group.

Thus, the message is that using teams is an effective management tool, but the manager will be responsible and accountable for the team's performance. Therefore, spending time mentoring/coaching the team and assuring that it has the resources and authority to accomplish the assignment is part of the management task. A key element of mentoring/monitoring is for everyone to understand her/his responsibilities. Table 4.1 is a team responsibility chart that the Loyola Marymount University Library uses for its OCLC PromptCat activities (outsourced cataloging).

Making Teams Work

The two types of work-related teams—temporary and permanent—have the same basic requirements for success, but there are some important differences to keep in mind. We will describe the basics and note where differences arise.

Labeling a work group a *team* carries some particular implications for working together. The more significant of these include the following:

- Each person on the team must share a sense of common purpose and of a goal that all are working to achieve.
- Each must have a sense of, as well as an interest in, how the members interact and have a willingness to address relationship issues in an open manner.

In the best of circumstances:

- Each individual will serve as leader for certain activities/processes.
- There must be a willingness to listen and to try to understand various team members' points of view on issues, and to encourage the free expression of ideas and opinions.
- The group must face conflicts and take action to resolve them, or at least reduce them enough that the group can continue to work effectively.

Table 4.1 Team Responsibilities PromptCat

	Head Cataloger	Head of Acquisitions	Cataloging Assistant	Receiving Assistant	Invoice Assistant	Physical Processing
Establish PromptCat profiles and processing requirements with OCLC and vendors.	P	S				
Define cataloging review process, including definition and handling of errors and exceptions.	P		S			
Load PromptCat files into local system.	S	S		P		
Compare books to PromptCat records and approve payment	S		S	P		
Route errors and exceptions to appropriate staff	S		S	P		
Pay invoices		S			P	
Correct errors and exceptions	S		P			
Relabel books as necessary			S			P
Provide feedback to OCLC and vendors	P	P				

P = primary responsibility

S = supporting responsibility

- There should be a balance between the various roles so that group morale and cohesion are enhanced, or at least not impeded. While this should be true in any work environment, it is especially important in teams for mistakes to be treated as learning experiences, rather than opportunities for finger pointing and "blame games." When a problem arises, the focus should be on finding a solution, not on finding out who is to blame.

FOR FURTHER THOUGHT

What are some other characteristics of team or group work experiences that you have had?

While the above should come about as the team works together, managers will need to assist in the process from time to time, and it will certainly require a good deal of time and attention during the start-up period. The team will need and want guidance in setting up the goals and performance standards that their overall effectiveness will be measured against. An "outside'" mediator/negotiator also may be required for conflict resolution.

There are other conditions that must exist for teams to work. Middle and upper management must be committed to, and believe in, the importance and value of the team. They must recognize that, just like professional sports teams, work teams need a team leader. The manager and the team leader(s) must be willing to assess their roles in relation to the team, as well as understand the need to share roles. Team meetings, which are critical to building cohesiveness, are often misunderstood by outsiders and appear to occur too often and last too long. But without such meetings, the team will not really be a "team," nor will it be any more effective than a "traditional" work unit (see chapter 9). Team building is an ongoing process. Bennis, Parikh, and Lessem (1994: 133-134) wrote, "It is essential to absorb this concept of integrality of all in the group. It does not come easily, for its opposite, that of separateness, is deeply anchored in our western culture. You cannot do truly good work, fulfill your function of effectively organizing the task of your group, unless you yourselves connect with your members on the basis of reciprocation." While their research was not based in the information sector, we believe that their ideas are general in character, and most, if not all, can be applied to services managed by information professionals (see table 4.2).

Table 4.2
A Comparison of Competitive Ethos with Group Ethos

Individual Competitive	Group Communal
• Profit for me is derived from self-interest	• Profit to me is a vote of confidence my society gives me for service rendered to that society
• I am mutually exclusive from my fellow-man	• I am mutually inclusive
• I prefer to be a self-actualized person	• I prefer to be a social person
• The more I have the more I am	• I am, therefore the more I am prepared to share and give
• I demand productivity from people	• I prefer to create a climate in which people will be willing to be more productive
• I am actually an aggressive kind of person	• I am actually a receptive kind of person
• I look you in the eye and challenge you	• I bow my head and show you respect
• My concern is for production	• My concern is for people

Neither approach is always correct in every circumstance, and the challenge for managers is to be able to correctly assess which is best for a given set of circumstances.

Team-based milieus impact other middle management activities beyond those already mentioned. Some—quality control, communication, and fiscal responsibilities—are discussed in later chapters. While middle and senior management both have responsibility for organizational morale and motivation, they have less involvement at the level of the individual staff member. An individual's motivation becomes primarily a team matter, with outside input on request. Staffing responsibility lies more with the team than upper management, within funding limits. This is especially true in the

Table 4.3
Diagnostic Questions to Assess Appropriateness of Empowered Teams

Organizational Level

1. Is the organization fully committed to aligning all management systems with empowered work teams including leaders behaviors, team-based rewards, and open access to information?

2. Will top management support such a change and the requisite system changes?

3. Does the organization have sufficient resources to invest in significant training and development of both managers and employees?

4. Is human resources ready/equipped to commit to changes in pay systems and performance management systems and to give up control over traditional selection and evaluation functions?

5. Are organizational goals and the expected results from empowered teams clearly specified?

6. Will the organization share strategic/competitive information and have systems (e.g., an enterprise-wide information system) accessible to empowered team members?

7. Does the organization have a plan to manage the transition including timetables for the transfer of managerial responsibilities and known boundaries or limits on the level of team empowerment expected or desired?

8. Will the organization support continued monitoring and adjustment of team empowerment implementation by team members (or as Chris Argyris states, will the "do your own thing—the way we tell you" mentality prevail)?

Team Level

1. Are the teams designed to be long-term, permanent work teams?

2. Will the teams have access to the resources they need for high performance?

3. Will team members carry out interdependent tasks (i. e., for tasks that require a high degree of coordination and communication?)

4. Are team tasks complex and nonroutine in nature? If not, can the tasks be enlarged or enriched to get optimal benefits from team empowerment?

Individual Level
1. Will employees be receptive to, and benefit from, cross-training?

2. Do employees have the necessary maturity levels to effectively carry out peer evaluations, selection, and discipline decisions, conflict management, and other administrative tasks?

3. Are employee ability levels currently sufficient for handling increased responsibility and, if not, will more training result in appropriate ability levels?

4. Do employees intended for empowered teams have appropriate personality characteristics such as high growth needs, preferences for autonomy, preferences for teamwork, a high tolerance for ambiguity, and an internal locus of control?

5. Will employees be open to examining their own behavior in the context of empowered teams?

Table 4.4
Organizational Levels of Team Empowerment

External Leader Behavior

1. Make team members responsible and accountable for the work they do.

2. Ask for and use team suggestions when making decisions.

3. Encourage team members to take control of their work.

4. Create an environment in which team members set their own team goals.

5. Stay out of the way when team members attempt to solve work-related problems.

6. Generate high team expectations

7. Display trust and confidence in the team's abilities.

Production/Service Responsibilities

1. The team sets its own production/service goals and standards.

2. The team assigns jobs and tasks to its members.

3. Team members develop their own quality standards and measurement techniques.

4. Team members take on product/service learning and development opportunities.

5. Team members handle their own problems with internal and external customers.

6. The team works a whole product or service.

Human Resources Management System

1. Pay the team, at least in part, as a team.

2. Cross-train team members to handle various jobs within their team.

3. Cross-trained team members to handle various jobs on other teams.

4. Make team members responsible for hiring, training, punishment, and firing.

5. Require that team members use peer evaluations to formally evaluate each other.

Social Structure

1. The team gets support from other teams and departments when needed.

2. The team has access to and uses important and strategic information.

3. The team has access to and uses resources of other teams.

4. The team has access to and uses resources inside and outside the organization.

5. The team frequently communicates with other teams.

6. The team makes its own rules and policies.

area of performance assessment and discipline. Areas where upper management retains most of the traditional roles are organization-wide in character, such as marketing and facilities and technology management.

Kirkman and Rosen (2000) are major academic researchers of team-based work units and have produced two excellent summary tables of what is necessary for successful team-based work. Table 4.3 lists questions that the organization must answer *before* starting a shift to such a model. A number of questions require answers based on expectations rather than known facts but still are critical to think about. Table 4.4 covers steps specific steps required of the organization if the teams are to be effective.

DECISION-MAKING

Like change, decision-making is part of everyday life, and yet it is not something that is easy for everyone—"just make up your mind" is a phrase one often hears. However, on the job indecision can be a serious matter, especially if the decision-maker is a manager.

The basics of decision-making are constants, whether in a traditional or team-based environment—what changes is the number of people involved. In a traditional setting, a manager can, and often does, decide upon an issue without any staff input. While there are times when that is appropriate (e.g., in a crisis or other situation demanding immediate action), it's normally preferable to involve other group members (or even the whole group) in important decisions. The manager *must* show evidence of valuing and acting upon staff views, because team-based situations require group decision-making.

Decision-making, choice-making, and problem-solving are interrelated. Decision-making involves nine processes.

1. Define the organizational objectives relevant to the problem/issue.
2. Classify the objectives according to their relative importance.
3. Develop a list of options/solutions that could resolve the problem/issue.
4. Evaluate each option/solution in terms of the relevant objectives.
5. Select the options/solutions that meet most of the highest objectives.
6. Explore the consequences, positive and negative, of each option/solution.
7. Select the option/solution with the highest positives and lowest negatives as the tentative "decision."
8. Determine how/if the negative consequences can be overcome.
9. Implement the decision.

Figure 4.1
Decision-making, Choice-Making and Problem-Solving

Decision Making

Choice Making

- Activities dealing with problem identification, definition, and diagnosis
- Activities dealing with generating alternative solutions
- Activities dealing with evaluation and choice among alternatives
- Activities dealing with implementation of the chosen solution
- Activities dealing with maintaining, monitoring, and reviewing the solution alternatives

Problem Solving

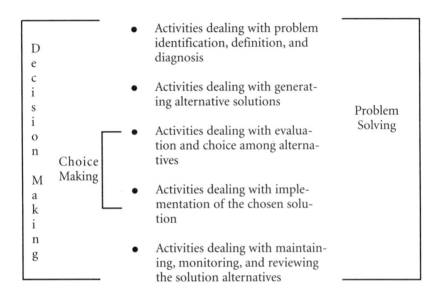

Figure 4.2
Decision-making Styles

Systematic Thinking	Intuitive Thinking
•Plan for solving a problem •Be very aware of process •Discard alternatives only after careful analysis •Conduct careful search for additional information •Complete any discrete steps in process once started •Jump from one step to another and back again	•Keep problem in mind •Rely on hunches and non-verbal cues •Define the specific construction immediately •Defend solution in terms of fit •Consider alternatives or options simultaneously •Explore and abandon alternatives very quickly

The process does *not* need to be lockstepped; however, for good decision-making all of the processes do need to occur.

Decision-making in the workplace falls into two broad styles—systematic and intuitive (see Figure 4.2 for how the styles differ). While some individuals may be very effective intuitive decision-makers, the systematic process is most effective and saves staff time in a team-based environment—as long as the team members understand the process.

FOR FURTHER THOUGHT

Are you naturally an intuitive or systematic decision-maker?

How could a team leader or monitor handle a team with one or more naturally intuitive decision-makers?

What are some situations where intuitive thinking might be the most effective approach?

PLANNING

Planning principles remain the same regardless of your level in the organization. However, as one moves upward, the amount of time spent on the activity, the timetable, and the scope increase. The planning process is a forward-looking, anticipatory series of related decisions, and plans should set out what needs to occur if the organization is to be successful.

All plans are based on a series of decisions about an uncertain future, and as the plan's time-line increases, so does the uncertainty. As with decision-making, the uncertainty that comes with planning can be a source of fear for a newcomer who is afraid of making a wrong decision. But a poor plan or decision is always better than no plan or decision.

FOR FURTHER THOUGHT

Think about where you are today in terms of work.

Where would you like to be in three, five, and ten years?

How will you get to those places?

What plans have you made for achieving those goals?

Think about where you are today. Is it where you wanted to be three, five years ago?

Did you plan for it or for something else? What role did chance/uncertainty play in the outcome?

While all middle managers must develop, review, comment on, and approve plans, the traditional manager develops plans (objectives, policies, procedures, and perhaps rules and programs) for her/his area of responsibility. Unless he/she is told to make changes sooner, a new manager should observe unit operations for some time to determine how well the existing plans function before initiating changes, and then only with staff input

The middle manager must have a broad understanding of the planning process and how plans interrelate. Front-line staff should be encouraged to develop plans for their areas of work in anticipation of senior management's drafting of organization-wide plans and requests for feedback and comments. Of course, supervisors must review and approve plans made by staff.

In a team-based environment, day-to-day and short-range planning (twelve to eighteen months) are the responsibility of the team. More of the middle manager's time will be spent reviewing team plans and working on intermediate and long-range planning.

Public libraries have perhaps committed more time and resources to planning as a group than any other service in the information sector, and their activities and efforts could be a model for other information services.

DIG DEEPER

Planning activity in public libraries

Barrish, Alan, and Dennis Carrigan. 1991. "Strategic Planning and the Small Public Library." *Public Libraries* 30 (2): 283-287.

McClure, Charles. 1993. "Updating Planning and Role Setting for Public Libraries." *Public Libraries* 32 (2): 198-203.

Sutton, Brett. 1994. "The Modeling Function of Long-Range Planning in Public Libraries." *Public Libraries* 33 (2): 151-160.

Stephens, Annabel. 1997. "The Public Library Planning Process." *Public Libraries* 36 (20): 110-116.

Saxon, Mathew, and Ruth Grenier. 1998. "Public Participation in Strategic Planning of Library Services." *Public Libraries* 37 (2): 126-132.

Elsner, Edward. 2002. "The Evolution of PLA's Planning Model." *Public Libraries* 41 (4): 209-215.

These papers demonstrate achievements over two decades.

Strategic Planning

Strategic planning is a system of organization plans that acts as part of the vision that the organization has for its future. There are several reasons why it is necessary to engage in this activity, especially for nonprofit organizations:

- to assign priorities to conflicting demands.
- to clarify what is done well, decide how to improve upon it, and determine what new things should be done
- to develop the clear sense of direction necessary to reinvent an organization

- to handle long-term downturns in economic outlook and funding
- to address private or for-profit sector competition
- to request funding from a funding authority or governing board for such a plan.
- to collaborate with other organizations
- to utilize the plan to educate, inform, involve, and revitalize the governing board, staff, service community, funding authority, etc.

As Bryson (1995) notes, a strategic plan is neither a panacea nor a substitute for leadership. He focuses on the political aspects of decision-making that are so much stronger for nonprofits such as libraries: "Public and nonprofit organizations (and communities) are *politically rational*. Thus, any technique that is likely to work well in such organizations must accept and build upon the nature of political rationality" (Bryson, 1995: 10). As further testimony to the value of Bryson's book, read "Strategic Planning: Politics, Leadership, and Learning" (McClamroch, Byrd, and Sowell, 2001), which describes the use of the Bryson model at the Indiana State University-Bloomington libraries.

WORTH CHECKING OUT

Strategic planning

Bryson, John. 1995. *Strategic Planning for Public and Nonprofit Organizations*. San Francisco: Jossey-Bass.

McClamroch, Jo, Jacqueline Byrd, and Steven Sowell. 2001. "Strategic Planning, Politics, Leadership and Learning." *Journal of Academic Librarianship* 27 (5): 373-378.

FOR FURTHER THOUGHT

What are some other reasons for engaging in strategic planning?

Why is important that middle managers be involved in strategic planning?

LEADERSHIP FOR TWENTY-FIRST CENTURY MANAGERS

Mintzberg (1998) summed up leadership of professional organizations: "Leadership is clearly a tricky business in professional organizations....I saw a lot of more of *doing* than what we conventionally think of as *leading*" (Mintzberg, 1998: 144). His comment suggests that covert rather than overt leadership is more important in information organizations.

There are three levels of leadership—individual, group, and organizational. At the individual level, the leader is a mentor, coach, and motivator. At the group level, the leader focuses on team-building and conflict resolution. Finally, at the third level, the leader builds an organizational culture.

Much has been written about leadership, but Bennis has contributed more to the subject through his consistent message and emphasis on human relations. According to Bennis (1998), great leaders—whether born or trained—must remember that leadership is not reserved only for those at the top, and is not about control or manipulation.

WORTH CHECKING OUT

Leadership

McLean, J. W., and William Weitzel. 1991. *Leadership—Magic, Myth, or Method?* New York: American Management Association.

McLean and Weitzel (1991) debunk twelve myths about leadership and discuss six leadership principles and six skills. The myths are:

1. Charisma is a necessary leadership quality.
2. Leaders can never be wrong.
3. Leadership means being consistent.
4. Leaders should always know the goal in advance.
5. It is usually more stressful to lead than to follow.
6. Leaders must be able to perform the jobs of the followers.
7. A leader in one environment should lead in others.
8. Leadership is an opportunity only for those who have strong support from "higher ups."
9. Followers resent being manipulated.
10. Leadership is often incidental because the success or failure of most group efforts is determined by outside events.
11. Leaders are an endangered species.
12. Leadership is too complicated for me.

Their basic message is that need to understand and apply effective leadership skills. According their principles, "To the individual armed with this knowledge and ability, leadership no longer need involve a reckless leap of faith" (McLean and Weitzel, 1991: xi).

MCLEAN AND WEITZEL'S LEADERSHIP PRINCIPLES AND SKILLS

Principles

1. Leadership begins with greater self-knowledge.
2. Leadership is not simply good management.
3. Leadership must be earned.
4. Motivation begins with the "G" word—goal—and ends with the "P" word—participation.

5. Planning is not all there is.
6. Building relationships is a leadership imperative.

Skills

1. Situational discretion
2. Communications
3. Motivation—try "inward marketing"
4. Assessment of risks and related factors
5. Unexpected problem solving
6. Relational renewal

Research carried out by Bennis and Nanus (1985) identifies four abilities that leaders need to develop: attention, or creating a compelling vision; meaning, or communicating the vision through analogy, metaphor, and vivid illustrations; trust, or the emotional glue that binds followers to leaders; and finally, "deployment of self," or the application of knowledge, persistence, risk-taking, commitment, and challenge, along with the ability to learn from failure. It is not surprising given this research that some gurus write of storytelling as a powerful means of communication.

The four things that people want are *purpose, trust, optimism, action* and *results*. In order to provide these wants, leaders must have a positive view of themselves, and not expect constant approval and recognition.

> WORTH CHECKING OUT
>
> **Managing people**
>
> We highly recommend Bennis, Warren. 1998. *Managing People Is Like Herding Cats.* London: Kogan Page.
>
> Among other points, Bennis focuses on some of the distinctions between managers and leaders. Often the differences are a matter of emphasis.

Perhaps the reason why we enjoy working with a particular leader or manager relates to the chemistry in the relationship. Two fantastic leaders influenced the writer's career and approach to leadership, and both gave their staff freedom to do their job, took a personal interest in staff and their families, and had strong and outgoing personalities. Neither was universally popular. Many of their staff were innovators and made things happen, but they were also "allowed" to make mistakes along the way, as long as those mistakes resulted in "learning"—and did you learn!

Other bosses didn't have a "presence"; staff didn't see them often or know what they were thinking about the organization or the staff. At another extreme were "control freaks" who left staff unsure of their "boundaries," or their tolerance for innovation or suggestions. We're sure some of their staff would have been happier working with a quieter leader who guided them more closely.

TRY THIS

Think of organizations you know; you can probably identify someone at a lower level who takes a leadership role. This is common in the information sector, where support and para-professional staff play a major role in the functioning of the service.

Think of the managers you have known—the good and the bad—both in the work situation and in clubs, societies, sports teams, etc. Draw a line down a sheet of paper. On one side write down all those things that you think make a "good manager," and on the other write down all those things that you believe to define a "bad" manager.

FOR FURTHER THOUGHT

What are the principles you use to lead your team?

How do you think others perceive your leadership and communication style?

What specific qualities do you want to add or change to be an excellent leader?

What behaviors would you change to increase rapport and leadership effectiveness?

NEGOTIATION SKILLS

Frontline staff in traditional organizations do not have the opportunity to develop negotiation skills other than the few they develop working with unhappy users. Even then, policies and rules limit the range of options for the staff. All staff will engage in "negotiations" with their supervisors over work schedules and perhaps performance assessments, and with colleagues about switching holiday, evening, or weekend hours. However, all these "negotiations" are highly informal and do not call on the skill set needed for formal negotiations.

Negotiations take on several forms in a service environment. Customer relations and intradepartmental or team negotiations are two important areas. Almost any collaborative project with other organizations will involve some negotiating. Middle managers may negotiate with vendors on a daily basis, senior managers negotiate between the library and governing boards and/or funding agencies, and there will be union contract negotiations in some settings.

One must keep in mind the differences between *influence, negotiation,* and *coercion.* Influence employs a strategy of *shared power;* negotiation employs the strategy of *trading* power; and coercion uses power *imposition.* While the first two methods are most common and desirable in either a traditional or team-based environment, there are a few times when managers must resort to coercion.

First, a successful, influential manager must build and maintain a reputation for reliability by remaining consistent in what he/she asks of the staff and in his/her own actions. Reliability means following through on all commitments and being clear about how a decision will be made. Second, an influential manager must demonstrate flexibility by adjusting to the person he/she manager is dealing with in order to make the individual more comfortable and willing to consider what is being said. Three components of the adjustment are language usage, tone of voice, and nonverbal behaviors.

Negotiation is a strength when one tries to reach an agreement between two parties that have some interests in common and some in opposition. Keep in mind that it is people, not organizations, units, or teams, that negotiate; successful negotiations are more dependent on the negotiators than on the parties they represent. Misunderstandings, intended or not, often trigger emotions or reactions that sabotage a negotiation, so it is essential to know the others as much as possible and to ensure shared understandings of terms and concepts (see chapter 5 for more information).

There is a Native American saying that you should not criticize someone else "until you have walked in his moccasins." Indeed, the ability to see, think, and feel, the issues as though you are on the other side, is as valuable to negotiation as facts and figures. Getting all relevant emotions out in the open is essential, as unexpressed feelings become barriers to the process. Defeat the problem, not one another.

What are the skills/characteristics of an effective negotiator?

- Patience: Take your time. Negotiations have an element of conflict as well as uncertainty, and many people try to deal with these factors quickly because they are uncomfortable. A patient negotiator has an advantage.
- Preparation and knowledge: Work to understand your needs and issues *and* those of the other side.
- A good sense of organization: Know the implications (funds, people, time, etc.) for your side and the requests the other side is likely to make.
- Tolerance for conflict, uncertainty, and ambiguity—Be willing to leave an issue unresolved and move on to another issue when necessary, and remember that resolutions you make will affect those unresolved issues. The negotiator who is best able to handle these factors has an advantage.
- Willingness to take some reasonable risks: Know that every negotiation/agreement involves a greater or lesser degree of risk. Being unwilling to take some risk almost always results in a failed negotiation.
- Ability to relate to the people "on the other side of table"
- Good listening skills
- High self-esteem: Possess a sure sense of your abilities and be

able to take on personal responsibilities without allowing the other side to gain something your side did not want to concede. Wanting everyone to like you is not a good trait for an effective negotiator.

- A sense of humor
- Integrity
- Physical and mental stamina: Have the mental and physical stamina to handle long negotiations and avoid making mistakes. Dealing with labor contracts or the purchase of new software can take —15 to 18 hours at a time.
- Persistence: Know when to continue and when to walk away. Many people are not persistent enough in negotiations, either taking the first rejection as final, or conceding something too soon.

Having the appropriate skills/characteristics is important, but of equal importance is the preparation and understanding of the negotiation process. The process consists of:

- developing knowledge of the other side;
- setting the goals for your side;
- developing alternatives (what is negotiable);
- identifying and test your assumptions;
- developing a strategy and set of tactics;
- rehearsing;
- identifying your "take or leave it" point; and
- establishing a timeline for reaching agreement.

In summary, a successful negotiator should:

- differentiate between wants and needs for both sides;
- ask high and offer low, but be realistic;
- make it clear that he/she was not "giving in," but that the object conceded was of value; and
- strive for a profitable agreement for both sides.

An agreement that is completely win-lose is unlikely to last for any length of time.

FOR FURTHER THOUGHT

How many of the negotiator skills do you think you have?

TRY THIS

This exercise presents you with the chance to be in the other person's moccasins. Think about how you would respond to the following objections to some proposal you "put on the table."

"Your fees are much higher than firm B's."

"We have only a limited budget for this. What can you do to reduce the cost?"

"This idea has a number of implications for other departments. How do you plan to address them?"

"Your proposal seems designed to meet an abstract ideal that does not relate to how customers actually behave and think. Why is that?"

"It seems your concept calls for two units doing very similar, if not identical, work. Why can't it all be in one unit?"

PROJECT MANAGEMENT

Many middle managers are selected because they have had success with some type of special project that was undertaken in addition to their regularly assigned duties. Whether or not a new manager has such experience, it is certain that in the new post they will be asked to handle special projects. So it is a matter of self-interest to gain an understanding of project management.

A project can be divided into four broad phases—initiating, planning, execution and control, and closing. Most projects will require the creation of teams, so keep in mind that the project manager must influence and negotiate with these teams rather than coerce or direct.

Because there will be staff from other units involved in the work and the team, the project manager must supervise by influencing and guiding rather than directing the activities. Most of the projects will be added on top of existing duties, meaning that the project manager will need to negotiate for the time of project team members and other unit heads.

Within the initiation phase, much of the work is the project manager's responsibility. Let's take an example from records management: the assignment to relocate some 20,000 yet-to-be-identified files to a remote storage facility.

The project manager begins with an *analysis of the situation*—which files should go, how to transport them, whether any work needs to done at the remote site before anything is moved, etc. The next step is to *identify the people/department with an interest* in what happens. In this example, it would certainly be more than just the person/department responsible for the storage facility. Once the project manager has these facts in mind, it is time to outline a *feasibility study(ies)* for handling the project.

Upon completion of the feasibility stage, the project manager assembles a "*core team*" by approaching the unit heads for the individuals not his/her supervision and choosing at least one member from each of the interested units. The project manager and core team then develop evaluation criteria for measuring the success of the project and then make the final step to prepare and submit to senior management a requirements document outlining the work plan, staffing, funding, and other needs of the project, including a tentative timeline for completion.

In phase two, detailed planning drawn on earlier work now begins in light of the resources made available for the project. At this point, the core team may be expanded. The team then identifies the project tasks, and determines work activities, and decides who should carry out the activity.

Newcomers sometimes overlook the process of identifying critical tasks (those that must be done before other activities can go forward) and determining options for handling potential problems. The final activity is to create the timeline that will serve as a control mechanism in the next phase.

Phase three—execution and control—requires the project manager to monitor the activities, with an emphasis on resolving problems as quickly as possible. A weekly team meeting to review progress, the status of activities, and make adjustments to the time line is another essential control device that is important to maintaining good relations with the units that are contributing staff and in some cases adding more staff at critical points in the project. Knowing well ahead of time that staff will be needed sooner or later than originally expected keeps conflicts to minimum. It is also a good idea for the project manager to prepare status reports for senior management during this phase.

The final phase—closing—is the point when many people think it is time to celebrate a job well done. Certainly celebration is a part of successfully finishing a project, but there is still some important paper work to complete.

A team review and evaluation session to identify what did and didn't work, as well as an assessment of the project in terms of the evaluation criteria that the team established during phase one, provides useful information for future projects. The process may also help improve collaboration between units outside the project context. Project managers usually prepare a final written report for senior management that incorporates ideas and lessons learned during the project.

FOR FURTHER THOUGHT

What are some other questions the manager of the relocation project should ask?

What departments would expect to be involved in the project?

What are the major issues to consider in such a project?

> WORTH CHECKING OUT
>
> **Project management**
>
> Lewis, James P. 1998. *Team-based Project Management*. New York: American Management Association.

MANAGING ONESELF

Managers have both a personal and organizational responsibility to manage themselves by understanding their strengths and weaknesses in terms of work activities, learning to manage time, and understanding and dealing with causes of stress. Understanding strengths and weaknesses, discussed in earlier chapters, is an integral part of developing a personal management style.

Tips for Effective Time Management

Managing your time effectively not only assists in "getting more work done," but also can help reduce personal work stress (and sometimes that of colleagues as well). For some, it may also assist in delegating activities or reduce the tendency to "put off until tomorrow whatever one can do today." Our tips are relatively easy to implement; what is more difficult is to follow them long enough to make them habits rather than special activities. Paperwork, e-mail, telephone calls, and personal interactions all create time management challenges.

"If it weren't for all the interruptions I'd be fine," is one of the most common laments of many staff members. Interruptions cost time, even when they are warranted, because it always takes a few minutes to get back to where you left off in a task or thinking after the interruption is over. The two most frequent sources of interruptions are the telephone and colleagues "dropping by."

SIX TIME-SAVING TIPS

1. Avoid the "paper shuffle" game.

    Some of the paper flowing steadily into the "in" basket is informational in nature—read it, file it, or recycle it as appropriate. Don't "get back to it later"—read and dispose of it or file it.

    Some material will require an action or response by a given date. Again, an immediate action will save time in the long run, since you will not have to reread the material later. In addition, since many issues arise unexpectedly, having completed an expected project ahead of time allows for more flexibility in responding to "rush" projects that suddenly appear.

2. Build a filing system based on action time requirements.

    Prepare a folder—either paper or electronic—for each day of

the week and weekly folders to provide coverage for a full month, and place action items in the appropriate folder to establish work priorities. Handle the few items that may be complex, difficult, or overwhelming projects by establishing a "finish date" that is slightly earlier than the required date. Break the activity in small, daily actions, to give yourself the sense of progress and a measure of success.

3. Create "to-do" lists.

    Each day, just before leaving work, go into the next day's folder and set up the priorities for the items in the folder (the next day's "to-do" list). That way, you will come into work with clear items to attend to and their priorities.

    It is a good idea to have as the first item something that is of high interest and relatively easy to accomplish. This gives a positive sense of achievement that may carry over into less interesting but necessary activities.

    At the end of the last day of your working week, go through the next week's folder, sorting the material into the appropriate folder according to the day you should work on it.

4. Manage your telephone calls.

    Batch the outgoing calls and spend a few minutes planning the call; ask yourself what it is you need to convey or learn. Make a list for each call and stick to it. Use a large writing pad—not a lunch napkin, business card or empty envelope— to keep all the notes, lists, etc., together.

    A typical business call usually only requires four to five minutes to cover the business content. For complex or detailed issues, it is often best to use a combination of providing something in writing and having a follow-up telephone conversation. This is a useful guideline for the vast majority of calls, but there are exceptions, especially when developing or maintaining a working relationship with someone in another organization, such as a library vendor.

    A useful approach to handling incoming calls, at least from other library staff and those one works closely with on a regular basis, is to tell people "the best time to call me is between x and y." While this does not, and should not, stop calls from coming in at other times, it does eventually lead to a batching of many, if not most, incoming calls. During this calling time frame, one can engage in activities that take less concentration, making the interruptions less of a problem.

    Voicemail is a great boon to handling calls, but remember to indicate if you are likely to be out of the office for a few days. Take a training program on how to use the system effectively.

5.   Manage your e-mail.

Use the same approach to e-mail as with the telephone. Batch the reading of and responding to these messages. Don't fall into the pattern of leaving your e-mail active all day or frequently checking to see if you have mail if you want to make the most effective use of your time.

6.   Establish time frames when "drop-in" visits are, or are not, welcome.

For supervisors, it is a little easier to establish times when staff can just come by with questions, as well as some time during the day when "the door is closed," even if there is no physical door to close. In smoothly running units, establishing such times for everyone is relatively easy.

In times of change or uncertainly, creating such time is problematic, but even in those circumstances having some private work time can be beneficial. However, supervisors need to make it clear that a "closed-door time" does not mean they are not available for unusual or emergency situations.

There are some people who like to engage in "small talk" before and after getting to the purpose of their visit. Frequently they are also individuals who, if allowed, will spend more time on the informal/social aspects of the "visit" than on the issue in question. Setting time limits and sticking to them—"I can give you x minutes"—is a sound method for handling this or any other kind of interruption—unless, of course, the person in question is one's supervisor. In this case, your supervisor should be as concerned about effective time usage and take no more time than necessary.

Finally, there is nothing wrong in politely asking the person what it is they want to discuss if they are having trouble getting to the point.

Helen Gothberg, who has written extensively on management and public libraries, reported on a survey of public library directors' practices in the area of time management (Gothberg, 1991). Her findings have implications for managers of other types of information service.

Meetings and Time Management

Meetings can be significant time wasters if they are not properly organized. While a manager can do little about how others run their meetings, it is possible to control the meetings you call and make them as efficient as possible. Encourage those you supervise to follow the ideas given below.

Meetings are necessary because they provide valuable interaction; allow for group decisions; help in team building for team-based environments; and distribute information *that may require clarification*. However, everyone has, at some time, sat through a meeting and left thinking, "Why was this necessary?"

For straightforward distribution of information, there are better methods than calling a meeting—memos, e-mail, telephone calls, and one-on-one exchanges, for example. Use the meeting thoughtfully and attendees will come to know that there *is* a reason for the meeting and expect it to positive, with the time spent on an important issue.

What are some of the most common pitfalls that prevent a successful meeting?

- too many participants
- the wrong participants
- unequal participation
- fear of personal attack among participants
- inadequate preparation by leader and/or participants
- lack of meeting focus
- mismatch of meeting topic and resolution authority
- poor meeting environment
- poor timing of meeting—right after a meal, for example
- routine/prescheduled meetings without a solid agenda

Why you are having the meeting should be a key concern—remember that just having a topic, time, and place does not assure that the meeting will be successful. There are seven broad categories of reasons for having a meeting:

- to create or develop new ideas
- to make decisions;
- to delegate work;
- to share work;
- to persuade or involve;
- to consult; and
- to give and/or exchange information.

The last category is probably the most over- and misused reason for having a meeting. While there may be a need to give and exchange information, such meetings should be employed judiciously.

A good meeting agenda should provide the meeting topic, the purpose, who called it, who should attend, the location and time, the *ending time*, the agenda items, and any special attachments participants should review prior to the meeting.

Proper preparation goes a long way toward having productive meetings, but in the final analysis the chair must keep the meeting on track, on time, and on topic, if the time is to be well spent. Properly managed, meetings are essential and productive; improperly handled, they are major time wasters.

FOR FURTHER THOUGHT

Think about how you might handle each of the following people challenges, if you were a meeting chair.

- a perpetually late person (asks to be "brought up to date")
- a perpetually early leaver (creates disruption)
- a perpetual point maker (makes the same point over and over)
- a perpetual doubter (doubts everything, creates negative feelings)
- a perpetual "side talker" (talks to neighbors and not about topic)
- a perpetual "big mouth" (talks too much and often off the topic)
- a perpetual attacker (asks hostile questions, makes personal challenges)
- a perpetual "in and outer" (slips in and out to "handle business")
- a perpetual interrupter (jumps in, cuts people off)
- a perpetual "dropout" (is physically present but doe not participate)

WORTH CHECKING OUT

Time management

Allen, David. 2001. *Getting Things Done: The Art of Stress Free Management.* New York: Viking.

Morgenstern, Julia. 2000. *Time Management From the Inside Out.* New York: Henry Holt.

Personal Stress Management

Perhaps stress was always an issue, but it seems an even greater one at present. Each of us faces the stress of personal/family issues and community/society issues as well as work-related issues. Perhaps if we could face only one set of stressors it might not be so difficult, but most of the time we must attempt to handle all three simultaneously. Few of us are capable of setting aside personal stressors upon going to work and leaving work stress behind when we go home.

The director at the first library Ed Evans worked at suggested he purchase a punching bag and hang it by the garage door, saying, "Punch it out before getting in the car to come to work and beat the devil out of it before going into the house." His advice has some scientific merit—physical activity can be a significant tension and stress reducer. Unfortunately, activity is not always an option; nor is it the sole solution.

What are some of the major sources of workplace stress? In the U.S. workplace, stress is such an issue that the National Institute of Occupational Safety and Health has identified six categories of risk factors—workload and pace, work schedule, role stressors, career security, interpersonal factors, and job context. Stressor triggers are the same in personal and work life.

- any life change or life event (such as promotion, maternity/paternity leave)
- threats to our person or self-esteem (such as a performance review)
- loss of someone or something we care for or depend on (such as a retirement)
- conflicting or ambiguous demands or expectations (such as a project on top of regular duties)
- pressure of deadlines, too much work, and confused priorities
- conflict or difficulty with other people
- frustration or threats to our personal needs (such as seeking a promotion)

The following are more specific triggers that may affect information professionals:

- lack of professional autonomy
- user expectations that constantly rise and need to be met
- role conflicts, such as those between professional and para-professional staff
- lack of control over service operations
- high idealism
- perfectionism
- over commitment
- technology that doesn't work as expected

The reader will recognize and relate to many of the above triggers. As a middle manager, you will find that they all take on greater importance. Other than physical activity, what can you do to control or reduce the stressors? Taking *direct action* by removing the stress factor is sometimes a possibility. In the workplace, however, this is often difficult at best. Talking to a supervisor about a specific issue is the best hope for most staff members in terms of direct action. There is, of course, the direct action option of resigning, but that is really the last resort for most people.

Setting realistic goals for yourself and for performance appraisal purposes, rather than idealistic/perfectionist goals, can be helpful.

A use of the word "no" is probably one of the best techniques for reducing stressors. The judicious balancing of "yes" and "no" will go a long way toward reducing stressors and keeping the workload reasonable while maintaining a reputation of being a highly effective performer.

Take some time to learn a few short- and long-term *relaxation techniques*. One problem the authors have noted in their younger colleagues is that they have to learn to *take time off*. Vacation/leave time exists in organizations for the benefit of both the individual and the organization. In U.S. libraries, as well as in other organizations, you hear people talking about "taking a mental health day." It is usually said in jest, but the reality is that people do require time away from the job or they will "burn out."

Having a good *support network* inside and outside of work is another mechanism for reducing stress, even if it is only three or four individuals you can "vent" to about work, who understand the environment, and who may even have some useful suggestions. Stress and burnout are very real concerns.

WORTH CHECKING OUT

Stress and burnout

Jaffe, Denis and Cynthia Scott. 1984. *From Burnout to Balance: A Workbook for Peak Performance and Self-Renewal.* New York: McGraw-Hill.

Caputo, Janet. 1991. *Stress and Burnout in Library Service.* Phoenix: Oryx.

TRY THIS

Think about the following eight items in terms of how often they are true of your work. Answer using "always" (worth 4 points), "frequently" (worth 3 points), "sometimes" (worth 2 points), and "never" (worth 0 points).

- Office politics interfere with my work
- I cannot get the information I need for my work
- What is expected and how to do things are not clear to me
- There is a competitive, backbiting atmosphere
- I do not have the resources I need to get my job done
- I can not participate in decisions that affect my work and job
- Things are changing too fast at work
- My work does not provide clear or reasonable pathways for advancement

If your total score was above 20, check out a book on stress management.

> AFTER READING THIS CHAPTER YOU SHOULD BE AWARE:
>
> - that managers have to balance a number of roles
> - of the importance of responsibilities, roles, accountability, and trust
> - that you will be managing a collaborative working environment
> - of ways to create productive teams
> - of what is involved in the planning process
> - that there are differences between leading and managing
> - of ways to handle negotiations and achieve the best outcomes
> - that project management is a valuable tool for managers
> - that self-management is an important key to success

REFERENCES

Agyris, Chris. 1973. "Personality and Organization Theory Revisited." *Administrative Science Quarterly* 18 (3): 141-167.

Allen, David. 2001. *Getting Things Done: The Art of Stress-Free Productivity.* New York: Viking.

Barrish, Alan, and Dennis Carrigan. 1991. "Strategic Planning and the Small Public Library." *Public Libraries* 30 (2): 283-287.

Bennis, Warren, and Burt Nanus. 1985. *Leaders.* New York: Harper & Row.

Bennis, Warren, Jagdish Parikh, and Ronnie Lessem. 1994. *Beyond Leadership.* Oxford: Basil Blackwell Ltd.

Bennis, Warren. 1998. *Managing People Is Like Herding Cats.* London: Kogan Page.

Bryson, John. 1995. *Strategic Planning for Public and Nonprofit Organizations.* San Francisco: Jossey-Bass.

Caputo, Janette S. 1991. *Stress and Burnout in Library Service.* Phoenix, Ariz.: Oryx Press.

Deming, W. Edwards. 1986. *Out of the Crisis.* Cambridge: MIT Press.

Diaz, Joseph, and Chestalene Pintozzi. 1999. "Helping Teams Work: Lessons Learned from the University of Arizona Library Reorganization." *Library Administration and Management* 13 (1): 27-26.

Elsner, Edward. 2002. "The Evolution of PLA's Planning Model." *Public Libraries* 41 (4): 209-215.

Fayol, Henri. 1967. *General and Industrial Management.* Translated by Constance Storrs. London: Pitman.

Giesecke, Joan. 2001. *Practical Strategies for Library Managers.* Chicago: American Library Association.

Gothberg, Helen. 1991. "Time Management in Public Libraries." *Public Libraries* 30 (6): 350-357.

Hanson, Philip G., and Bernard Lubin. 1995. *Answers to Questions Most Frequently Asked about Organizational Development.* Thousand Oaks, Calif.: Sage Publications.

Herzberg, Frederick. 1959. *Motivation to Work.* 2d ed. New York: Wiley.

Jaffe, Dennis, and Cynthia Scott. 1984. *From Burnout to Balance.* New York: McGraw-Hill.

Kirkman, Bradley L., and Benson Rosen. 2000. "Powering Up Teams." *Organizational Dynamics* 28 (3): 48-65.

Lewis, James P. 1998. *Team-Based Project Management.* New York: American Management Association.

Maslow, Abraham. 1943. "Preface to Motivational Theory." *Psychosomatic Medicine* 5 (1): 85-92.

McClamroch, Jo, Jacqueline Byrd, and Steven Sowell. 2001. "Strategic Planning: Politics, Leadership, and Learning." *Journal of Academic Librarianship* 27 (5): 373-378.

McClure, Charles. 1993. "Updating Planning and Role Setting for Public Libraries." *Public Libraries* 32 (2): 198-203.

McGregor, Douglas. 1960. *The Human Side of Enterprise.* New York: McGraw-Hill.

McLean, J. W., and William Weitzel. 1991. *Leadership—Magic, Myth, or Method?* New York: American Management Association.

Mintzberg, Henry. 1973. *The Nature of Managerial Work.* Englewood Cliffs, N.J.: Prentice-Hall.

Mintzberg, Henry. 1975. "The Manager's Job: Folklore and Fact." *Harvard Business Review* 53 (4): 49-61.

Mintzberg, Henry. 1998. "Covert Leadership: Notes on Managing Professionals." *Harvard Business Review* 76 (6): 141-147.

Morgenstern, Julia. 2000. *Time Management from the Inside Out.* New York: Henry Holt.

Munsterberg, Hugo. 1913. *Psychology and Industrial Efficiency.* New York: Houghton Mifflin.

Ouchi, William. 1981. *Theory Z.* Reading, Mass.: Addison-Wesley.

Saxon, Mathew, and Ruth Grenier. 1998. "Public Participation in Strategic Planning of Library Services." *Public Libraries* 37 (2): 126-132.

Scholtes, Peter. 1988. *The Team Handbook: How to Use Teams to Improve Quality.* Madison, Wis.: Joiner Associates.

Stephens, Annabel. 1997. "The Public Library Planning Process." *Public Libraries* 36 (20): 110-116.

Sutton, Brett. 1994. "The Modeling Function of Long-Range Planning in Public Libraries." *Public Libraries* 33 (2): 151-160.

Launching Pad

Bennis, Warren, and Robert J. Thomas. 2002. *Geeks and Geezers: How Era, Values, and Defining Moments Shape Leaders.* Boston: Harvard Business School Press.

Dearstyne, Bruce W., ed. 2001. *Leadership and Administration of Successful Archival Programs.* Westport, Conn.: Greenwood.

Farson, Richard, and Ralph Keyes. 2002. "The Failure-Tolerant Leader." *Harvard Business Review* 80 (8): 64-71.

Rockman, Ilene. 2002. "Establishing Successful Partnerships with University Support Units." *Library Management* 23 (4/5): 192-198.

Tam, Lawrence W. H., and Averil C. Robertson. 2002. "Managing Change: Libraries and Information Services in the Digital Age." *Library Management* 23 (8/9): 369-377.

Tyree, Michael, and Mary Jo Hansen. 2001. "Reasons, Not Excuses: Lessons from Elizabeth I, CEO on Leading, Not Managing Libraries." *The Bottom Line: Managing Library Finances* 14 (4): 202-206.

Weech, Terry. 2002. "Back to the Future: When Resource Sharing Seemed to Work. The Rise and Fall of a Successful Consortial Resource Sharing Network." *Interlending and Document Supply* 30 (2): 80-86.

Young, Naomi Kietzke, Josephine Williamson, and JoAnne Deeken. 2002. "Tact and Tenacity: Dealing with Difficult People at Work." *Serials Librarian* 42 (3/4): 299-304.

5: MASTERING THE COMMUNICATION RESPONSIBILITIES

"Communication is never as good as you think it is."

IN THIS CHAPTER YOU'LL DISCOVER:

- why you need to be an effective communicator
- how to communicate with senior management, supervised staff, and people outside the organization
- how to communicate with users
- the advantages and disadvantages of different modes of communication
- that listening is the key to effective communication
- the basics of making presentations
- the key points for effective communication
- how to manage conflict
- the connection between communication and ethics

EFFECTIVE COMMUNICATION

Managers must be effective communicators. Berlo (1960), in his study of how much time managers spent on all aspects of communication, found that, on average, 70 percent of work time involved communication in some form—reading, writing, and listening. In today's electronic environment, that percentage is likely somewhere in the 75 percent range, if not higher.

Everyone communicates in some fashion from shortly after birth until death—so why have the management gurus always suggested that 60 to 65 percent of all management problems are in some way related to communication issues? The answer probably lies in the fact that we do communicate all the time, but do not consider communication as something that requires study or understanding—we just do it.

Perhaps it is not surprising that *USA Today* (2002) reported 68 percent of human resources directors identified communication as the leading cause of workplace stress. Their data suggests that while we may be communicating all the time, we are not doing it all that well in the workplace. This indicates that perhaps managers must devote some time to learning how to be *effective* communicators.

DEFINITION

Effective communication takes place when the person receiving the message interprets it with the identical meaning that the sender had in mind.

What appears to be a simple, straightforward concept is, in fact, highly complex and seldom 100 percent achieved. Remember that communication is a two-way process—between sender and receiver(s)—and that an important component is the feedback from the receiver to sender that completes the cycle and brings the intended and interpreted meanings closer to being identical. However, for a great many issues, a 50 or 60 percent similar meaning is sufficient to accomplish the work.

There are a number of challenges in the communication process. In today's culturally diverse workplace and service community, even when two individuals share the same first language, meanings and interpretations are not always the same if they are from different countries. Two examples based on the authors' experience illustrate the point. When someone in the U.K. asks "how did you find X?" more often than not they are not asking if a person had difficulty finding X (as someone from the U.S. might think) but whether the person liked X. This is a minor matter quickly resolved by feedback.

However, if someone in the U.S. says to a person from the U.K. "my job is redundant," an English person might respond with expressions of concern and even sympathy, thinking the other had lost her/his job. In fact, the U.S. meaning is that the job is tedious, repetitive, and/or boring. It could be some time before the actual meaning became clear, as concern and sympathy might be what the sender expected to the news that the job was repetitive. The challenges increase when the individuals in the communication process have different first languages and cultural backgrounds.

FOR FURTHER THOUGHT

Can you think of some common words that information professionals use in a technical way that may cause misunderstandings between users and staff members? What steps could be taken to reduce those risks?

> WORTH CHECKING OUT
>
> **Gender differences in communication**
>
> Deborah Tannen has conducted extensive research into what differences exist in how U.S. men and women communicate among themselves and how that can impact intergender communication. Her studies demonstrate that there are significant gender differences in communication, and behaviors learned as a child become the underlying, subconcious patterns impact communication in adulthood and impact one's actions without being aware of the patterns. We strongly recommend reading the following title, because those communication differences do carry over to the workplace.
>
> Tannen, Deborah. 1994. *Talking from 9 to 5: How Women's and Men's Conversational Styles Affect Who Gets Heard, Who Gets Credit, and What Gets Done at Work.* New York: Morrow.

We will return to the question of the challenges to effective communication after a brief review of the groups a middle manager will work with on a regular basis.

COMMUNICATION GROUPS

There are three broad categories of people a middle manager must communicate effectively with—supervised staff, senior management and those who are not information professionals. Within each group there are subgroups, each of which holds some special challenges. The subgroups include new and existing employees; the middle manager's direct supervisor, other unit heads, and senior managers; and the largest and most diverse group— the primary service community, non-library support staff (facilities, computing services, and security/public safety staff), vendors and suppliers, colleagues in related services, and members of the general public.

While the basics of good communication are constant, there are variations for each subgroup. One broad variation is that technical jargon (thesaurus, MARC, CALM, GroupWare, ISAD [G], for example) has a very good chance of being misinterpreted by anyone not working in the service. Even within a service, the use of unit-specific short phrases (MARC field 805, encumber, til forbidden, for example) can be a hindrance to good communication. Use jargon only when you are *certain* the receiver knows the meaning.

> ### DIG DEEPER
>
> **Communication with unions**
>
> In mid-2002, Hampton (Skip) Auld put together a series of contributions from various public librarians on dealing with unions. Almost all of the issues raised by the contributors have implications for any information service manager who works in a service that has union employees in any capacity.
>
> Auld, Hampton. 2002. "The Benefits and Deficiencies of Unions in Public Libraries." *Public Libraries* 41 (3): 135-142.

Communicating with Senior Management

Effective communication with your direct supervisor should be the easiest to achieve, as there are only two people involved. Shared experiences and length of time working together should lead to close to 100 percent correlation between meaning and interpretation.

However, even in this area it takes an effort. After ten years as the senior manager, Ed Evans hired an administrative assistant with over twelve years of experience in the same type of job for a large medical library—clearly someone with substantial experience with library operations. During the performance assessment session (six months into the job), when asked what Evans could do to make her job easier, she responded, "It's taken me a while to get use to your shorthand communication style. I think I'm catching on, but try to fill me in more. It will save us time in future, but for now give me more to work with." Five years later, she still occasionally reminds Evans to "expand on that." The key point is that timely, accurate feedback from both parties is critical for good communication.

Some other elements to keep in mind for good communication with the "boss" are:

- taking responsibility for the process—don't wait for her/him to take the lead;
- sharing both good and bad news quickly (bosses do not like being "blindsided" by an issue); and
- remembering that, while it is not necessary to always agree with what the boss says or does, you should do your disagreeing privately rather than publicly.

We emphasize that timely, accurate feedback *in both* directions is perhaps the most critical aspect of effective communication with the boss.

A new manager needs to learn the organization's communication style. Some organizations, even those with teams, may be very formal and expect anything of substance to be in written form; others are highly informal and almost everything is discussed orally. Most organizations fall somewhere in between, which presents a learning challenge for a newcomer. What must be recorded what isn't, and what are the exceptions? Are there differences between how things are handled when communicating with senior managers versus other unit heads?

Communicating with Staff

Remember that there are two major subgroups for staff communication—new and existing.

Very often, a manager's communication with other unit staff (in team settings, with cross-trained staff, and with those sharing holiday, weekend, and evening hours, for example) occurs through the person's direct supervisor, adding another dimension and level of complexity to communication. While your message may be fully understood by the other supervisor, you have little, if any, control over what may be conveyed to the staff member. Direct communication reduces the risks of filtering, —leveling, sharpening, and assimilation—but organizational culture and communication style may make direct communication inappropriate.

If new hires are given a good orientation and receive an early sense of how communication and interactions in the unit take place during their first few days on the job, their adjustment to the new conditions will be easier. If nothing else, they can spend more time mastering the work and less attempting to ascertain how the workgroup communicates and interacts.

Keep in mind the major purposes of supervisory communication outlined by Conroy and Jones (1986).

- To inform: convey both information and understanding.
- To gather information: collect input from others to help make decisions and solve problems.
- To motivate: change or reinforce behavior, and prompt specific action.
- To instruct and/or train: enable another to carry out instructions, tasks, or procedures appropriately.
- To coach and/or discipline: foster growth and prevent disciplinary action, help another learn how to do a specific task better, and improve attitudes or behavior.
- To counsel: help someone with a personal problem that affects work productivity or morale.
- To mentor: help another succeed, usually by imparting better understanding of organizational policies, practices, or politics.
- To develop staff: guide staff progress and growth with performance appraisals and goal-setting sessions.
- To build teams: help work groups establish interpersonal rapport, build esprit de corps, and develop cohesion.

Graham and Valentine (1973) point out that the communication problem is even more complex when the "established" or "official" channels are involved, because staff see these channels as manipulative and receive the messages—if they receive them at all—with considerable cynicism.

But the fundamental problem is even more serious, because the act of communicating itself is seen as inherently manipulative and attempts at communication are often evaluated in terms of observed change in behavior on the part of the receivers of the message.

Since the staff may perceive a manipulative intent, the manager should always remain aware that a degree of hostility could be present. There are means to counteract this hostility:

- Try to establish authenticity by achieving rapport with the staff—engendering an atmosphere wherein staff are free to discuss problems without fear of reprisal.
- Shorten the period of time between work activities and their evaluation. The process is less threatening when it involves the immediate situation rather than a review of a person's year's work.
- Involve the staff in all processes of the unit, giving each person an opportunity to see that each job is important to the unit's success.

All of these steps assist in achieving better communication through feedback and shared experiences.

The middle manager should take the lead in the feedback by asking for it rather than waiting to see if it materializes. How that request is made, as well as overall manager-staff relations, will determine the accuracy of the feedback. For it to be useful, the manager *must* make it clear that questions, clarifications, etc., are welcome and that the goal is to assure that everyone is "on the same page."

With a multicultural staff, the manager should be aware of possible cultural values that may prevent some individuals from expressing confusion or contradicting the "boss."

TIP

Listen to staff as much as you talk to them. As Maurice Line said, "Feelings are facts; ignore them at your peril."

Communicating Outside the Organization

VENDORS AND SUPPLIERS

The two groups that middle managers most often communicate with are members of the service community, and vendors and suppliers. Working with vendors is more like working with staff, because any vendors who have been in the business for any length of time have learned the jargon related to their area of interest—if they haven't contributed the jargon themselves. Also, it is to the benefit of the vendor to make sure their representatives are cognizant of service-related terms and their meanings.

One of the balancing acts for the middle manager working with vendors is knowing what to share and not to share while trying to maintain honest and open communication. Based on the authors' experiences, there are a few vendor representatives who seem to thrive on "picking up the latest" about service X and sharing with all their other customers. Vendor "reps" can be a useful source of relatively current information about how other services are addressing a problem or issue, or what new product is or isn't working.

Maintaining the proper balance between under- and overcommunicating information about the service can be a challenge. How relevant is information about funding levels, staffing changes, and so on? Again, time with the various "reps" and chats with colleagues, as well as with your supervisor, will help you sort out the important from the unimportant information.

PROFESSIONAL COLLEAGUES IN OTHER SERVICES

Communicating with colleagues in other services has two aspects—working situations in professional groups or collaborative projects, and networking with former classmates and others you regard as friends, at least on a professional level.

Working in professional groups is similar to contact in the workplace, but with less shared time or experiences. This results in a very formal communication style (especially when individuals know little about each other), more jargon use, and little feedback beyond formal comments on proposals or documents.

Middle managers, especially newcomers, should develop a support network of professional colleagues, ideally consisting of a number of peers in terms of age, experience, and responsibility, and one or two older individuals who act as mentors. Having one or two people in the network from your service can be advantageous, as they more fully understand the local environment. While such groups are useful in stress control, they also have advantages for communication.

The peer group provides a mechanism for talking through issues outside the organizational framework and addressing concerns about the consequences of what is said. Peer networks can be effective tools for "thinking out loud" without worrying about what people think, for seeking advice when you want it, and for sharing work experiences and "horror stories" as well as personal issues.

Mentors are also good for these reasons, but the relationship is more formalized, like that of a student and teacher, and often there is an unspoken expectation that the mentor *will* offer advice, thoughts, or opinions. Mentors may also assist in advancing one's career.

COMMUNICATING WITH SUPPORT STAFF

Communicating with support staff who are employees of the parent organization (academic, city, corporate, etc.), but not part of the service can be complicated. Facilities staff tend to be tradespeople and union members whose contracts often have detailed work rules spelling out who can request whom to do what and what will and will not be done (housekeeping staff may not be permitted to dust the book stacks, for example). For someone without prior experience with union staff, trying to communicate with them can be like walking into a minefield blindfolded.

A new manager coming into a union environment is well advised to find time early on to read the terms of the contract in order to avoid unexpected consequences. Remember the danger of indirect communication—sometimes all communication regarding work issues must go through a union representative, who usually is not the person who will do the work.

The technology support personnel, especially those who are not staff members of the service, pose another communication challenge. When information professionals and systems support personnel get together, jargon seems to be all anyone can speak. Part of the issue, at least in the U.S., is that all too many of the "techies" don't understand that information professionals do have some grasp of technology and most information professionals *know* that the techies don't understand the needs of their service. When both sides have doubts about the other side's understanding of the issues, lots of words will be said but little information will be gained by either side.

One of the difficulties is the clash of the "service" goals of the two professions. A major goal for systems people is network security, which usually translates into trying to keep the incoming and outgoing data flow from the local system as low as possible. Information professionals have just the opposite goal, wanting the "pipe" to be as wide open as possible to assure the access to all the electronic resources outside the local system. Both sides must recognize this conflict and address it head-on before there can be any meaningful communication.

> TIP
>
> Jargon is a barrier to effective communication. Use it with great care.

COMMUNICATING WITH USERS

There are times when we, the information professionals, forget that users are the reason our services exist and meeting their needs requires effective communication. Are our OPACs and databases really user-friendly? Are we offering services that users truly want and need? Are our collections, regardless of format, appropriate for user needs? The list could go on, but the point is that we need clear user feedback to answer these questions.

All communication rests on a number of assumptions, several of which have special significance in service provider-user communications. Ford (1989: 8-9) offers five of the most significant assumptions:

- communication has verbal and nonverbal components;
- communication has content and relationship components;
- communication is influenced by context;
- communication is transactional; and
- communication requires cooperation.

Service providers send both *verbal and nonverbal* messages during a service transaction. When the two are congruent, users easily understand the message(s); however, when they are incongruent the customer becomes confused and tends to believe the nonverbal message(s).

Service providers establish content and relationship messages that are informational and attitudinal in character during the transaction. The definition of the transaction arises from the content side of the message, while the interpersonal aspect comes from the relationship-oriented message.

The service context is influenced by the physical surroundings during the transaction (an open environment with other people present vs. a one-on-one office setting, for example). The context is influential in determining the approach to the service—courteous, manipulative, or personalized (more about these later). Service interactions are highly transactional in character—both provider and customer constantly exchange both verbal and nonverbal messages while interpreting and reacting to messages received.

Part of the cooperative character necessary for successful transactions comes from the provider and customer developing accurate role expectations and following expected behavior patterns.

WORTH CHECKING OUT

Communicating with users

Ford, Wendy Zabava. 1998. *Communicating With Customers: Service Approaches, Ethics and Impact.* Creskill, N.J.: Hampton Press.

Here is a taste to tempt you to check out Ford's book. Ford (1998) identified three broad categories of service approaches based on empirical research from the fields of communication, psychology, sociology, marketing management, and organizational behavior. They are:

- courteous service,
- manipulative service, and
- personalized service.

Rapport is the starting point of service transactions and a key element in the courteous service approach, which almost everyone thinks of as *customer service*. However, it very often shifts to either the manipulative (think about the last time you purchased an automobile) or personalized service approach. The courteous approach should be the *basic* approach, as it is based upon the provider and customer having fully understood their roles in the transaction process.

There are three important elements of the courteous approach:

- phatic speech,
- nonverbal immediacy, and
- verbal immediacy.

By using simple words and phrases, basic pleasantries ("good morning," "nice day," etc.), and "small talk" (non-transaction conversation) the provider engages in *phatic speech* (DeVito, 1970).

Research by Higgins, Rholes, and Jones (1977) indicated that people are most influenced by the first and last information they receive. In our experience, services are very good about the way they open a transaction but give little thought to the closing. An important fact to keep in mind is that too much phatic speech can be detrimental to a person's perception of good service, primarily when the speed of the transaction is an important customer value.

FOR FURTHER THOUGHT

Consider some of the call center services you use in your personal life.

- How do the operators open the contact?
- What do they use to close?
- Do these change if the call becomes difficult, i.e. a problem is not being resolved?

Haase and Trepper (1972) found that *nonverbal immediacy* (eye contact, body orientation, etc.) contributed more to a customer's sense of empathy during the transaction than did verbal behaviors. If there is incongruity between the two, the customer usually perceives the phatic/courteous speech as false. Keep in mind that most of the research in this field took place in the U.S., which means some of the findings may not apply elsewhere.

Verbal immediacy is achieved through subtle stylistic speech differences. For example, saying "we" rather than "you" ("Let's see if we can find what you need") can create a sense of psychological closeness. Other more immediate language forms are "here," "these," and "this" rather than "there," "those," and "that." One issue in creating and maintaining courteous service is the degree to which the provider shows responsibility for what transpires. Using conditional statements distances the provider from the user—say "It is evident that your books are overdue" rather than "I see your books are overdue." Part of the effective process is to share responsibility; for example, saying "Here are some options for handling the fine" is better than "How are you going to pay the fine?"

Manipulative service occurs in a variety of forms and is *not* always negative. It is a strategy for achieving the provider's objectives, and sometimes that objective is to provided user- centered service. You must be certain that you are, in fact, working for the benefit of the user and not the organization.

Bureaucratization is one form of manipulative service that information services often slip into after a courteous opening. The communication/behavior norms that govern this approach are *affective neutrality, specificity,* and *universalism.*

As the term suggests, affective neutrality results in a detached communication and behavior pattern by maintaining a neutral tone of voice.

Specificity means limiting communication to the business at hand, avoiding as much as possible any nonessential conversation with the user.

It is easy to see why universalism, which calls for equal treatment of users regardless of status or other variables, is a common approach for information services and those serving high numbers of users. Limited staffing and heavy customer demand puts pressure on staff to quickly focus on one user's needs so that they can move on to the next person. Further, professional training and values make neutrality and universalism the appropriate modes of provider-user interaction in services with high numbers of users. The response will be very different in information and knowledge management services where the staffing/user ratio allows in-depth service for specialist users with known information needs.

Interaction control occurs in situations where the service provider/organization wants to exercise some control over transactions in terms of timing, content, and perhaps purpose. For example, today a great many information desks must attempt to handle in-person, telephone, and electronic inquiries, but their staffing situation allows only one person on duty to handle all queries. Services with little available staff support must "control" interactions by putting lower priority requests on hold in order to handle higher priority requests; a common hierarchy is first to handle in-person, then telephone, and finally electronic requests. Another way services attempt to control interactions is by trying to "teach the user" to be more independent and thus place fewer demands on the staff. Such techniques are similar to compliance gaining.

Compliance gaining has the goal of influencing customer/user behavior, which can be positive (medical staff attempting to achieve patient compliance) or negative (automobile salesperson attempting to force the customer to buy now). There is a large body of literature on this topic.

WORTH CHECKING OUT

Compliance gaining

Marwell, Gerald, and David R. Schmitt. 1967. "Dimensions of Compliance Gaining Behavior." *Sociometry* 30 (3): 350-364.

Personalized service is what most libraries and information centers wish they could achieve—but the problems of staffing, funding, and space make this an ideal which is only achievable in specialist services. Suprenant and Soloman defined personalized service as "behaviors occurring in the interaction intended to contribute to the individuation of the customer" (Suprenant and Soloman, 1987: 87). But, in truth, in almost every service there are a few users who are "more equal than others." An inquiry from the office of the president, mayor, or school superintendent demands personalized service, followed by some of the "regular heavy users." The reality is that services employ elements of all three approaches.

There are four communication strategies associated with personalized service—*customer orientation, interaction involvement, information sharing, and social support*. Without question, the service philosophy of the information professional is to provide user orientation and to assist with their *information needs.*

FOR FURTHER THOUGHT

How many of the following user orientation behaviors were covered in your qualifying course work?

- Help the user make satisfactory decisions.
- Help users assess their needs.
- Offer products that satisfy the user's needs.
- Describe products and services accurately.
- Match presentations to user's interest(s).
- Avoid manipulative influence methods.
- Provide the user with "thinking time."

Interaction involvement is the degree to which the service provider becomes fully engaged with the user, both cognitively and behaviorally, during the inquiry. Involvement requires full attention (nonverbal cues often give away lack of attention), perceptiveness, clarification, and finally interpretation.

Information professionals have expertise beyond that of the customers, and users expect such individuals to share that expert information. How much is shared and the method employed takes place through use of framing techniques.

WORTH CHECKING OUT

Framing techniques

Guinan, Patricia J., and Joseph N. Scudder. 1987. "Client-Oriented Interactional Behaviors for Professional Client Settings." *Human Communication Research* 15 (3): 444-462.

Framing methods are means the provider uses to present information or questions to the customer in a way that the customer can easily understand. Guinan and Scudder (1989) describe seven framing methods—outcome, backtrack, pointer, metaphor, metacommunication, as-if, and metaframe.

Social support is a basic element in the so-called "helping professions" that may be a simple extension of phatic speech patterns, or may involve demonstrating sensitivity to customer uncertainty and/or increasing the customer's self-esteem, or providing the customer with a sense of social connection with others.

Communicating with the Unhappy User

No matter what approach(es) a service employs, they will sometimes need to handle customers who are confused, upset, angry, or disruptive. The first level, and the most common, is the *confused* and/or *upset* user who may not understand a policy or rule. With these users, as well as those at other levels, attentive listening is the starting point. Asking for additional information is often helpful: "Tell me more." "What have you tried so far?" "I do not quite understand, please tell me about…" Paraphrasing the person's comments tells the upset user that he/she is being listened to. This is one of the times when distancing is appropriate, so avoid making the response a personal choice ("I wish I could…") and keep the answers within the realm of service policy and practice. Your focus should be on determining what the situation is, keeping the user from becoming angry, and finding a proper solution, do not let it become a personal matter between user and staff member.

Level two—the *angry* user—is more complex and less common, or at least it should be. Angry users fall into one of three categories of anger: controlled, expressed, and irrational.

Occasionally the user who appears confused is really in a state of controlled anger, so a wise approach is to treat any person with a complaint or problem as if they are at some level of controlled anger. Such an assumption, if steps one and two of the following method are utilized, should keep the situation under control Step three is only for individuals clearly in a controlled anger state.

The steps are to:

- rephrase/paraphrase the user's statement of concern;
- always treat the user with respect and her/his concern as important;
- clearly state the position of the service on the concern, once the nature of the concern is fully understood; or
- present firmly and clearly the possible consequences of action contrary to the position of the service.

When rephrasing the user's statement/concern, choose your own words; do not "parrot" (repeat word for word) the user's comments. In some cultures, parroting someone's comments is seen as a form of ridicule. A key element in restating is not to talk down, use professional jargon, or use elaborate words. Using jargon and/or complex terms and words may also offend some users. By paraphrasing, you give the user an opportunity to clarify any misunderstanding and it suggests that you are attempting to understand the situation. However, using phrases that represent the service as the "authority" and the user as "subordinate" is almost certain to escalate the situation.

Another way to show your commitment to finding a solution and your respect for the individual is to acknowledge her/his emotions regarding the situation—even if you don't agree with her/his argument.

Explain the policy or issue from the perspective of the service and the limits on what can immediately be done. Presenting the position of the service clarifies the situation and establishes the issue(s) that need addressing in order to reach a solution.

An alternative approach, if the situation appears to be escalating, is to outline the possible consequences if the user persists, allowing the user to make a decision about her/his behavior or position with full awareness of the possible outcomes and demonstrates trust in the user's decision-making capability.

While this step may make the user angrier or be read as an ultimatum, the demonstration of concern and respect for the person's rational decision-making capability more often than not leads to a successful resolution.

When the user is openly angry, there are some slight differences in how to respond. Begin by acknowledging the user's anger. As with the controlled-anger user, the goal is validation and understanding of anger and feelings Be certain that you have clearly identified the problem; rephrasing the expressed concern allows the person to verify that there is or is not agreement as to the nature of the problem.

Explain how the user's behavior affects you. Focusing on the behavior and its effect keeps the focus off the person and leaves little room for the user to argue, especially if you have already acknowledged that this person's anger is justified. Saying "This behavior..." rather than "You..." usually makes the person much less defensive and consequently easier to handle. Avoid sweeping generalities about the behavior's impact.

Asking specific questions about the problem or issue and letting the individual fully respond usually narrows the scope of the problem and helps identify possible ways to resolve it.

Level three, the *disruptive* individual, is irrationally angry, and the first step is to allow the person to vent her/his emotions. Although it is not enjoyable to listen to someone "rant and rave," there is a better chance of resolving the situation if you begin by letting them release their anger. A person who is irrationally angry will not be very likely to hear anything until they have "had their say." It may be difficult to be patient and listen for clues as to what is the issue is, but it is essential in such situations. There is little point in a long explanation or in apologizing unless it is clear that there was an obvious service error.

After the person finishes expressing the anger (one indication of this is when there are repetitive statements), the steps for dealing with expressed anger can be followed. All too often it is necessary in such situations to use direct confrontation: "Your behavior is disruptive to our work (and perhaps to other people here). If you do not stop, then we must..." (call the security office/police, for example). Try to present the statement in a non-emotional manner. The statement sets clear limits and states what the consequences will be but leaves it to the user to decide what to do.

> TIP
>
> **You have a user who is upset**
>
> - Listen first; watch for nonverbal clues as to the emotional state of the person.
> - Rephrase the person's concern in order to clarify the issue.
> - Maintain a non-emotional state, if possible.
> - Acknowledge the emotions and don't try to calm the user just to assure your own comfort. The goal is to find a solution.
> - Avoid being defensive; it usually does not help to resolve the situation.
> - State clearly the options and consequences in institutional, rather than personal, terms, and, if possible, allow the user to decide which option to take.

SELECTING THE CORRECT CHANNEL AND MODE

Earlier in this chapter, we described the directions in which communication flows. Let's now turn to the channels that can be used to communicate with the various constituencies. Selecting the correct channel and mode for a particular group of people enhances the chances of achieving an effective communication, but the selection process is somewhat more complex than you might expect.

There are three channels—written, spoken, and pictorial. Each one has its advantages and disadvantages for the various constituencies, and each has a number of associated modes.

Modes of Communication		
Written	**Spoken**	**Pictorial**
• Letter	• One-on-one	• Slides
• Telex/cable	• Small groups meeting	• Film
• Memo	• Presentation	• TV/Video
• Major circulation	• Film publication	• Overhead projection
• Small circulation	• TV/Video publication	• Photographs, charts, drawings, etc.
• Fax	• Telephone (one-on-one)	• Quantitative data
• Advertising	• Telephone (conference call)	
• Electronic (e-mail)	• Radio	
• Quantitative data	• Videoconferencing	

The greater part of the management literature relating to channel and mode selection tends to reflect Anglo communication priorities—speed and efficiency, relatively high individualism with narrow power distances, legalistic approach to relationships, and the importance of planning for the future.

In the near future, we expect that new research will emerge to address the changing structure of organizations. The existing literature on the subject presupposes a command and control system that has been, and is, changing rapidly, and it tends to oversimplify the complexity of contemporary organizations. That said, there is useful information on the factors to consider when selecting a channel and mode.

CHANNEL AND MODE SELECTION FACTORS

- Number of receivers
- Identity(ies) and needs of receivers
- Relationship with receiver(s)
- Complexity of the message
- Importance of the message and the need for impact
- Routine/original quality of the message
- Complexity of the language used
- Need for pictorial/quantitative data
- Function of the message (persuade, sell, inform, etc.)
- Distance/location of the receiver
- Need for speed—urgency
- Need for accuracy
- Need for legal protection
- Need for receiver feedback
- Availability of communication technology
- Cost
- Precedent

Written Communication

Deciding when to write and when to talk is a matter of fine judgment, and the judgment extends to deciding whether to write on paper or use an Intranet or e-mail. At times, it is best to provide written statements and then clarify them orally through question-and-answer exchanges.

Policies should always be written, and it certainly helps if instructions and procedures are clearly written. It is essential, however, that the managers follow up written documents with an oral presentation that allows the staff to ask questions.

Every letter and memo, whether electronic or paper, is to some degree a "sales" letter. Fine directional hinting is best for persuading readers—avoid overtly blunt statements. It is vital that memos receive careful attention as to wording; all too often managers spend too little time on memos, thinking they are not as significant as letters and other "formal documents." All written material is important in that it conveys an image of the sender. Careless memos suggest to some people that the writer is careless or, worse, that the writer does not respect the receiver(s) enough to prepare a sound document.

Shared vocabulary is essential for any on-the-job communications, whether with workers or with superiors. Consider the degree of abstraction of the material under consideration and use simple sentences. Restrict inspirational flights of prose to situations that are general in nature and concrete in subject matter. Jargon or shoptalk is all right if the reader understands it and if it does not actively interfere with (complicate) the message's content. The problem with many memos lies in not planning or not thinking about the factors appearing in the Channel and Mode Selection box above.

Obviously, two important aspects of written communication are readability and structure. An effective document includes a frame of reference (established at the beginning), a clear, well-thought-out statement of what is meant or desired, and an explanation of how, when, and where the staff is to meet the expectations.

Electronic Communication

By providing Intranet access for all staff, a manager creates a more democratic working environment. The range of information sources provided is only limited by the manager's imagination. Some possibilities are:

- policy documents needed for reference by staff;
- replacements for hard-copy staff handbooks;
- internal information, e.g., dates, times, and agendas for meetings; and
- access to external databases.

The advantages are that:

- updating can be done speedily;
- managers can be sure that staff have access to the most recent information;
- information can be quickly disseminated;
- internal discussion groups can be established;
- the volume of paper circulating can be reduced; and
- the work of the secretarial staff can be examined to produce a more interesting workload.

The disadvantages are that:

- every member of staff needs access—hardware, a password, and training;
- there is the real danger of an information overload;
- chaos may reign and information will not be systematically updated if there is no single person responsible for Intranet management.

It is essential that one person have responsibility for the management of the Intranet, ensuring that updates and deletions take place promptly. The design and layout of the Intranet needs attention so that it is easy to navigate and locate information and is visually attractive.

Useful external information sources may be identified that could make the work of staff easier. For personnel staff, this may be the provision of relevant legislation online; for management, the management checklists published by the professional management bodies; for specialist inquiry staff, the subject-focused databases, etc.

The aim of the Intranet is to provide easy access to up-to-date information required by the staff in their daily work. In a service where the staff work shifts, making it difficult to get everyone together, an Intranet can ensure that everyone has equal access to needed information.

E-MAIL

Electronic communication has been technically possible since the early 1970s, but really started in earnest in the 1990s with the growth in the number of Internet service providers. In some ways, it has been a great blessing, resulting in ease of communication around the globe. E-mail, like letters, allows the receiver time to think before replying, unlike a telephone call, particularly one that involves a mobile phone.

However, there is also the danger of an information overload. There may be a perceived sense of urgency about attending to e-mail on the part of both sender and receiver. For example, business executives report that they have difficulties keeping up with their mail, and e-mail now follows middle and senior mangers home and on vacation. And when the service goes down just when we are expecting a quick answer to a query, our stress level rises.

Perhaps one of the greatest concerns is the way in which the developed world takes e-mail for granted, while in the less-developed countries, access to hardware, software, and reliable telecommunications may prevent access to the Internet. In some developed countries, local telecommunication companies may not time-charge local calls, making access to an ISP inexpensive; in other countries, all calls are time-charged, adding to the bills at home or in the office.

Guidelines and procedures for the use of electronic communication technology are a must. First, decide the legitimate uses of e-mail and Internet access at work. Second, decide what electronic records are to be archived, where, and for how long. Make the guidelines clear to all members of staff within the organization, and require departing staff be restricted from purging their files without consultation with the nominated responsible officer.

WORTH CHECKING OUT

Netiquette

Ross, Catherine S., and Patricia Dewdney. 1998. *Communicating Professionally.* 2d ed. New York: Neal-Schuman.

There are a few basic points to bear in mind when using e-mail:

- Include your address, phone number, and fax number so that you can be identified and a reply can be sent in a different format if preferred by the recipient.
- Ask yourself if your message is really necessary or if it is more of a "chat." Don't use e-mail for passing on gossip.
- Make it short.
- Think before you write, and think before you send—it is easy to write in haste and have later regrets (perhaps over style or content of the message).
- Give an indication of the subject to allow the receiver to prioritize their messages.
- Make sure the receiver will understand the content—avoid using an abbreviation unless you know it will be understood.
- Check the spelling.
- Remember the legal constraints, and that a message sent outside the library may be taken to represent the view of your employer.
- Observe the organizational policies and procedures for filing electronic mail.
- Select the discussion lists that you join carefully—they can be time-consuming—and observe the same courtesies as you would in joining a discussion around a table.

TIP

Ensure that your service has guidelines for the use of e-mail, the Internet, and Intranet that are revised regularly and communicated to all staff. They need to know what is expected of them and what can and cannot be done.

FOR FURTHER THOUGHT

Reflect on your use of e-mail and the Internet.

Drawing on this experience, list six benefits and six problems.

Oral Communication

A new middle manager should keep the following points in mind regarding oral communication.

Do:

- let other people talk;
- keep the discussion from wandering aimlessly;
- keep it simple and straight; and
- get to know the level of understanding of the person you are talking with.

Do not:

- take the supervisory position too seriously;
- become overcommitted to an idea; or
- argue.

A speaker's position naturally affects the way people listen and respond to that person. If someone who holds a superior position acts in a superior manner, that person will have problems talking with subordinates.

New managers (as well as for the experienced manager) should not fall into the trap of becoming an instant expert on everything. An instant expert never hears anything that others say, unless it provides her/him with a springboard, and subordinates of such a person stop listening.

Total commitment to one idea—to the exclusion of entertaining a discussion of the idea's possible defects—is another way to lose an audience. When the manager believes that there is only one right way, and the workers know from experience that it is not working, the workers usually remain quiet until the system collapses.

Arguments seldom solve problems and do not lead to understanding, but the line between discussion and argument is often quite fine. To say "I disagree with that!" or "You are dead wrong!" is a very good way to turn a discussion into an argument. Managers who cut off (or cut down) subordinates in this way almost guarantee themselves serious personnel problems.

Although there are times when the direct approach is best, an indirect approach using a third party or hypothetical situations (based on actual knowledge of circumstances), is usually best when discussing personal feelings and behavior. However, if the indirect approach is not followed up by a more direct discussion, the entire point may well be lost or serious misunderstandings may occur. Always focus on the issue or situation, and not on the individual.

FOR FURTHER THOUGHT

Which is your preferred method of communication, and why?

Do you need to brush up your skills in using any methods?

LISTENING—THE KEY TO EFFECTIVE COMMUNICATION

We were given one mouth and two ears, perhaps to suggest that we should listen twice as much as we speak. When people discuss good communication, more often than not there is little or no time given to the "art of listening." Like any art, listening requires practice, and few us have really mastered it.

Listening is harder than most people realize. We hear about four times faster than most people speak; that leaves about three-quarters of our listening time free for the mind to wander, and it will unless we concentrate on listening.

Think back to a recent speech or lecture you attended. Can you honestly state that you did not think about where to eat afterwards, errands to run, letters to write, something you want to say to someone in the audience, or a host of other matters unrelated to what the speaker was saying? If you can, then you are one of the few who really practice the art of listening, and have no need to join the rest of us who need more practice.

According to communication researchers, we also "filter" what we do hear and later communicate via three major types of filtering: leveling, sharpening, and assimilation.

Leveling occurs when the recipient of a message omits certain elements of the original message and essentially changes its meaning. For example, suppose that a children's librarian is told that a vacant position will not be filled until the level of usage of children's services increases. There has been a decline in the number of children getting library cards and attending story hours and the department head wants time to develop a plan to increase the use of the services. The department head, in a leveling situation, might report to the department staff that the position was withdrawn because of a declining number of children using the library. While part of the original content comes through the filtering process, the meaning has been changed through significant omissions.

Sharpening is a process in which a part of a message receives greater emphasis than in the original message. Suppose that during a staff development review, a supervisor tells a staff member, "Your performance is excellent. If you continue at the present rate of development you may be considered for a new position that we expect to have in the next year or so." What the staff member tells others is, "I have been chosen for the new position the department will get next year." In essence, the person emphasizes what she/he wants to hear and plays down, or filters out, the qualifying elements.

Assimilation retains all of the original message and adds elements to it, thus expanding the original meaning. Suppose a university president told the university archivist, "I am talking with a potential donor who is interested in making a major contribution to the new archives building fund. I expect we will have an answer soon." The archivist reports to the staff, "The president is very supportive of a new archives building—it is a priority. The president is working with a prospective donor at present and a new building will be started very soon—as soon as the donor makes the major contribution." All of the elements of the original message are present, but there are many added elements that essentially change the meaning.

Barriers to Effective Listening

One of the most common problems in "hearing" a message is the listener's assumption that she/he already knows the subject, it is uninteresting, it is of no concern, or the topic is unimportant. As a listener, the best way to overcome this problem is to make a conscious effort to suspend judgment and keep an open mind from the outset.

Similarly, some listeners may be prone to spending so much time assessing or criticizing the speaker's method of presentation that they cease listening to the content—especially if they regularly give presentations themselves. Keeping an open mind will help, but the real issue is to stop focusing on the "how" of the message and to switch to the "what" of the presentation.

Jumping to conclusions is something most people do, at least occasionally. Listeners begin to think, assume, or feel that they know where the speaker is going with her/his talk, and listening either decreases or ceases entirely. To avoid jumping to conclusions, consciously reflect on what is being said; focus on the current words and not on assumptions about the ultimate purpose of the message.

Each of us has a set of phrases and words that we really do not like hearing because they carry special meanings based on one or more past experiences in which someone used them in a manner that caused us discomfort, harm, or emotional distress. Frequently these are relatively common words and phrases that have no special meaning for other people. In the workplace, we must be cautious about overreacting to any message, especially when we hear words or phrases from our personal meaning set.

Becoming overstimulated when questioning or opposing an idea also creates barriers to understanding. In such situations, the natural pattern is to plan one's response while the other person is talking. Needless to say, little of what the person says is heard, as the mind is focusing on the opportunity to respond. Overcoming this barrier requires practice and a substantial amount of self-awareness.

It may be difficult to paying attention to elements of agreement, but practice may improve one's ability to listen to areas of disagreement and may serve as a valuable starting point for resolving the conflict.

FOR FURTHER THOUGHT

Are you a talker or a listener—have you got the balance right?
Test this out with someone who knows you well.

FORMAL PRESENTATIONS

Upon moving into a middle management position, a newcomer may be surprised at how often she/he must give a presentation. A person with information literacy instruction (IL) experience whose training included the development and delivery of presentations has "a leg up."

For a number of people—even those who have had experience—giving a formal presentation is *very* stressful. There is a world of difference between presenting material to a group of students or users, some of whom have "completely tuned out" and most of whom are only partly paying attention, and presenting something to colleagues and senior managers who will be paying more or less close attention. In the case of senior management, they may even being making judgments about the individual's potential for higher posts.

While the following points may not reduce the stress felt at the prospect and at the time of delivery, they will help ensure that the presentation is well structured. For many people, just knowing this is a stress-reducer. The key is preparation; the more time spent on preparations, the more likely the presentation will be good. Following the checklist is no guarantee of success, but it will enhance the chances.

PRESENTATION CHECKLIST

- Define your objective—write a single sentence about your goal.
- Define your audience—analyze their level of knowledge of the topic, likes and dislikes, what they expect from the presentation.
- Define your approach—write a single sentence describing the thought or message that best leads into your topic.
- Develop your opening—you have thirty seconds to grab their attention; does it lead to your objective, relate to your audience, relate to your approach, and does have both verbal and visual impact?
- Develop the body—does it explain the point(s) you want to make, describe what you've done, use language appropriate for the audience, and deliver the message in the fewest possible words?
- Develop the closing—does it summarize your point in two or three memorable sentences and ask for the action you want from the audience in terms of specific steps and a timeline?
- Create visual aids—are they related to your point, helping you make your point, *readable* from all points in the room, and compatible with the time allotted?
- Time the presentation—is it 10 percent shorter than the time allotted?
- List dreaded questions—have you developed a list of potential difficult/dreaded questions and thought about how to answer them?
- List general questions—have you listed expected questions and your answers for them?
- Check the room layout—are the room and expected audience size compatible?
- Check the lectern—is it the right height for you, and is there a glass of water?
- Consider other distractions—have you checked out lighting, temperature controls, and possible noise sources? Are there any trailing cables to avoid?
- Check PowerPoint/projectors/visual equipment—if you are using equipment, have you checked it out in terms of operation, is there backup in case of failure, and do you have a number to call for technical assistance, if required?

- Rehearse—have you rehearsed the presentation a number of times from start to finish, using your visual aids if appropriate?
- Test PowerPoint/slides—have you tested your presentation/slides, are they in the correct order and right side up?
- Develop choreography—have you thought about how you will move to and from the visuals?
- Plan audience participation—is there an element where you can gain audience participation in the presentation?
- Plan questions for the audience—are there questions you could ask the audience during the presentation, and have you factored into your timing their involvement or lack thereof?
- Plan handouts—are there handouts that you want the audience to have, and when should the distribution take place—before, during, or after the presentation? If the distribution is before or during, have you considered how that might impact on your timing or verbal presentation?
- Consider attire—if in doubt, tend toward the conservative, but have a bright scarf or tie that is visually attractive. Check in a mirror before going to the room.
- Analyze post-presentation—after the presentation, analyze, with a participant if possible, what worked, what didn't work, and presentation time vs. rehearsal time.

KEY POINTS FOR EFFECTIVE COMMUNICATION

Communication is a complex activity at the best of times, but when issues of cultural and gender diversity are added, it becomes an even greater challenge. The content of this chapter is strongly focused on the U.S./U.K. work environment.

> WORTH CHECKING OUT
>
> **Cross-cultural communication**
>
> Mead, Richard. 1990. *Cross-Cultural Management Communication.* New York: Wiley & Sons.

There are key points for managers to keep in mind if they want clear and effective communication.

- Know what to communicate.
- Know who needs to know what.
- Know who should communicate with whom.
- Know how to time messages.
- Know how to listen and read.
- Don't judge and evaluate the other person.
- Demonstrate empathy and understanding.

- Ask open questions.
- Check your perceptions of what others are saying.
- Check the perceptions of others of what you have said.
- Concentrate on the other person, even when your mind wants to go elsewhere.
- Give timely, effective feedback.
- Be open to receiving feedback, without reacting emotionally.
- Evaluate both verbal and nonverbal signals.
- Be certain your verbal and nonverbal signals are congruent.
- Be conscious of and control the nonverbal signals you send.
- Use language that is understandable to the other person.
- Look beyond the appearance of the person—seek the message.
- Be enthusiastic.

AND

- Be very generous with praise that is deserved!

For further thought

Reviewing *your* communication skills:

- Which mode of communication are you most comfortable with?
- Which mode of communication are you least comfortable with?

Now:

Thinking about communication in general:

- What are your strengths?
- What are your weaknesses?

Some key points for managers to remember:

One of the factors that influences preferred communication practices is personality—for example, being outgoing or reserved.

Another factor can be experience in using, for example, e-mail. This may affect your preferred mode of communication.

Understanding our strengths and weaknesses identifies our training needs.

MANAGING CONFLICT

Although we all probably wish it were not true, that fact is that conflict is a part of life. It has been said that conflict is a growth industry, and, unfortunately, we believe that is correct, in part, because of the growing use of teams. Teams can be stressful because they require a high degree of cooperation and consensus to function, but they are beneficial because they allow greater participation in decision-making. Individuals tend to enjoy that participation—until they are the "odd person out" on a decision.

In a traditional work environment, a staff member has to convince only the supervisor/manager that a problematic decision needs modification, whereas in a team, probably more than half the members supported the problematic decision in the first place. Changing several people's mind about something is much more difficult than changing one person's mind. Thus, the seeds of conflict are planted and often grow quickly. (**Note:** this is *not* meant to suggest that conflict only arises in a team setting; nothing could be further from the truth. The point is only that the team environment has added another element to conflict development and resolution.)

Watching for signs of conflict that will impair team activities is one of the monitoring responsibilities of a middle manager. Thus, knowing something about conflict management and resolution is essential for success.

Not all conflict is bad. In fact, it can produce innovative, or at least new, ideas that allow the organization to move into other useful areas. Sorting out the useful from dysfunctional conflict is one of the hallmarks of an effective manager.

Conflict resolution and negotiation are interrelated, and the basics of negotiation are addressed in chapter 4. In the current chapter, the focus is on those aspects of negotiation that relate to resolving dysfunctional conflict.

Models of conflict are based on two axioms: conflict invariably involves more than one person, and it involves a negative intersection/interaction of values, beliefs, etc. Some years ago, Ken Jones wrote the following:

> Conflict with others is the strongest and most disturbing way in which organizational change may be experienced, and its successful resolution appears as one of the most intractable and difficult problems. Objectively, conflict appears as a disagreement about what should or should not be done. Subjectively, and less consciously, it is experienced either as a threat and challenge to the needs, status, authority and even sense of identity of oneself or one's group, or as an opportunity for stronger self-confirmation. The significance and relative force of these two facets of conflict will, of course, differ from one situation to another, but they are as integrally related as the two sides of this page. (Jones, 1984: 235)

Although Jones's focus was on change and conflict, his points apply to any conflict situation.

There are three "modes" of conflict—fight, flight, and flow.

Fight is the most difficult mode for the manager to address, because the fighter sees the issue(s) as right or wrong, and naturally her/his position is right. Fighters tend to have high energy levels, strong personalities, and a tendency to use intimidation to gain control or resolve the issue in their favor and produce an "I win, you lose" outcome. Often, at least in the U.S., there is the unspoken but clear threat of litigation. Fighters generally can only accept the facts that they have decided are correct, making it difficult for a third party to mediate.

Flight is the other end of the spectrum; some have said that this can be a typical mode in the information sector. The authors have seen more occurrences of flight or denial than fight; however, the fighters stand out in our memory. People in flight/denial modes tend to see issues as good or bad and prefer to avoid the discomfort of confrontation, even if it means "giving in" or compromising integrity and truth out of fear. These people will often even forego good performance if it might in some way create or increase conflict. Mediators have almost as big a challenge with the "fleers" as with the "fighters," because often they are ready to yield too quickly to any suggestion; the mediator knows that, in the long run, this will not resolve the issue.

If everyone would just go with the *flow*, conflict management would be easy. People in "flow" mode are willing to seek out what will in fact work; they are inclusive in their perspectives on issues and are willing and able to engage in dynamic exchanges with others in the search for a solution. They can take correction as well as give it without taking offense, because they separate the issue(s) from the person, which makes it easier to identify potential solutions.

FOR FURTHER THOUGHT

Think about some of the work conflict situations you have been in. Which mode is your typical response? As a person called upon to act as a third party, how would your typical conflict mode impact your efforts to reach a resolution?

The legal meaning of the word "mediator" carries a very specific meaning in the U.S., and mediating is even a profession. While the middle manager does not have to develop the skills of a certified mediator, some understanding of way professionals handle the process may save the library a substantial amount of money. (A professional mediator's fees are typically in the range of $5,000 U.S. per day; the fee quickly escalates with the complexity of the situation.). Mediation is informal as opposed to legalistic, facilitative rather than impositional, and its goal is to get the parties to find a mutually agreeable resolution.

The process begins with some fact-finding on the part of the third party, prior to any meeting with the parties involved in the conflict. How did the issue reach the level of needing third party intervention? Who are the individuals involved? Is there some history associated with the parties that may be relevant to the current situation?

Background information of this type helps the mediator prepare to probe and ask questions that will provide information, draw out issues, assists in anticipating where tensions may arise when the parties meet, and aids in developing a plan for reducing tensions. In addition, the information will help the mediator keep the parties on track, as well as develop a basis for rapport between the parties.

Effective mediation takes place in a "neutral" setting, which should be as pleasant a physical environment as possible. Obviously the space *must* be private both visually and audially. It is best not to have any telephone available, and participants should be told to turn off any cell phones—the idea is to have uninterrupted time with the focus solely on the issues in dispute. This also means that supervisors of the parties must not, to every degree possible, impose work deadlines that overlap with the meeting times.

Many mediators find it useful to employ tables when note-taking is necessary, but dispense with them when the goal is to achieve maximum interaction without a "barrier" between the parties. If you need a table, a round table is best, since it gives the sense of equality and there is no "head of the table."

Opening the session is the task of the mediator, and it is often the event that makes or breaks the process. The goal is to create a "safe" environment for the parties, to establish the mediator's credentials and role in the process, to explain what is and is not going to take place, and to answer questions. After the introductory activities are finished, the mediator's next goal is to get a commitment from the parties to be full participants in the process—this is one place where the modes of handling conflict show themselves. The opening session is also where the ground rules of behavior are established and agreed upon. If one or more of the parties are fleers and the other(s) are fighters, the mediator will have to spend some time on stress reduction.

If the process is to continue the same day, there should be a substantial break after the opening session to vent stress and other emotions. The mediator must be skillful enough to achieve emotional release while keeping personal attacks at bay. This is a fine line, and many managers do not have the background or skills to make this happen.

After the opening, the parties set forth their perceptions of the conflict, and the mediator clarifies the issues. A goal is to find areas of agreement on the nature of the issues, not the solution, as often even the nature is not mutually understood. If differences do exist, the mediator encourages the parties to explain why this is so.

Upon reaching agreement about the issues, the parties each are asked to say what it is they want and need in order to resolve the conflict. Almost always there are multiple issues and a need to establish a priority sequence for addressing them. The goal is for the participants to reach agreement, rather than the mediator making a decision for them; even small agreements are useful to show that the parties are able to agree, and that a satisfactory resolution is possible.

A successful mediation normally results in a written memorandum of understanding, even if only the parties to the dispute have copies. The memorandum should cover, for both parties:

- who is to perform which tasks;
- what specific performance is expected;
- when the performance is to occur;
- how the performance is to be handled;
- how much is expected; and

- what outcome will result from failure to perform.

The above are only highlights of the process, and reading about the subject is recommended, as conflicts will arise and must be dealt with. Simply using some of the techniques may keep the situation from escalating to the point of requiring the full process or a professional mediator.

WORTH CHECKING OUT

Conflict management

Leviton, Sharon, and James Greenstone. 1997. *Elements of Mediation*. Pacific Grove, Calif.: Brooks/Cole Publishing.

Wilkinson, Margaret, and John Wilkinson. 1997. "Plotting Conflict." *Library Administration and Management* 11 (4): 205-216. (This presents several conflict scenarios and possible solutions for each).

TRY THIS EXERCISE

Identify situations when you felt as if you were "being hassled" or "getting the runaround." Did you sometimes find that the person who was frustrating you did not have any authority to solve the issue/dispute? Did you fight, flee, or flow? Could you have settled the dispute more easily in some other way?

Consider your personal beliefs about what you think is right or wrong. List five of those beliefs that you are unwilling to compromise. How can you discover the beliefs/values that others are unwilling to change?

ETHICS AND COMMUNICATION

Having a code does not always translate into behavior reflective of the code. Most professional associations have a code of conduct, and while the vast majority of their members know that a code exists, few have actually studied the code.

What you say and actually do in reference to the code may be different, and you may not even be aware of it. Remember that people tend to read and believe the nonverbal signals when there is incongruity between your words and actions; thus, communication and ethics are connected.

FOR FURTHER THOUGHT

Do you *know* what topics are covered in the code of the professional association(s) you belong to?

Is there a difference between a code of conduct and code of ethics?

Our unique backgrounds and life experiences make communicating with another person somewhat of a challenge if our goal is 100 percent understanding. The same factors create similar issues for us when we "do ethics"— that is, when we reflect critically on the character and actions of ourselves, our organization, and our community. We become more ethically perceptive and sensitive individuals when we see ourselves as layers of contexts and understand what creates and changes those contexts.

Central to ethical practice and the idea of a caring community is an understanding of important moral principles and values. We live in organizations and the morality of those organizations live in us; there is a constant interaction that adjusts our context. When we join a professional organization, further adjustments take place as we come to understand the values residing in the organization and the moral consequences of joining it.

Professional associations set standards and codes which are perceived as *guidelines* to generally accepted norms, at least in the information profession. That means that, unlike the U.S. legal and medical professions, there is no enforcement beyond the individual's willingness to abide by the guidelines and perhaps some organizational oversight of overall performance.

What follows are not answers to how to behave ethically, but rather a series of questions/issues that need to be considered as we perform our duties. As noted above, morals/ethics are relative as to time, place, situation, etc., and are subject to change.

Let's take one example of the "relative" nature of the American Library Association's 1995 Code of Ethics. It states that libraries should provide users with "equitable services policies; equitable access; and accurate, unbiased, and courteous responses to all requests" (Section I). Later, in Section VII, it states, "We distinguish between our personal convictions and professional duties and do not allow our personal beliefs to interfere with fair representations of the aims of our institutions or the provision of access to their information resources."

What would be appropriate ethical or moral behavior at the reference desk if someone came to the desk asking for information on how to build a bomb? Almost twenty years ago, Hauptman (1976) did this in a number of academic libraries, and all the librarians helped him with his search, even though he strongly hinted that he intended to blow up a house. Given the current terrorist environment, do you think there would be a different reaction today? Even in 1975, was it appropriate to go against one's personal belief that blowing up a building and perhaps people is wrong in the name of professionalism? , With the U.S. passage of the "Homeland Security Act"

in 2002, the issue may have changed from an ethical to a legal consideration— a further indication of changing norms.

On a less life-threatening level, there are shifts in professional values over
time, such as the idea of neutrality/unbiased treatment of users which is
reflected in many information professional codes. In the 1960s, it was an article of professional faith, as Foskett wrote in *The Creed of a Librarian—No
Politics, No Religion, No Morals*, that "[d]uring the reference service, the
librarian ought virtually vanish as an individual person, except as in so far as
his personality sheds light on the working of the library" (1962: 10). Starting
in the late 1980s, the notion of neutrality was being challenged (Gremmels,
1990; Froehlich, 1998), and today there is little belief that such service can or
should exist, at least in an absolute form.

Professional ethics/behavior, of course, extend beyond interactions with
users to areas where ethical behavior is invisible to all or most people, such
as selecting materials for the collection or vendor/dealer relations. Also, the
ethical or unethical interaction with staff members is often unseen by those
outside the unit, except when there is a major problem with the behavior.

WORTH CHECKING OUT

Ethical behavior

Zipkowitz, Fay. 1996. *Professional Ethics in Librarianship: A
Real Life Casebook*. Jefferson, N.C.: McFarland & Company.

Juznic, Primoz, et al. 2001. "Excuse Me, How do I Commit
Suicide? Access to Ethically Disputed Items of Information in
Public Libraries." *Library Management* 22 (1/2): 75-79.

Froehlich, Thomas. 1998. "Ethical Considerations Regarding
Library Nonprofessionals." *Library Trends* 46 (3): 444-467.

A<small>FTER READING THIS CHAPTER YOU SHOULD BE AWARE</small>
<small>THAT</small>:

- communication is complex—culture and gender differences matter;
- feedback is essential for successful communication;
- managers communicate with a number of groups—and in different ways;
- selecting the correct channel and mode for each group makes for effective; communication
- listening is the key to effective communication;
- making presentations requires planning and careful thought;
- conflict is part of life;
- ethics are important; and
- as Maurice Line said, "Communication is *never* as good as you think."

REFERENCES

Angell, David, and Brent Heslop. 1994. *Elements of E-mail Style: Communicating Effectively Via Electronic Mail.* Reading, Mass.: Addison-Wesley.

Auld, Hampton. 2002. "The Benefits and Deficiencies of Unions in Public Libraries." *Public Libraries* 41 (3): 135-142.

Berlo, David K. 1960. *The Process of Communication.* New York: Holt.

Conroy, Barbara, and Barbara Jones. 1986. *Improving Communication in Libraries.* Phoenix, Ariz.: Oryx Press.

DeVito, Joseph A. 1970. *Psychology of Speech and Language.* New York: Random House.

Ford, Wendy Zabava. 1998. *Communicating with Customers: Service Approaches, Ethics, and Impact.* Creskill, N.J.: Hampton Press.

Foskett, Douglas J. 1962. *The Creed of a Librarian—No Politics, No Religion, No Morals.* London: Library Association.

Graham, Roderick, and M. Valentine. 1973. "Management, Communication, and the Destandardized Man." *Personnel Journal* 52 (November): 962-979.

Gremmels, Gillian. 1990. "Reference Service in the Public Interest: An Examination of Ethics." *RQ* 30 (fall): 362-369.

Guinan, Patricia J., and Joseph N. Scudder. 1987. "Client-Oriented Interactional Behaviors for Professional-Client Settings." *Human Communication Research* 15 (3): 444-462.

Haase, Richard F., and Donald T. Trepper. 1972. "Nonverbal Components of Empathic Communication." *Journal of Counseling Psychology* 19 (5): 417-424.

Hauptman, Robert. 1976. "Professionalism or Culpability? An Experiment in Ethics." *Wilson Library Bulletin* 5 (8): 626-627.

Higgins, E. Tory, William Rholes, and Carl Jones. 1977. "Category Accessibility and Impression Information." *Journal of Experimental Psychology* 13 (2): 141-154.

Jones, Ken. 1984. *Conflict and Change in Library Organizations.* London: Clive Bingley.

Juznic, Primoz, et al. 2001. "Excuse Me, How Do I Commit Suicide? Access to Ethically Disputed Items of Information in Public Libraries." *Library Management* 22 (1/2): 75-79

Leviton, Sharon, and James Greenstone. 1997. *Elements of Mediation.* Pacific Grove, Calif.: Brooks/Cole Publishing.

Marwell, Gerald, and David R. Schmitt. 1967. "Dimensions of Compliance Gaining Behavior." *Sociometery* 30 (3): 350-364.

Mead, Richard. 1990. *Cross-Cultural Management Communication.* New York: Wiley.

Ross, Catherine S., and Patricia Dewdney. 2002. *Communicating Professionally.* 2d ed. New York: Neal-Schuman.

Surprenant, Carol F., and Michael R. Soloman. 1987. "Predictability and Personalization in the Service Encounter." *Journal of Marketing* 51 (2): 86-96.

Tannen, Deborah. 1994. *Talking from 9 to 5: How Women's and Men's Conversational Styles Affect Who Gets Heard, Who Gets Credit, and What Gets Done at Work.* New York: Morrow.

"Factors Causing Workplace Stress." 2002. *USA Today.* (14 June): business section.

Wilkinson, Margaret, and John Wilkinson. 1997. "Plotting Conflict." *Library Administration and Management* 11 (4): 205-216.

Zipkowitz, Fay. 1996. *Professional Ethics in Librarianship: A Real Life Casebook.* Jefferson, N.C.: McFarland & Company.

Launching Pad

Anderson, Virgil A. 1977. *Training the Speaker's Voice.* New York: Oxford University Press.

Bliq, Ron, and Lisa Moretto. 2001. *Writing Reports to Get Results.* Piscataway, N.J.: IEEE Press.

Brownell, Judi. 2002. *Listening: Attitudes, Principles, and Skills.* Boston: Allyn & Bacon.

Disanza, James, and Nancy J. Legge. 2000. *Business and Professional Communication: Plans, Processes, and Performance.* Boston: Allyn and Bacon.

Hill, Nigel, Bill Self, and Greg Roche. 2002. *Customer Satisfaction Measurement for ISO 9000:2000.* Oxford: Butterworth-Heinemann.

Radford, Marie L. 1998. "Approach or Avoidance? The Role of Nonverbal Communication in the Academic Library User's Decision to Initiate a Reference Encounter." *Library Trends* 46 (4): 699-717.

Radford, Marie L. 2001. "Encountering Users, Encouraging Images: Communication Theory and the Library Context." *Journal of Education for Library and Information Science* 42 (1): 27-41.

Riggs, Donald. 1991. *Library Communication.* Chicago: American Library Association.

Tannen, Deborah. 1990. *You Just Don't Understand: Women and Men in Conversation.* New York: Morrow.

Yuling Pan, Suzanne Wong Scollon, and Ronald Scollon. 2002. *Professional Communication in International Settings.* Malden, Mass.: Blackwell.

6: ASSUMING THE CONTROL RESPONSIBILITIES

"When problems occur, look for causes and solutions, not for people to blame."

IN THIS CHAPTER YOU'LL DISCOVER:

- the basics of money, budgets, and planning
- how to establish costs and standards
- the basics of assessing quality, performance, and outcomes
- the need for risk and crisis control

A major responsibility of a middle manager is to assist senior management in the control of the organization's resources—fiscal, human, equipment, and time—allocated to their specific area.

This chapter will explore some of the key control areas: monitoring spending, which is the work of the manager; monitoring teams, which involves staff; monitoring quality, which involves people, time, and equipment; and monitoring effectiveness/demonstrating accountability, which involves everything. Finally, you will learn how to protect your organizational assets.

MONEY, BUDGETS, AND PLANNING

Moving into a middle management post generally brings with it the first significant experience with funding matters, beyond sharing a staff's general concern about next year's budget and possible salary increases. How well you do in handling the funding responsibilities will be a significant factor in how well you succeed as a manager and your chances of further advancement. When in doubt ask for assistance/information; guessing or assuming is not a good tactic when it comes to financial matters.

FOR FURTHER THOUGHT

What are your prior experiences with organizational fiscal matters? Is that experience likely to be a benefit in your new role?

What are the four most common types of library/information center budgets?

What are some of the types of funds a middle manager might typically oversee? A head of a reference unit in an academic or public library might use part of the acquisitions budget for selecting materials for the departmental collection. It then becomes the head's responsibility to ensure that the funds are spent—but not overspent—within the timelines required by the acquisitions unit. A head of an archives service may have a fixed sum of money for the year to pay for the conservation of documents. The manager in charge of online services in a knowledge management or information management environment may have a budget allocated for licenses. Within a records management service, a middle manager may be allocated a sum for the purchase of equipment and files.

Many, if not most, units within services have expenses associated with their activities, and effective senior managers usually give the heads responsibility for monitoring those expenses. This happens for two reasons. First, because senior managers usually have enough "on their plate" that it is difficult to track all the unit's costs in enough detail while still allowing time for all their other activities. And, more importantly, it provides useful money management opportunities for middle managers, a skill they must master if they are to achieve a senior position.

Services may also have income expectations; for example, there may be "target figures" for income from copying fees, usage fees, document delivery fees, or sale of publications. Thus, heads of income-generating units have two budgetary responsibilities—generating income and monitoring expenses.

Often, senior managers are more interested in how the income picture looks than they are about expenses. Because funding authorities often factor in the anticipated income from library-generated "revenue," and failure to generate the expected money means that the library has that much less money to operate with.

SOME BUDGET/FISCAL BASICS

A budget is an *estimate* of the costs for some activity over a given time frame. People tend to forget that a budget is a plan because, once approved, budgets, at least in nonprofit institutions, typically become fixed for the budgetary period—usually twelve months. The consequences of going "over budget" can be devastating for future budget requests, as funding authorities always review past spending patterns as part of the approval process. It may result in a reduction of the following year's allocation by the amount of the overexpenditure. You can see, given the potential "cost" of overspending, that senior managers who delegate some budgetary responsibility to junior managers are taking a risk, and the junior managers do need to develop an understanding of fiscal matters.

People forget that budgets are merely plans because there is essentially no planning in budgeting methods like the line-item method employed by the majority of U.S. libraries. Costs for salaries, materials, supplies, maintenance contracts, etc., each have their own line and object code. Line-item budgets are generally "incremental" in character; that is, each year each budget line receives an increase of some amount—frequently the amount is some percentage of the past year's general inflation rate. Requestors may be asked for their budgetary needs, service enhancement costs, etc., but they know that the chances are slim to none that they will receive any increase above the inflation factor—if they are lucky.

At the time of writing, deflation is affecting some countries, and may well spread to others. Such a situation is outside the experience of anyone working in the U.K. or U.S. today, and it is difficult to predict how, if it becomes necessary, a budget may be managed in deflationary times. However, information professionals in a number of countries have had to work with swinging exchange rates that make it difficult to budget and obtain funding for items that have to be purchased from countries with unfavorable exchange rates.

Spending time on long-term budget planning in a line-item budget environment may be a waste of time. However, in the authors' experience, the truly successful services—even those with the line-item budget format—continue to engage in budget planning, because there are always surprises in the budget process, and requests repeated often enough may suddenly get funding when least expected.

What is the budget process? The ideal process consists of several phases that should be the same for the service and each of its subunits.

- Examine current economic trends and projections and review the parent organization's long-range goals and plans. Periodically assess the user's attitudes toward the service.
- Examine the goals of the service in terms of the parent institution and the changing needs and wants of users. Based on those assessments, develop projected program needs.
- Examine the current operating costs and projected needs, as well as past fiscal performance (under, on, or over budget), and prepare a funding request.
- Examine the rationales for the requests for new/additional funding and prepare a "budget request defense" plan. Present the request to the funding authorities.
- Examine on a regular basis the actual operating costs in comparison to budgeted allocations. Make any necessary adjustments in order to stay on budget.
- Examine any variances between projected and actual costs to determine if there is a problem or just a change in workload.
- Examine variances for possible adjustments in current operations and implications for future budget requests.

A combination of top-down and bottom-up planning, in which senior management provides the information about the external environment and unit heads provide the internal current operating data, is an ideal budgeting situation. If senior management creates a fiscal planning environment, establishes a fiscal planning team, provides the team with requisite data, sets realistic time schedules and sequencing of team activities, and oversees the results. In addition, middle managers must engage in the budget process within their units.

Turock and Pedolsky (1992) produced a useful fiscal management plan for libraries.

USING THE FINANCIAL PLAN

- Define and quantify the service's long-term and short-term objectives in monetary terms.
- Assess progress in meeting financial goals and objectives.
- Establish indicators that will identify significant deviations in the use of assets.
- Provide direction in safeguarding the assets.
- Allocate technical, human, organizational, and financial resources to support service priorities.
- Attract potential funders.

After Turock and Pedolsky (1992: 16).

Fund-Raising

As a result of recent and increased difficulty in securing the necessary fund from their parent organizations, more and more public sector services have turned to fund-raising from other sources. Clay and Bangs (2000) wrote, "Since 1993, fund-raising and development has become a mainstay in the budget mix of libraries. According to *Library Journal's* '1999 Budget Report' find-raising activities for libraries has risen by 228 percent in the past six years" (Clay and Bangs, 2000: 606.). (Note: In U.S. fund-raising parlance, "development" refers to the *process* of fund-raising.) Having a long-term fund-raising effort, which is often necessary for adequate funding, requires staff, effort, and a large amount of time. The experience of libraries will be of particular interest to archives seeking external funding.

WORTH CHECKING OUT

Fund-raising

Steele, Victoria, and Stephen D. Elder. 1992. *Becoming a Fundraiser: The Principles and Practice of Library Development.* Chicago: American Library Association.

Steele and Elder (1992) make it clear that effective fund-raising is a slow process. First one must identify potential "prospects," which can be a challenge, as academic institutions, a host of fine arts and cultural organizations, and other charitable groups are all seeking donors. Next, the "development cycle," which may require years of effort that may or may not result in a significant gift, consists of six stages—identification, involvement, cultivation, solicitation, stewardship, and resolicitation (1992: 24-25).

One of the first points Steele and Elder make, which is restated in all subsequent articles on library funding, is that the senior library manager must take the lead.

> Major donors are not interested in talking to fundraisers; they want to talk to the library's CEO [chief executive officer]. Money wants to talk to power. Professional fundraisers—development officers— are like Sherpa guides: they get the leaders to the top of the mountains by leading the way and carrying the bulk of the luggage. But library leaders must climb the mountain with them—fundraising can not be delegated. (Steele and Elder, 1992: 2)

While major fund-raising is always in the hands of the senior manager, a significant development program often results in middle managers having more day-to-day operational responsibilities, as the CEO will not be on site or will be engaged in fund-raising duties. (For example, one of the authors is currently involved in trying to raise $40 million (in U.S. dollars) for a new library building. The university's president expects that fifty percent of the library director's time will be spent on fund-raising. This means that the assistant and middle managers will be on their own much of the time.)

Susan Kent, city librarian for Los Angeles, commented in an interview for *Library Administration and Management* that there was initial staff concern about how much time the director would have to commit to fund-raising, but that there was more staff involvement than anyone had expected, with staff meeting with a donor when the gift was for a branch or department of the main library (Johnson, 1998: 130–131).

DIGGING DEEPER

Dennis Carrigan reported on a study of public library private fund-raising activities in the early 1990s, which was a growing and a relatively new endeavor for a great many public librarians. While the data is now dated, the majority of the essay addresses the fundamentals for a public library private fund-raising program.

Carrigan, Dennis. 1994. "Public Library Private Fund-Raising: A Report Based on a Survey." *Public Libraries* 31 (1): 31-36.

While middle managers and staff may not be involved in all phases of the development cycle, they play key roles at various point in the process. They may suggest a prospect's name; they may identify a significant fund-raising opportunity in their unit; often they will be key players in the stewardship phase, interacting with the donor in terms of how the funds were/are being used. The Los Angeles library's fund-raising program was effective and the city now has a splendidly refurbished Central Library.

Fund-raising in the sense of seeking out donors has been and is becoming more and more of a job requirement for senior managers in the U.S. Many state libraries in the U.S. have annual funding opportunities through a grants program. Top management may have to approve of and sign off on such funding possibilties involving middle management, but more often than not it is the mid-level staff who write the proposal, based on their detailed knowledge of the operations and how the funds would be used. In addition to state libraries, there are foundations and other government bodies (for example, the National Endowment for the Humanities) that have grant opportunities for archives and libraries. However, such money typically is for start-up costs or one-time expenses, and it is rare for a service to receive ongoing expense funding from such sources.

Grant writing is an art, and a newcomer should seek out assistance and guidance in preparing a grant proposal. Many parent organizations have staff members whose job it is to assist individuals in preparing a proposal because, especially in the academic environment, the parent organization takes part of the funds secured from a successful proposal as "overhead costs."

The practice arose because researchers were doing research for outside agencies that was not directly related to the parent institution's purpose, but using organizational resources. In the case of archives and libraries, this rationale is seldom valid, and the grant writer may need to negotiate a lower overhead rate with the parent organization in order to secure enough money to do the project within the funding limits set by the granting agency.

TIP

Writing grant applications

- Seek out grant opportunities from journals and Web sites.
- Get the necessary documentation and application forms in good time.
- Examine the offer, the requirements, and your eligibility.
- Seek out those who have made successful bids for grants and ask for their experience and advice.
- Identify the advantages and disadvantages to making an application.
- Discuss it with the team and get their commitment and ideas if the result is on the plus side.
- Rough out the proposal.
- Check it out with the finance office.
- Get the approval of senior management.
- Submit the application in good time by courier or registered mail.

Remember is that, whether it is fund-raising or grant writing, the monies secured are supplemental in character. As Steele and Elder stated, "Define your aspirations in terms of definite, forward-looking goals. By forward-looking goals, we mean positive projects that advance the library. Do not conceive of a development program as a deficit-closing mechanism. Your neediness will not motivate donors" (Steele and Elder, 1992: 53).

TRACKING THE BUDGET AND CONTROLLING OPERATIONS

Your budget activities may seem difficult to handle at first, but they are manageable, especially since it is likely the parent organization will have an online financial management system available to budget holders. If this is not available, or if the manager needs to track finer details of the unit's budget, then a spreadsheet program such as Microsoft Excel will be helpful. Setting up a budget form will take a little time, but it is well worth it Strive for a projection of where you'll be at the end of the budget period—not simply a record of what you had and what you spent.

Being able to run a program anytime senior management asks, "How is your budget doing?" and provide an up-to-date, accurate answer (e.g. "We're right on target" or "We're probably going to have a little left by year's end") will enhance your reputation, especially if you hand them a printout showing the figures. However, in order to do that you must have the projection capability.

WORTH CHECKING OUT

Monitoring costs

Paul Eriksen and Robert Shuster provide a good case study on the value of monitoring costs. While their case is from an archival setting, the value of such activities is clear for any type of information or library setting.

Eriksen, Paul, and Robert Shuster. 1995. "Beneficial Shocks: The Place of Processing-Cost Analysis in Archival Administration." *American Archivist* 58 (winter): 32-52.

Once you have addressed the control issues of productivity, quality assurance, efficiency, and effectiveness there are still benchmarking, accountability, and, at times, outcome assessment activities to consider.

What follows is a discussion of some of the interrelated measurement tools that you will need to accomplish the tasks associated with the concepts. Whatever the activity may be, it is worth remembering a statement by Turock about measurement systems and control that applies to all types of service:

Measurement systems based upon productivity are only worthwhile when:

- they reflect the key tasks of the library, decided upon in cooperation with the library staff;
- they are based on precise definitions of key tasks to ensure consistent data gathering; and

- they result from measuring the time required by qualified staff working at normal pace to complete the key tasks.

If all three conditions are met, the resulting productivity measures can be used by the financial manager to improve operations and increase or defend continued resource development (Turock, 1984: 5).

A number of elements go in to a measurement system, not just costs and time—though these two are key. Whatever the system, the process will involve (a) observing staff engaging in the work, (b) asking team leaders to provide the data, or (c) asking staff members to self-report data. Each of the methods has its advantages and disadvantages. No matter what approach is taken there will be staff concerns and, as noted above, it is important to have staff input and understanding of what is being collected, why it is being done, and how the data will be used.

> ### REMEMBER...THE HAWTHORNE EFFECT?
>
> The Hawthorne effect takes its name from a work analysis project conducted at the Western Electric manufacturing plant in Hawthorne, Illinois, in the 1920s. It was originally designed to investigate the relationship between workplace lighting and worker efficiency. The full implications of the research were realized when researchers studied the effect that the observer had on the workers being observed. When applied to managing people, the Hawthorne effect indicates that higher productivity results from using an engaged management style that encourages worker participation.

The observed person will not perform in a typical manner for some time, if ever, because of the presence of the observer. Also, there is no way to know exactly what the effect will be: workers may become nervous and perform very badly; they may work harder than they normally do; or they may see the observer as a threat and respond with the type of performance most likely to remove the perceived danger. Work analysis is necessary to effectively manage any work unit, but the supervisor or manager must be fully aware of the potential implications of this phenomenon on the data collected.

> ### FOR FURTHER THOUGHT
>
> Think of some situations where your work was being observed. How did you react? What were your feelings about the process?
>
> What did you think might be the outcome of the observation(s)?
>
> What lesson can you draw from that experience that might be useful in your efforts to study work activities in your unit?

CONTROL, WORK ANALYSIS, AND EVALUATION

These activities consist of several components: establishing costs and standards, measuring performance, comparing/evaluating performance against the standards, and correcting deviations from the standards. Typical issues relate to quality, quantity, time, and cost. The following sections describe some of the methods that managers use to establish standards and how services engage in various types of evaluation activities.

Keep in mind the difference between the concepts of efficiency and effectiveness.

DEFINITION

Efficiency is doing something with the least possible effort in the least amount of time for the lowest possible cost.

Effectiveness is doing the "right" thing.

A manager's goal is for her/his unit to be both efficient and effective, but while this sounds simple, it can be very difficult to achieve. Often, focusing on one concept has a negative impact on the other.

KNOWING THE COST OF DOING BUSINESS

It is the middle manager's control responsibility to be accountable and to know what the various activities cost to perform. No matter what unit you are responsible for, there are costs that you should know so you may predict funding needs as workloads change. Answering a reference question, searching a database, sending files to storage, accepting a deposit, cataloging an item, etc., all have a cost per item.

When done properly, cost accounting is a powerful tool in preparing a budget, determining staffing needs, planning new services, arranging new service locations, or deciding if unit costs are high enough to consider outsourcing.

Kusack was correct when he wrote, "Cost finding is not hard, and it certainly doesn't involve higher math. A bit of simple arithmetic and a dollop of logic will suffice. Basically all the task requires is to add up each of the costs and then divide that total cost by the number of people served or number of transactions performed" (Kusack, 2002: 152). It is slightly more complicated than the quotation suggests, but it is not all that complex.

There are a number of decisions to make before the summing and dividing activities can occur. The major decision is what costs you are going to calculate and why. If it is just something you wish to do for your unit, then some discussion with the staff about what and why should be sufficient. On the other hand, if the exercise involves other units or is service-wide, the discussions of what and why will involve many more people and may take some time.

Next, resolve which elements should be included in the cost categories; a common way is to divide costs into labor, supplies, and overhead. Supplies such as pens, paper, forms, books, files, documents for the collections, and printer ink cartridges are easy to identify, but what about the upgrading and maintenance of computers, desks, chairs, etc.? Are they supplies or overhead? Do you depreciate equipment cost over a fixed period and use only a given year's cost? Do you use the original purchase price or the cost of replacing the item? There are various methods and rationales used to decide these questions. If you overlook such issues, you will ignore some real organizational costs. Keep in mind that how you categorize expenses impacts your ability to compare your budget with that of other units or libraries.

You will almost always want to use all the direct costs, such as salaries and supplies. The major question is whether you should include indirect costs such as equipment, equipment maintenance, utilities, physical space, and senior administration, and if so, how many.

Only a percentage of the total indirect costs can be assigned to the unit cost. Determining those numbers can be time-consuming, so it is important to know *why* you are doing the calculations. For comparative purposes and benchmarking activities, there must be a clear understanding of what and what not to include in the unit cost if the data is to be useful.

The ease of calculating labor costs depends on how accurate you must be. Seldom is it as simple as multiplying the number of persons by their total salaries. For example, for persons who work in more than one area, you must accurately determine the percentage of time and work for each of their activities. Do you count vacation time and an allowance for sick/special leave toward the unit's production cost, even if the vacationer will have nothing to do with production? Then there is the question of employee benefits—they certainly are an organizational cost. The point is that the type of data sought depends on its intended use. Simple figures may be adequate for internal planning in a unit; however, service-wide or system-wide planning normally requires more detailed information.

Overhead (indirect) costs are those not directly attributable to the production of a particular product or service, such as administrative salaries, building maintenance, utilities, travel expenses, and insurance. Because publicly funded activities usually take place in public buildings that are tax- and rent-free, some writers suggest that not taking these factors into account produces unrealistic cost data, particularly if a loan was raised to finance the land acquisition and building costs. They suggest treating the building as private for accounting purposes, but is it worth the time and effort to calculate it?

In today's environment of privatization, these calculations may become necessary, regardless of the time and effort required. In the private sector, the overhead costs of the space occupied by the service will almost certainly be part of a budget, and the location of the space may determine the costs. For example, locating the service at the center or in a prominent place in the offices may incur higher costs than setting up elsewhere in the same building. And costs will also be affected by the location of the parent organization in a prestigious building or city.

An expert should assist in establishing a proper cost-accounting system. However, for "quick and dirty" purposes—that is, for the manager's use in funding problems that call for careful examination—rough cost accounting is not that difficult. Use staff salaries as labor costs, the annual supplies budget as the supplies cost, and administrative salary as overhead. This provides the total cost, which is then divided by the number of units of service or products produced by the unit in a year. The figure will probably be surprisingly high.

FOR FURTHER THOUGHT

What are some of the reasons you might want to calculate a unit cost?

One obvious reason would be to compare the differences in cost for alternative ways of doing work in your unit. You might want to use the data to establish some unit standards or to compare your unit costs against those of other similar services. Costs are a part of the issue of overall productivity and optimal methods of operation; thus, the process may be part of a larger assessment activity.

Establishing Standards

Cost accounting and standard-setting are very closely related. When engaging in a cost-accounting study, you are gathering data that is useful in setting standards and vice versa. A standard serves as a target for performance; to be useful, it should be measurable. The typical measures of quality, quantity, time, and cost are useful individually and even more so in combination: cost/benefit, unit cost, and time/quantity.

Standards assist in monitoring organizational performance. The key question becomes, how does one establish the standards? Four broad data categories exist that can assist in establishing standards: historical, comparative, engineered, and subjective.

Historical data, which records past performance, is of some help in establishing a standard, as long as the components making up the activity are likely to remain constant. A problem with using past performance measurements is that there is no assurance that the activity was done efficiently, effectively. Just because something has always been done one way does not always mean it is the best, or the only, way. And what if they best way for one activity causes performance problems in other areas? Remember, too, that part of the control/operations function is to coordinate activities and view the whole.

Data can also be gathered from comparisons to the same activities in a number of like organizations—benchmarking. A problem with collecting data from a number of institutions is that, despite common definitions of cost categories, there is a wide range of interpretations of what to include.

Often, it is not a matter of interpretation but one of time, and "guesstimates" are reported as if they were hard data. Also, how identical must two organizations be in order to compare or extrapolate data? Perhaps it is best to look at one's historical performance and that of comparable institutions early in the process of establishing standards.

Airline companies reviewed the questions of standards of service in 2002 following the downfall in travel after 9/11. The question was whether to run a low-cost, no-frills operation or a premium service—i.e., Southwest vs. United Airlines—as it was not possible to do both. There is evidence that airline passengers are taking the low-cost, no-frills option, even for business travel in Europe.

Benchmarking

With funding agencies and other organizations growing ever more concerned about cost containment, there is an increasing use of *benchmarking*—a tool for comparing operations for either internal or external purposes. The goal is to provide data that can help managers answer the following questions:

- How well are we doing compared to others?
- How good do we want to be?
- Who is doing the best?
- How do they do it?
- How can we adapt their practices to our organization?
- How can we be better than the best?

While there are four basic types of benchmarking—internal, competitive, industry, and best in class—it is the first two that are most commonly used in publicly funded services. In the corporate sector, industry or best in class is generally used.

As the name suggests, *internal benchmarking* looks at the internal practices of an organization, such as the cost of creating a purchase order in various departments across a campus. A *competitive benchmarking* project might collect data on the cost of creating purchase orders in various departments in a number of institutions. *Industry benchmarking* would collect data from all or a representative sample of all organizations within an "industry." *Best in class benchmarking* collects information across industries, essentially seeking the most effective practices.

Internal benchmarking may also vary between vertical and horizontal projects. A *vertical project* seeks to quantify the costs, workloads, and productivity of a defined functional area—for example, handling accounts payable. A *horizontal study* analyzes the cost and productivity of a single process that crosses two or more functional areas—for example, database searching in acquisitions, cataloging, and interlibrary loan departments.

When developing a benchmarking project, make sure all the participants have a clear understanding, of what each benchmark will measure and what the data collected—time, staff salaries, equipment costs, staff benefits, etc—will include. A common problem for first-time projects is misunderstanding what staff costs should and should not include—just salary, salary and directed benefits such as health insurance, or all of those plus vacation and sick leave costs. The data will be essentially useless for comparative purposes unless there is a single, clear approach.

Work Analysis

Engineered standards—those which use hard data collected from work analysis—are, in many ways, just a different label for "scientific management." By learning and applying work-analysis techniques, managers can make the work environment much more pleasant, but only when there is a broad-based staff understanding of what is being analyzed and why the analysis is taking place. Work analysis can also assist in making effective use of physical space, choosing a sequence for doing work, and finding ways of performing tasks more efficiently. Most work-analysis techniques relate in one way or another to time or money, and as a result, they provide much of the data needed for budgeting and planning.

To illustrate work analysis and standard-setting, imagine that you are the head of an acquisitions department. You have been asked to establish performance standards for your unit. For example, you have six persons in the department; who verify an average of 1,250 order requests per week. This effort keeps the work up-to-date, but you might wonder if Parkinson's Law is in effect here—that is, the work expands to fill the time available. You have applied for a grant to acquire large quantities of material in a new subject area; will those six people be able to handle a 10 to 15 percent increase in the workload or will you need to hire additional staff?

The two-part work-analysis technique will help you determine what needs to be done—establish realistic workloads (standards) and compare those to the staff's performance.

Sampling is a part of any work-analysis project; if your knowledge of statistics is a little rusty, glance over college notes or a textbook.

WORTH CHECKING OUT

Statistics

Hafner, Arthur. 1998. *Descriptive Statistical Techniques for Librarians.* 2d ed. Chicago: American Library Association.

In statistical terms, the current workload in the example above is the universe, or population, that you need to study. In order to know with almost complete certainty what is being done, you would have to study *all* steps in the verification process for *all* requests for *one* year. Even then, you could not be absolutely confident that there were no unusual characteristics that made that year's work atypical. Fortunately, you can achieve almost the same level of confidence with much less work and in less time. A reasonably small, properly selected sample of the work will provide results comparable to those of a comprehensive study.

The use of sampling techniques rests on the assumption that there is a *distribution pattern* of natural phenomena (in this case, work activities) that will resemble a *normal distribution* (bell-shaped curve). Normal distributions are those in which the characteristics under study cluster around a central point. As you move away from the central point, there are fewer instances of those characteristics.

A *random sample* drawn from a normal population will probably display a pattern that is similar (although not identical) to the pattern displayed in the entire population from which it was drawn. Repeated samples from the same population would eventually duplicate the actual pattern.

In the example, the actual times for processing might range from five minutes to one hour, with most of the requests being finished in twenty-seven minutes. The requests represent one variable in the study. The other variable is the skill of the staff, which will not be identical; therefore, you should sample both the requests and the staff.

A *random sample* means that every member of the population has an equal chance of being selected. For instance, to draw a random sample from the requests for new materials, you might consider putting each request into a large container and then drawing out the number of requests that you wish to study or assigning each request a number as it arrives and using a random number table to select the sample. The random character of the sample is a *key* factor in having confidence that sample results mirror the results of studying the entire population.

Sampling is necessary in work analysis as well as in research. While doing it takes time, it requires much less time than examining the entire population. If you do not have the statistical background yourself, secure the help of someone who does.

Not all of the work analysis techniques relate directly to establishing standards. In some cases, they improve the flow of work, after which one should set the standards. Some help the manager visualize the interrelated nature of some of the activities and thus improve coordination or establish that the present system is, in fact, the best. Others help managers control complex projects that may not be part of the normal activities. All of them serve to assist the manager in controlling and monitoring organizational work activities.

The *block diagram,* the most elementary form of work analysis, provides a simple overview of the relationships among various units or activities within an organization. The *flow diagram* allows a finer level of analysis, as it gives a graphic view of both the work area and the movement of personnel or materials within that area. A *flow process chart* indicates the movement of an object of study, but does not relate the movement to a physical space. The *decision flow chart*—typically used in systems analysis for computer application—is a method for analyzing workflows in which numerous decisions occur.

Such charts and diagrams allow managers to track every step/process that an object of study (request, book, or form) goes through. This, in turn, permits the supervisor/manager to accurately assess the process and determine if this is the best sequence or if steps could be combined or altered. These charts also help ensure that one does not miss a step in the process.

Form analysis can be of great value in libraries, where forms and files seem to multiply rapidly and a unit can easily lose control of them. To avoid causing unnecessary work for the department, each form should be regularly reviewed in order to determine whether it still serves a function and does so efficiently. Naturally, the first question to ask is whether the form is actually necessary at all. What does it do that is not already done? Can some forms be combined? Do all items on the form need to be there? Is there a less-expensive form available serving the same purpose? Should it be in paper or electronic format? Can the department shorten its retention time?

The answer to the last question will vary, and you may have no control over that policy. Governments often set certain minimum time limits for retaining records, especially fiscal and personnel records. Auditors may require the retention of additional records or longer timelines. If you have control over the use of forms used outside the library, double-check to make certain that they are easily understood by non-library personnel.

Other Useful Concepts

Many of the following techniques require a mathematical background. If you lack the necessary background, you may be able to find someone who has the training needed to gather and interpret the necessary data.

Linear programming can help determine the best use of scarce resources to achieve a specified goal. It can help in:

- improving the use of all organizational work resources,
- keeping the costs of an operation or activity to a minimum,
- determining volume-cost relationships, and
- selecting the optimum mix of customer services.

Queuing theory provides models for deciding the optimum number of service points for waiting lines of people or things. We have all gone to a bank, a store, or a library and stood in line for one of a few operating service points. Customers who wait too long can become frustrated, angry, and perhaps, ultimately, non-customers. Using queuing theory will helps reduce this problem as much as possible given specific levels of resources.

Libraries have a surprising number of waiting lines for users: security checks at entrances, waiting lists for popular materials, and lines for book check-out, reserve services, and in-person, telephone, and e-mail reference service, to name a few. Documents and files spend time in line for processing of one sort or another—everything from ordering to shelving. Such waiting involves two types of cost: the cost of additional service points, and the cost to the institution in terms of customer frustration. The task is to balance the two.

Other prominent theories that might be of use include *game theory* (for the allocation of resources between competing demands), *search theory* (for the optimum means of locating information), and the *Monte Carlo method* (for accounting for chance occurrences). The appropriate application of these and the many other techniques will help to enhance the image of the organization as effective and cost-conscious.

FOR FURTHER THOUGHT

Now that you have read the section on work analysis, take each technique and give two additional examples of how it could be used in a service with which you are familiar.

One key factor to keep in mind is that efficient, and even effective, components must work well as a system. Consider the integration not only within your unit but as part of the overall service.

TIP

Many organizations are subject to quality checks, often for the purpose of accreditation.

Make sure your service is not only included in the process, but plays a prominent part.

Take advantage of the increased understanding of the importance and value of information.

QUALITY AND PERFORMANCE

The foregoing concepts focus on providing efficient service—but it is possible to be very efficient while doing the wrong thing. It is even possible to efficiently produce high-quality products or services but still not be doing what you should. This section reviews quality and performance, as well as assessment.

TIP

This is one of the fastest-moving areas of management in general, but it is particularly so in the information sector. We discuss concepts and provide some examples, but check out what is happening now in your sector.

Quality Management

A distinction must be drawn between quality control and quality management.

DEFINITION

Quality control refers, most often, to a product or service (item/transaction); for example, producing error-free document records or error-free reshelving or filing.

Quality management is broader based—it looks at the total operation (mission, goals, objectives, etc.).

You can have perfect quality control with error-free document records——but that almost always comes at the cost of the number of records produced. For your users, quality may mean having a greater quantity of records with less perfection.

What is "quality"? Quality is an elusive and indistinct concept. People often talk about it using rather imprecise adjectives like "good," "right," and "correct," or words giving cues to its characteristics, such as "style," "label," "feel," and "elegance." As suggested above, there are several perspectives about what constitutes quality. It is important to start any definition of institutional quality with definitions of goals and objectives and how the staff are to achieve them.

WORTH CHECKING OUT

Writers on the importance of quality

We encourage you to check out one of the books by the best known proponents of the importance of quality: W. Edwards Deming (1986), Philip B. Crosby (1979), Armand V. Feigenbaum (1985), Kaoru Ishikawa (1985), and Joseph M. Juran (1974). Each has published extensively and others have expanded on their work. We encourage you to follow up with one of their books.

It is somewhat difficult to define quality in the service setting, where there is no physical product as an output. What standard defines quality service in an information or library setting—Is it just user satisfaction? A person may be satisfied with the information provided and not be aware that the information is incomplete, or even incorrect. In time, the person may determine that the information was less than satisfactory, which gives rise to the question—when should we measure user satisfaction?

FOR FURTHER THOUGHT

How do you judge the elusive concept of quality as a customer of any service—information or otherwise?

What is the most important factor to you?

How is it evident?

By their very nature, most services are intangible. Shaughnessy (1987) enumerated three points that help explain "service intangibility."

- Services are often performances or processes rather than products, and unspecified (unarticulated) user expectations are the typical criteria by which they are evaluated.
- Most services are heterogeneous. Performance varies from producer to producer, from user to user, and from day to day.

Services are generally open long hours each day, and often every day of the week. Staffing varies because of the need to cover all hours of operation; thus, uniform quality is more difficult to assure.

- Frequently the production and consumption of many services are inseparable. Evaluations of quality are not solely based on the outcome of a service; they also involve evaluations of the process of service delivery and comparison of performance with user expectations.

Previous research on service quality reveals ten dimensions that, to a greater or lesser degree, determine the quality of a service:

1. reliability or consistency,
2. responsiveness or timeliness,
3. competence,
4. access or approachability,
5. courtesy,
6. communication,
7. credibility,
8. security (including confidentiality),
9. understanding the customer needs, and
10. tangibles (such as physical facilities, appearance of personnel, and tools or equipment).

(Parasurman, Zeitaml, and Berry, 1987)

All of these elements apply to the work of the information professional and can serve as a starting point for defining quality in a given environment. We will return later in this chapter to the ideas that have influenced developments in some U.S. academic libraries.

Understanding users is the key element for assessing the quality of services. Information professionals have a firm understanding of what their services and products are, as well as what constitutes their primary service population, but what they may not fully understand is what constitutes the entire user base.

One of Deming's widely quoted statements about TQM (total quality management) is: "Quality has no meaning without reference to the customer" (1986). The idea that quality equals customer satisfaction appears to be simple and straightforward. As noted earlier, however, quality is a complex idea and satisfaction varies with circumstances over time. Sirkin (1993) suggests that some indications of a satisfied user are repeated usage of services, referrals of the service to others, and public praise of the service.

> TIP
>
> One simple way to find out the user's view of the service is to use unobtrusive testing, known in the retail trade as the "mystery shopper." One example is given in:
>
> Czopek, Vanessa. 1998. "Using Mystery Shoppers to Evaluate Customer Service in the Public Library." *Public Libraries* 37 (6): 370-375.

Newcomers to quality management are sometimes surprised that there are two classes of customers to consider— the external customer and the internal customer. The external customer is the person who is, in fact, the ultimate owner or consumer of the product or service—the end user. The internal customer is the direct recipient of one's work output. It is essential that both classes of customer be satisfied in order to have a "quality environment."

> WORTH CHECKING OUT
>
> The importance of internal marketing strategies in the information and library sector is evident in papers reporting a survey that examined employee satisfaction and customer orientation.
>
> Broady-Preston, Judith, and Lucy Steel. 2002. "Internal Marketing Strategies in LIS: A Strategic Management Perspective." *Library Management* 23 (6/7): 294-301.
>
> Broady-Preston, Judith, and Lucy Steel. 2002. "Employees, Customers and Internal Marketing Strategies in LIS." *Library Management* 23 (8/9): 384-393.

Performance and Quality

Users, staff members, funding authorities, and other interested groups have different views of the definition of a performance indicators. Practitioners and researchers have produced a variety of manuals and articles designed to help measure/ascertain what constitutes library and information center effectiveness. (See Abbott, 1994; Adams, 1993; Bannister and Rochester, 1997; Brophy and Coulling, 1996; Childers and Van House, 1989, 1993; Cook, 2002; Cullen and Calvert, 1995, 1996; Giappiconi and Carbone, 1997; Hernon and Altman, 1996, 1998; Joint Funding Council, 1995; Kyrillidou and Heath, 2001; Morgan, 1995; Van House, et al., 1990; Walter, 1992; and Zweizig, et al., 1996.)

Beware the temptation to measure anything that can be measured. For example, the number of fiction titles borrowed in a public library would tell us nothing about the number of books that are available to read. If the stock is small and someone has already read all of the titles in the genres that interest them, their borrowing rate will go down. Conversely, if the number of books available is larger, a person visiting the library may take out more books than they are likely to read, allowing them to make a further choice at home. The person borrowing the books may also pass them on to someone else to read. From these examples, it is easy to see that there are several factors that lie beyond crude borrowing statistics.

The impact of the reading of a document and the degree of "value" or satisfaction to the reader may be greater for some readers than others. Similar questions can be posed in relation to the use of documents and Web sites in, for example, a law firm, where immediate access to a specific document can be critical.

When looking at data and information about performance and quality, ask yourself:

- What is being measured?
- What does it indicate?
- What is not being measured?

PUBLIC LIBRARY PERFORMANCE MEASURES

We will illustrate performance measures with a public library example from the U.S. and U.K.

In the U.S., the American Library Association's Public Library Association set in place a study whose aim was to produce a strategy for public library change by replacing standards with goals (Martin, 1972).

De Prospo, Altman, and Beasley (1973) examined the question of performance measurement and proposed four criteria for selecting "meaningful indicators."

- Data collection must be amenable to the use of sampling techniques.
- The measurement criteria must differentiate between libraries.
- The measurement tests, while objectively based, should be constructed in a manner suitable for interpretation by practicing librarians.
- Data collected should provide administration with a tool for internal management and decision making.

These criteria still have relevance today, and the last criterion has become even more important as a greater emphasis is placed on evidence-based practice (Davies, 2002).

Effectiveness measures for public libraries emerged following concern about standards for service and the development of the public library planning process. They did not prescribe levels of achievement, but offered options, so that individual libraries could define effectiveness based on their own missions. At the outset of the American Library Association project, some 257 separate indicators of effectiveness had been identified. The task of the U.S. Public Library Effectiveness Survey was to list the measures proposed and reduce it and test the reliability and validity of the remaining measures.

The indicators that scored highest in the survey were:

- convenience of hours;
- range of materials;
- staff helpfulness;
- community services;
- materials quality;
- materials availability;
- awareness of services; and
- convenience of location.

FOR FURTHER THOUGHT

We have listed the preferred indicators from the U.S. Public Library Effectiveness Survey. Take the eight indicators and rank them in the order that they would be important to you as a public library user.

The librarian respondents rated the performance of their libraries; the criteria on which library performance was rated most highly were:

- support of intellectual freedom;
- the extent to which library services are free;
- staff contact with users;
- staff helpfulness;
- interlibrary cooperation;
- users variety;
- range of materials;
- public opinion;
- circulation; and
- equipment usage.

Librarians were asked to rank the importance in their libraries of eight standard public library roles. Their ranking was:

- reference library;
- popular materials center;
- preschoolers' door to learning;
- community information center;
- formal education support center;
- community activities center;
- independent learning center; and
- research center.

(Van House and Childers, 1993)

The Public Library Association moved to develop a guide providing a tested, results-driven planning process which would enable public libraries to respond to rapidly changing environments. It starts from three basic assumptions:

1. Excellence must be defined locally—it results when library

services match community needs, interests, and priorities.
2. Excellence is possible for both small and large libraries—it rests more on commitment than on unlimited resources.
3. Excellence is a moving target—even when achieved, excellence must be continually maintained (Nelson, 2001: 1).

EXAMPLE

One example of output measures is given in:

Immroth, Barbara F., and Keith C. Lance. 1996. "Output Measures for Children's Services in the Public Library." *Public Libraries* 35 (4): 240-245.

Work on performance measures carried out in the U.S. influenced those adopted for use in U.K. public libraries. As is the case in the U.S., the U.K. indicators have gone through several stages of development. This illustrates a point made in chapter 1—the influence of the external operating environment.

In the 1980s, the U.K. government agency responsible for public libraries—the Office of Arts and Libraries—commissioned a manual which, among other things, differentiated between inputs, outputs, service effectiveness (or outcome), and domain. These factors are important for the definitions they provide and their ability to adapt to any aspect of service. A *performance indicator* is the relationship between two or more measures of operational performance. *Operational performance indicators* are concerned with resource allocation and the internal efficiency of a library, and relate library inputs to outputs. *Effectiveness indicators* are concerned with performance from the perspective of the user, and relate outputs to outcomes. *Cost-effectiveness indicators* express the outcomes of investing resources, relate inputs to outcomes, and consider how much use is being made of the service and the costs of the use. *Impact indicators* compare actual use and potential use as a guide as to how well the service serves the community. These definitions overcame the problems with blurred distinctions between indicators and measures.

The draft manual was tested and the results indicated that, not surprisingly, the measures most often used were those that were easiest to collect and were quantitative rather than qualitative. There was the caveat that while these measures might be aids to decision making, the "constructive use of them depends very much on the skill and knowledge of the decision maker...the responsibility for providing the correct context, interpreting the results, and exercising judgment, remains with librarians" (Bloor, 1991: 49). And this holds true for the development and use of all performance measures.

The Audit Commission, a U.K. national body that examines the efficiency of public organizations, set down performance indicators from public libraries for which data were collected in 1996–97:

- issues per capita of books and of other items
- the number of books and recordings available in libraries per capita

- number of public libraries open 45 hours or more per week, open 10–44 hours per week, and the number of mobile libraries
- number of visits per capita
- expenditure per capita on books and other materials
- net expenditure per capita

Later other measures relating to efficiency, access, and usage were added to the initial list.

Part of the U.K. government move to modernize involved performance measurement, with each public library being required to produce an Annual Library Plan. All public services, which include public record offices and libraries, are currently required to demonstrate that they provide Best Value by gathering management information and feedback from users to help improve services (Liddle, 1999; Favret, 2000).

These programs have been backed up by a new set of principal service objectives, standards, and assessment measures for public libraries against which progress can be monitored (Department for Culture, Media and Sport, 2001). Library authorities must:

- enable convenient and suitable access for users of libraries;
- provide adequate opening hours of libraries for users;
- enable electronic access for library users;
- ensure satisfactory services for the issuing and reserving of books;
- encourage the use made of the public library service;
- ensure user satisfaction with the services provided;
- provide choice in books and materials made available to users; and
- provide appropriate levels of qualified staff.

Each objective is linked to between one and four standards, and each standard has an associated measure or target. For example:

OBJECTIVE: Library Authorities must ensure user satisfaction with the services provided.
PLS 12. Percentage of library users reporting success in obtaining a specific book:

i. adults
ii. children

To be based on the National PLUS standards (Public Library User Surveys).

The target for the three-year planning cycle commencing in April 2001 will be 65 percent for both adults and children. Authorities may also inform this measure with information about the number of searches for books leading to reservations, and satisfaction with the outcome in the measure. Many of the standards are based on the collection of simple data, for example, "aggregate opening hours per 1,000 population for all libraries."

The assessment of all services provided by public funds has resulted in some criticism, particularly in the fields of education and healthcare. There has been comment about the difficulty of measuring some aspects of the services and of the "massaging" of data to produce the desired outcomes. The standards have produced stress for managers and their staff, but have also motivated them to achieve publicly recognized high results that could bring enhanced funding. If the service that is perceived as a "failure," "successful" managers may move in to improve the situation.

For a manager who has to develop performance measures, the conceptual framework developed by researchers, together with manuals published by professional and commercial bodies, provide a good starting point. Paton, Foot, and Payne (2000) summed up the use of quality self-assessment:

> A particular value of quality models at the present time is their credibility in the wider society. The language of quality sustains a public discourse in terms that are specific, categorical, and definitive. At the same time it enables a private intraorganizational negotiation that recognizes the shifting, problematic, and multifaceted nature of quality in human services. This is advantageous, allowing managers both to address substantive (if often intractable) issues and to represent their organization externally as successful, client-focused, and abreast of the times. (Paton, Foot, and Payne, 2000: 31)

For FURTHER THOUGHT

Can you identify the problems that might be encountered in developing performance measures in a knowledge-management center, a school library, or an archives service?

Determining the Value of a Service

Many managers in the public sector around the globe are being asked to assess the value of the service they provide as local authorities become concerned about levels of local taxation. It is not an easy task, but the St. Louis Public Library in Missouri developed an approach that can be used in any type of information service in the public sector. A team consisting of two library staff members, the director, and the chair of the economics department of the University of Southern Illinois, Edwardsville, was asked "prove" that there was/is a net value of library services to their population.

The team used a number of economic analysis techniques, including economic impact and cost-benefit, and they explored the direct benefit (value to those using the service) and indirect benefits (third party/societal). One of the interesting results of their data was the suggestion that the lowest return on the tax dollar to users was two to one and that the highest was ten to one. Their approach could be modified for use in any type of information setting (Holt, Elliott, and Moore, 1999; Holt and Elliott, 2002).

Outcome Assessment

Over the years, the issues of accountability and measurement of quality have become more and more important, and sometimes even quality/effectiveness measures are not enough for funding and accrediting bodies. They are asking for evidence of an outcome. Typical resource questions were: "What is the size and currency of collections, budget, staff, and physical facilities?" "Does the service engage in periodic planning and program review processes?" "Are the collections, and access to them, adequate?" The new questions are harder to answer from statistics alone. For example:

- "How does the service collect and analyze data on its collections, staff, budget, etc.?"
- "Does the service identify learning goals for itself, and are they linked to institutional learning goals?"
- "Are satisfaction surveys *regularly* conducted and *used*?"
- "How *does* the service assess accomplishment of its learning goals?"
- "How are assessment results *incorporated* into planning and improvements?"
- "How are service learning goals *linked* with institutional learning goals?"

The above are examples of the ever-growing importance of "proving one's worth" to the community served and those who provide the funding. In the not-too-distant past, archives and libraries in the U.S. were right there with "the flag, Mom, and apple pie" in terms of overall public sense of societal value. Today, a great many people see social services—including libraries, archives, and even education—as too much apple pie, and they think that perhaps the country needs to cut its calorie intake. Rudd (2001) succinctly summed up the thoughts/feelings of many information professionals about "outcome assessment."

> For those of us who work in libraries, who educate those who work in them and who use and support them in a variety of ways, the value of libraries goes without saying. We believe they are a public good. We believe that libraries positively influence student achievement, contribute to the corporate bottom line, fuel research, support community development, improve quality of life, further education from cradle to grave and contribute to personal betterment. We've long held that one of the best investments of public funds is in libraries and that the key to personal improvement and success is a library card. But no matter how fervent our beliefs about the value of libraries, our belief system offers the weakest of responses when presented with the classic question: What difference does it make? (Rudd, 2001: 17)

Having an answer to that question will become increasingly critical to the long-term viability of publicly funded services, including almost every non-profit organization in the U.S. that depends upon either tax support or charitable gifts. In fact, it is one of the largest of charitable groups—the United Way—has led the way in creating a model for addressing this challenging area of evaluation faced by a variety of organizations (See www.unitedway.org/outcomes/publctns.htm#It0989). Unfortunately, this model and others cannot tell you what your outcomes ought to be; they just provide the framework for making the decisions about what may be right for your unit/organization.

Most of the models contain four components—inputs (resources), activities (what is done with the resources), outputs (results/products of activity), and outcomes (values/benefits for end users/society). An example might be goals for the outcomes of an undergraduate's interaction with the library:

- to understand the research process through which new knowledge is created
- to understand the cycle of scholarly communication and its relationship to research
- to understand how to evaluate information for creditability, scholarship, and bias
- to understand the differences between primary and secondary information sources
- to understand and have respect for the intellectual property of others

Coming up with similar outcomes takes some time and is often best done in group "brainstorming" sessions. But that is nothing compared to the time and effort needed to gather the data to demonstrate that the outcome actually took place.

Older data-collecting activities such as performance measures will be useful in providing clues as to what some outcomes might be and how to demonstrate that they did occur. Outcome assessment will of necessity be relatively slow; most outside agencies requesting outcomes understand the complexity and recommend starting with just two or three outcomes, developing a sound base for those, then adding additional outcomes.

One reason the process is slow is because the only way of determining any of the above outcomes is to test, or have access to information about, individual end-users and their behavior *before and after* their interaction with the library. Such information raises questions about ethics as well as personal privacy. Self-reporting by end users is another possibility, but it is filled with questions about reliability and validity. Begin with outcomes that are directly observable.

In addition, follow the United Way's three categories of outcomes: initial, intermediate, and long-term. Long-term outcomes may be the most problematic for some libraries, as only a small portion of the users will be "long-term. Academic institutions do track alumni and have longtime faculty members; public libraries have a few very long-term customers; and corporate libraries often have a core of long-term heavy users. Thus it may be possible to develop a few long-term outcomes, but the focus is always likely to be on initial and intermediate outcomes.

> WORTH CHECKING OUT
>
> **Outcomes assessment and service quality**
>
> Hernon, Peter, and Robert E. Dugan. 2001. *An Action Plan for Outcomes Assessment in Your Library*. Chicago: American Library Association.
>
> Hernon, Peter, and John Whitman. 2001. *Delivering Satisfaction and Service Quality*. Chicago: American Library Association.

Measuring Quality and User Expectations in Academic Libraries

In the U.S., a number of academic libraries have drawn upon the approach developed by Parasuraman, Berry, and Zeithaml (1988) named SERVQUAL, which is designed to measure service quality in the retail sector. Parasuraman (2002) describes how this series of empirical studies developed, tested, and refined a scale for measuring service quality as perceived by customers.

SERVQUAL is a two-part instrument that measures services along a range of attributes grouped into five dimensions:

- reliability,
- responsiveness,
- assurance,
- empathy, and
- tangibles, e.g. appearance of the physical facilities, equipment, etc.

Later refinement resulted in two levels of expectations being incorporated into the first part of the tool:

- desired service level
- adequate service level

The range between the two levels indicates the levels of service performance a customer would consider to be satisfactory.

From SERVQUAL emerged LibQual+^{TM}, which asks users to rate three service attributes on a nine-point scale. Their "perception of the service performance" can be rated between "desired" and "adequate" (Parasuraman, 2002). Journals have published special issues focusing on this approach, describing its use and outcomes in U.S. academic libraries (Kyrillidou and Heath, 2001; Cook, 2002).

DIG DEEPER

A series of international conferences focuses on performance measurement, and the proceedings are published; the latest at the time of writing is:

Stein, Joan, Martha Kyrillidou, and Denise Davies, eds. 2002. *Proceedings of the 4th Northumbria International Conference on Performance Measurement in Libraries and Information Services: Pittsburgh, 12-16 August 2001.* Washington, D.C.: Association of Research Libraries.

FOR FURTHER THOUGHT

Think about one of the services you have worked in; what are some realistic outcomes for that service?

How would you go about collecting the necessary data?

How would you go about involving the users in the process?

RISK AND CRISIS CONTROL

A manager is responsible for the well-being and safety of the staff and customers who work in or use the unit, as well as the equipment and other resources assigned to the unit. Besides handling budget, staffing, quantity and quality, and evaluation issues, a middle manager must monitor and control risks and, on occasion, handle a crisis.

Safety and security are interrelated, but not identical in meaning. Safety relates to the well-being of people, while security relates to that of people and things. If a safety audit is conducted on your unit, the report will address the physical aspects of the facility in terms of harm or health risks to people. A security audit will also provide information about the security of computer equipment, collections, etc., against such threats as theft and vandalism, which cost large sums of money annually.

While it is unlikely that a middle manager will have the authority to call for such checks, it is their responsibility to raise the issue if there is reason to believe that circumstances warrant a review. Generally, the local fire department conducts some basic safety checks of alarm systems and emergency exiting on a regular, if unannounced, basis. Although it is senior management's responsibility to have any deficiencies corrected, the unit manager is often in a better position to know if/when the corrections are completed and to maintain the proper conditions (such as making sure no objects obstruct sprinkler heads). Often the fire marshal will undertake a more comprehensive review of the facility and provide staff with training in handling facility evacuations.

One good—and often free—source of input is the risk manager for the parent organization. Risk managers are responsible for insurance coverage, and they are usually more than willing to come to a service to review all the risk factors.

The U.S. has a system of "tort law" that deals with mental, emotional, or physical injuries to individuals caused either by negligence or intentionally. Unfortunately, U.S. society seems to be more and more willing to file lawsuits over rather minor matters. Three key points to remember about U.S. tort law are: the cause of the injury must be a person, not an "act of God"; the person causing the injury has a responsibility/duty to the injured party; and the duty may be one of warning or one of action.

In a library, failure to put a sign that the entrance floor is wet on a rainy day is an invitation for a lawsuit if a user slips and falls. What responsibility does the public library staff have for "latchkey" children or the homeless?

FOR FURTHER THOUGHT

What are some other possible areas of injury, either physical or mental?

Part of a risk audit involves looking at service policies in order to ensure that the proposed action by the staff does not create a problem larger than the one the policy was to address. In the case of mental or emotional harm, the problem is often inadequate user knowledge of policies. Post policies at the entrance and train staff in how to carry out the policies.

A security audit addresses two other major concerns—the weakness of the existing operation and the implementation of present procedures/policies/rules. The auditor may ask are what evidence of theft exists; what type of deferred maintenance exists; what type of door key control system exists; what are the procedures for handling terminated staff and customers; if an emergency plan exists; if a disaster plan exists; and if there a security plan.

Observing the security procedures of any special collections or other restricted-access areas is a must. Auditors' observations might include issues of visual control from service points and staff offices. If there are "exit guards," how do they handle the work? Is there a discernable pattern to their checking? Does it vary with the volume of traffic? If there is an electronic exit control system, how does the staff handle "bypass" materials (that is, materials that cannot go through the system without damage)?

Checking on the security of any after-hours return facility is another important aspect of the audit. Staff members may be surprised when the auditor checks the efficacy of closing procedures. Some auditors have been known to succeed at hiding in the facility after the staff have "cleared and closed" it.

Why all this effort? By avoiding risks, you can avoid paying higher insurance costs due to claims. More often than not, insurance monies will not cover all the costs, so risk control can also help with the operating budget.

Insurance seldom covers the documents, books, journals, newspapers, files, videos, and even equipment that seem to "grow legs" and disappear, unless there is a major theft/loss. The cost of replacement is, in a sense, a loss to the service and its users, as funds used for replacement are funds not available for other purposes. But some items may be irreplaceable, e.g. archives and records, and the cost of others, such as vital standard textbooks, may be very high.

A security audit reviews the emergency plan and disaster preparedness plan—sometimes contained in the same document. These are vital plans to have and to understand when it comes to crisis control. The emergency plan deals with such issues as building evacuation (how it is done and who is responsible until assistance arrives) and which documents staff should or should not attempt to "rescue."

A disaster preparedness plan is more complex, draws on the emergency plan, and covers what to do after the problem occurs. You can almost count on being involved in at least one disaster at some time in your career. Broken pipes, floods, and fires can happen anywhere; some places are at high risk for hurricanes, earthquakes, or tornadoes; and terrorist attacks are more frequent in many countries.

WORTH CHECKING OUT

Disaster planning

Alire, Camila, ed. 2000. *Library Disaster and Recovery Handbook*. New York: Neal-Schuman.

Fortson, Judith. 1992. *Disaster Planning and Recovery*. New York: Neal-Schuman.

Lorenzen, Michael. 1998. "Security Issues in the Public Libraries of Three Midwestern States." *Public Libraries* 37 (2): 134-136.

The basic steps in preparing a plan are:

- Study the risk potentials.
- Establish a planning team—consult with risk, fire, and safety officers.
- Establish procedures for each of the likely problems.
- Establish a telephone calling tree, or other rapid notification system, for each type of problem. The calling tree establishes who gets notified and when. Top management may not be the first call or two, depending on circumstances.
- Develop salvage plans for collections, equipment, and other assets. Have facility floor plans marked with priorities. Setting the priorities may take some time, as team members may differ on what is critical to salvage first.
- Establish a list of recovery resources—people and vendors— who may be of assistance.
- Develop a list of recovery supplies that should be on hand,

and identify places to store them that are likely to be accessible in the event of a disaster.

- Establish a method for authorizing emergency spending that may be needed during the early hours of the problem.

Once you have a draft plan ready, it is time to work with other groups in the parent organization to coordinate the overall disaster plan. This may require some extensive rewriting of your plan when it comes to a major disaster such as an earthquake, hurricane, or terrorist attack, which can stretch parent institution resources to the maximum and can result in the service having to deal with matters in a less than ideal manner.

Naturally, some training and practice is vital in making a plan work. Ensure that some members of staff have undertaken professional training in search and rescue, others in first aid, and everyone in the use of the in-house fire suppression systems. Try to organize the firsthand experience of handling real water damage problems." Be prepared" is a very good motto, as that preparation will likely pay off at some point in time.

AFTER READING THIS CHAPTER YOU SHOULD BE AWARE THAT:

- knowing how to handle money, budgets and planning are essential managerial skills;
- fund-raising is of increasing importance in the public sector;
- it is essential to track budgets;
- knowing how to calculate costs, establish standards, and benchmark is important;
- there is a difference between quality control and quality management;
- assessing quality is a rapidly changing field and of is concern to decision-makers; and
- risk control and disaster planning are essential.

REFERENCES

Abbott, Christine. 1994. *Performance Measurement in Library and Information Services.* London: Aslib.

Adams, Roy, et al. 1993. *Decision Support Systems and Performance Assessment in Academic Libraries.* London: Bowker-Saur.

Alire, Camila, ed. 2000. *Library Disaster and Recovery Handbook.* New York: Neal-Schuman.

Bannister, Marion, and Maxine Rochester. 1997. "Performance Measures for NAW TAFE Libraries." *Australian Academic and Research Libraries* 28 (4): 281-296.

Bloor, Ian. 1991. *Performance Indicators and Decision Support Systems for Libraries.* British Library Research Paper No. 93. London: British Library Research and Development Department.

Broady-Preston, Judith, and Lucy Steel. 2002. "Internal Marketing Strategies in LIS: A Strategic Management Perspective." *Library Management* 23 (6/7): 294-301.

Broady-Preston, Judith, and Lucy Steel. 2002. "Employees, Customers and Internal Marketing Strategies in LIS." *Library Management* 23 (8/9): 384-393.

Brophy, Peter, and Kate Coulling. 1996. *Quality Management for Information and Library Managers.* Aldershot, England: Aslib/Gower.

Carrigan, Dennis. 1994. "Public Library Private Fund-Raising: A Report Based on a Survey." *Public Libraries* 31 (1): 31-36.

Childers, Thomas, and Nancy Van House. 1989. "Dimensions of Public Library Effectiveness." *Library and Information Science Research* 11 (3): 273-301.

Childers, Thomas, and Nancy Van House. 1993. *What's Good? Describing Your Public Library's Effectiveness.* Chicago: American Library Association.

Clay, Edwin S., and Patricia C. Bangs. 2000. "Entrepreneurs in the Public Library: Reinventing an Institution." *Library Trends* 48 (3): 606-619.

Cook, Colleen, ed. 2002. "The Maturation of Assessment in Academic Libraries." *Performance Measurement and Metrics: The International Journal for Library and Information Services* 3 (2): 37-107.

Crosby, Philip B. 1979. *Quality Is Free.* New York: McGraw-Hill.

Cullen, Rowena, and Philip Calvert. 1995. "Stakeholder Perceptions of University Libraries Effectiveness." *Journal of Academic Librarianship* 21 (6): 438-448.

Cullen, Rowena, and Philip Calvert. 1996. "New Zealand University Libraries Effectiveness Project." *Library and Information Science Research* 18 (2): 99-119.

Czopek, Vanessa. 1998. "Using Mystery Shoppers to Evaluate Customer Service in the Public Library." *Public Libraries* 37 (6): 370-375.

Davies, J. Eric. 2002. "What Gets Measured, Gets Managed. Statistics and Performance Indicators for Evidence Based Management." *Journal of Librarianship and Information Science* 34 (3): 129-133.

Deming, W. Edwards. 1986. *Out of the Crisis.* Cambridge: MIT Press.

De Prospo, Ernest, Ellen Altman, and Kenneth Beasley. 1973. *Performance Measures for Public Libraries*. Chicago: American Library Association.

Department for Culture, Media ,and Sport. 2001. *Comprehensive, Efficient and Modern Public Libraries—Standards and Assessment*. London: Department for Culture, Media and Sport.

Eriksen, Paul, and Robert Shuster. 1995. "Beneficial Shocks: The Place of Processing-Cost Analysis in Archival Administration." *American Archivist* 58 (winter): 32-52.

Bang, Tove, et al., comps. 1996. *ISO 9000 for Libraries and Information Centres: A Guide*. The Hague: International Federation for Information and Documentation.

Favret, Leo. 2000. "Benchmarking, Annual Library Plans and Best Value: The Implications for Public Libraries." *Library Management* 21 (7): 340-348.

Feigenbaum, Armand V. 1985. *Total Quality Control*. 3rd ed. Milwaukee, Wis.: ASQC Quality Press.

Fortson, Judith. 1992. *Disaster Planning and Recovery*. New York: Neal-Schuman.

Giappiconi, Thierry, and Pierre Carbone. 1997. *Management des Bibliothèques: Programmer, Organiser, Conduire et Évaluer la Politique Documentaire et les Services des Bibliothèques de Service Public*. Paris: Editions du Cercle de la Librairie.

Hafner, Arthur. 1998. *Descriptive Statistical Techniques for Librarians*. 2d ed. Chicago: American Library Association.

Hernon, Peter, and Ellen Altman. 1996. *Service Quality in Academic Libraries*. Norwood, N.J.: Ablex.

Hernon, Peter, and Ellen Altman. 1998. *Assessing Service Quality*. Chicago: American Library Association.

Hernon, Peter, and Robert E. Dugan. 2001. *An Action Plan for Outcomes Assessment in Your Library*. Chicago: American Library Association.

Hernon, Peter, and John Whitman. 2001. *Delivering Satisfaction and Service Quality*. Chicago: American Library Association.

Holt, Glen, and Donald Elliott. 2002. "Cost Benefit Analysis: A Summary of the Methodology." *The Bottom Line: Managing Library Finances* 15 (4): 154-158.

Holt, Glen, Donald Elliott, and Amonia Moore. 1999. "Placing a Value on Public Library Services." *Public Libraries* 38 (2): 98-108.

Immroth, Barbara F., and Keith C. Lance. 1996. "Output Measures for Children's Services in the Public Library." *Public Libraries* 35 (4): 240-245.

Ishikawa, Kaoru. 1985. *What Is Total Quality?* Englewood Cliffs, N.J.: Prentice-Hall.

Johnson, Eric W. 1998. "Fund-Raising and the Library Director: An Interview with Susan Kent." *Library Administration and Management* 12 (2): 129-131.

Joint Funding Council. 1995. *The Effective Academic Library: A Framework for Evaluating the Performance of U.K. Academic Libraries*. Bristol: HEFCE Publications.

Juran, Joseph M. 1974. *Juran's Quality Control Handbook*. 4th ed. New York: McGraw-Hill.

Kyrillidou, Martha, and Fred M. Heath, eds. 2001. "Measuring Service Quality." *Library Trends* 49 (4): 541-799.

Kusack, James M. 2002. "Understanding and Controlling the Costs of Library Services." *Library Administration and Management* 16 (3): 151-155.

Liddle, David. 1999. "Best Value—The Impact on Libraries: Practical Steps in Demonstrating Best Value." *Library Management* 20 (4): 206-212.

Lorenzen, Michael. 1998. "Security Issues in the Public Libraries of Three Midwestern States." *Public Libraries* 37 (2): 134-136.

Martin, Allie-Beth. 1972. *A Strategy for Public Library Change.* Chicago: American Library Association.

Morgan, Steve. 1995. *Performance Measurement in Academic Libraries.* London: Mansell.

Nelson, Sandra. 2001. *The New Planning for Results: A Streamlined Approach.* Chicago: American Library Association.

Parasuraman, A. 2002 "Foreword." *Performance Measurement and Metrics: The International Journal for Library and Information Services* 3 (2): 37-39.

Parasurman, Raja A. 2002. Valaria Zeitaml, and Leonard Berry. 1987. *A Conceptual Model of Service Quality and Its Implications for Future Research.* Report No. 84-106. Cambridge, Mass.: Market Science Institute.

Paton, Rob, Jane Foot, and Geoff Payne. 2000. "What Happens When Nonprofits Use Quality Models for Self-Assessment?" *Nonprofit Management and Leadership* 11 (1): 21-34.

Reading the Future: A Review of Public Libraries in England. 1997. London: Department of National Heritage.

Rudd, Peggy D. 2001. "Documenting the Difference: Demonstrating the Value of Libraries Through Outcome Measurement." In *Perspectives on Outcomes Based Evaluation for Libraries and Museums.* Washington, D.C.: Institute of Museum and Library Services. (Accessed January 2003.) Available: www.imls.gov/pubs/pdf/pubobe.pdf.

Shaughnessy, Thomas. 1987. "Search for Quality." *Library Administration and Management* 8 (1): 5-10.

Sirkin, Arlene. 1993. "Customer Service: Another Side to TQM." In *Integrating Total Quality Management in a Library Setting,* edited by Susan Jurow and Susan Barnard. New York: Haworth Press.

Steele, Victoria, and Stephen D. Elder. 1992. *Becoming a Fundraiser: The Principles and Practice of Library Development.* Chicago: American Library Association.

Stein, Joan, Martha Kyrillidou, and Denise Davies, eds. 2002. *Proceedings of the 4th Northumbria International Conference on Performance Measurement in Libraries and Information Services: Pittsburgh, 12-16 August 2001.* Washington, D.C.: Association of Research Libraries.

Turock, Betty J. 1984. "Productivity, Financial Management and the Public Library." *Public Library Quarterly* 5 (4): 3-7.

Turock, Betty J., and Andrea Pedolsky. 1992. "Financial Planning for a Stable Fiscal Future." *The Bottom Line: Managing Library Finances* 5 (3): 13-17.

Van House, Nancy, et al. 1990. *Measuring Academic Library Performance: A Practical Approach.* Chicago: American Library Association.

Van House, Nancy, and Thomas Childers. 1993. *The Public Library Effectiveness Study.* Chicago: American Library Association.

Walter, Virginia A. 1992. *Output Measures for Public Library Service to Children.* Chicago: American Library Association.

Zweizig, Douglas, et al. 1996. *Tell It! Manual: The Complete Program for Evaluating Library Performance.* Chicago: American Library Association.

Launching Pad

Ashley, Kevin. 2002. "The Costing of Digital Records Management." *Records Management Journal* 10 (3): 140-149.

Bundy, Alan. 2002. "Public and School Library Cooperation: Evaluation Checklists." *Australasian Public Libraries and Information Services* 15 (3): 100-103.

Coulson, Graham, et al. 2001. "Securing Funding in the Local Bidding Culture: Are Records Sufficiently 'Sexy' to Succeed?" *Records Management Journal* 11 (2): 83-95.

Cullen, Rowena, and Philip Calvert. 1993. "Further Dimensions of Public Library Effectiveness." *Library and Information Science Research* 15 (2): 143-164.

Dutton, Jane E., et al. 2002. "Leading in Times of Trauma." *Harvard Business Review* 80 (1): 54-61.

Eng, Sidney. 2002. "How Technology and Planning Saved My Library at Ground Zero." *Computers in Libraries* 22 (4): 28-32, 34-35.

Gadd, Elizabeth. 2002. "Meeting the Needs of Distance Learners Without Additional Funding." *Library Management* 23 (8/9): 359-368.

Hannabuss, Stuart. 2001. "Scenario Planning for Libraries." *Library Management* 22 (4/5): 168-176.

Harrop, Ken, et al. 2002. "Bidding for Records: Local Authority Archives and Competitive Funding." *Journal of the Society of Archivists* 23 (1): 35-50.

Healy, Susan. 2001. "ISO 15489 Records Management: Its Development and Significance." *Records Management Journal* 11 (3): 133-142.

Hernon, Peter. 2002. "Quality: New Directions in Research." *Journal of Academic Librarianship* 28 (4): 224-231.

Hill, Nigel, Bill Self, and Greg Roche. 2002. *Customer Satisfaction Measurement for ISO 9000:2000.* Oxford: Butterworth-Heinemann.

Jones, Virginia A., and Kris E. Keys. 2001. *Emergency Management for Records and Information Programs.* Lenexa, Kans.: ARMA International.

Kahn, Miriam B. 2003. *Disaster Response and Planning for Libraries.* 2d ed. Chicago: American Library Association.

Kostiak, Adele. 2002. "Valuing Your Public Library: The Experience of the Barrie Public Library, Ontario, Canada." *The Bottom Line: Managing Library Finances* 15 (4): 159-162.

Kusack, James M. 2002. "Understanding and Controlling the Costs of Library Services." *Library Administration and Management* 16 (3): 151-155.

Mayo, Diane, and Joanne Goodrich. 2002. *Staffing for Results: A Guide to Working Smarter.* Chicago: American Library Association.

Meraz, Gloria. 2002. "The Essentials of Financial Strength Through Sound Lobbying Fundamentals." *The Bottom Line: Managing Library Finances* 15 (2): 64-69.

Nicely, Donna D. 2002. "Private Funding for Capital Projects." *The Bottom Line: Managing Library Finances* 15 (4): 163-166.

Palmer, Marlize. 2000. "Records Management and Accountability Versus Corruption, Fraud and Maladministration." *Records Management Journal* 10 (20): 61-72.

Pickford, Chris. 1999. "Contract Cataloguing: An Opportunity or a Threat?" *Journal of the Society of Archivists* 20 (2): 169-176.

Singer, Paula M. 2002. *Developing a Compensation Plan for Your Library.* Chicago: American Library Association.

Seer, Gitelle. 2000. "Special Library Financial Management: The Essentials of Library Budgeting." *The Bottom Line: Managing Library Finances* 13 (4): 186-192.

Sherbine, Karen. 1994. *Libraries and Archives: An Overview of Risk and Loss Prevention.* Chicago: Society of American Archivists and Inland Marine Underwriters Association.

Shuman, Bruce A. 1999. *Library Security and Safety Handbook: Prevention, Policies, and Procedures.* Chicago: American Library Association.

Trinkhaus-Randall, Gregor. 1995. *Protecting Your Collections: A Manual of Archival Security.* Chicago: American Library Association.

Ward, Suzanne M., Yem S. Fong, and Damon Camille. 2002. "Library Fee-Based Information Services: Financial Considerations." *The Bottom Line: Managing Library Finances* 15 (1): 5-17.

Wellheiser, Johanna, and Jude Scott. 2002. *An Ounce of Prevention: Integrated Disaster Planning for Archives, Libraries, and Records Centers.* 2d ed. Lanham, Mass.: Scarecrow Press.

Whitmire, Emelene. 2002. "External Partnerships and Academic Libraries." *Library Management* 23 (4/5): 199-202.

Yong, Josephine, and Adrian Wilkinson. 2002. "The Long and Winding Road: the Evolution of Quality Management." *Total Quality Management* 2 (2): 101-111.

PART III: UNDERSTANDING THE PEOPLE FACTORS

7: MANAGING DIVERSITY

"Humor relaxes, creates bonds, gives perspective, and stimulates creativity."

IN THIS CHAPTER YOU'LL DISCOVER:

- what is meant by "diversity"
- your belief system about multiculturalism
- the aim of diversity management
- why diversity needs to be embedded in strategic planning
- organizational policies and practices that promote equal opportunities
- the challenges of managing a diverse staff
- ways of meeting the needs of diverse users; and
- how much your organization has achieved in managing diversity

COMING TO GRIPS WITH DIVERSITY

Pick up any management journal today and you will see that managing diversity is an issue of concern and importance in all organizations. The phrase "cultural diversity" is heard increasingly at conferences and professional meetings around the globe.

There are four important reasons why managers need to understand the concept and the implications it has for their service:

1   A number of colleagues will not have been raised in the society where they are now working.
2   Service is being provided to an increasingly multicultural and diverse community.
3   The skills of information professionals are transferable across national boundaries, so they can choose to work overseas on a long or short-term assignment.
4   As information professions operate on a global basis, it is essential to be able to communicate effectively with colleagues around the world.

Working in a culturally diverse situation is already challenging, and *managing* it presents even greater challenges—so it is not surprising that is sensitivity to issues of diversity heads a list of seven attributes that workforce trends indicate leaders will need in the future (Conger and Benjamin, 1999).

THE REASON WHY

"A diverse workforce, including different races, sex, age, skills, experiences, geographical backgrounds, may be politically correct....But I believe it is essential to competing in an uncertain environment. The objective is not just to have diversity of personal characteristics but to have a diversity of ideas, skills, and experiences that can add economic value to the organization. Because of the life experiences and different perspectives that can be brought to bear on a problem or challenge facing an organization, diverse people with very different perspectives may identify new and previously unconsidered options...."
(Fulmer, 2000)

But what do we mean by "diversity"? As a management topic, it developed from "equal opportunities," which focused on issues of gender and racial discrimination both in society and in the workplace. Today, the broader term "diversity" is a better description of the changing social and political environment. The term has widened to cover all visible characteristics such as race, gender, age, physical abilities, and weight, together with invisible characteristics of work experience, social and economic background, religion, access to educational opportunities, and sexual orientation.

Another change in the approach to diversity has been to focus on the individual rather than the group in society. This recognizes that the differences among staff in the workplace, if effectively managed, can be an asset in getting work done more efficiently and effectively.

IN A NUTSHELL

Diversity is:

A context-dependent concept—*no one can be defined as being different in isolation.*

A selective concept—*some characteristics are stronger indicators than others, e.g., color, gender.*

A relative concept—*women may be defined as more (or less) "feminine" than others.*

A criterion used by some for vertical or horizontal job segregation— *the unequal distribution of men and women in certain occupations.*

(Moore, 1999)

Hofstede has had a considerable influence on the way that managers think about culture today. He indicates that "every person carries within him or herself patterns of thinking, feeling, and potential acting which were learned throughout their lifetime. Much of it has been acquired in early childhood. As soon as certain patterns have established themselves (s)he must unlearn these before bring able to learn something different, and unlearning is more difficult than learning for the first time" (Hofstede, 1997: 4).

He makes a distinction between the several layers of culture people carry within them as a mental programming. They are:

- the national level (especially strong for immigrants);
- the regional, ethnic, religious, and/or linguistic level;
- the gender level;
- the generation level;
- the social class level; and
- the organizational or corporate level. (Hofstede, 1997: 10)

WORTH CHECKING OUT

Culture

Hofstede, Geert. 1997. *Culture and Organizations*: *Software of the Mind*. New York: McGraw-Hill.

Belief Systems About Multiculturalism

In working with users and colleagues, try to understand what lies at the core of a person's belief system; a helpful approach is based on the theories of perception and uses the idea of "lenses" that filter what we have been taught and what we have seen, heard and experienced. (Williams, 2001). Ten lenses have been identified through which differences such as race, culture, ethnicity and nationality can be examined. For those who are interested in taking a sociological approach to human understanding, this is well worth exploring.

> ## Dɪɢ ᴅᴇᴇᴘᴇʀ
>
> **Williams's ten lenses describe people and their belief systems.**
>
> - *The Assimilationist* submerges individual and cultural identities for nationalist ideals
> - *The Colorblind* person believes ignoring race and color has an equalizing effect
> - *The Culturalcentrist* encourages cultural pride and creates a support network
> - *The Elitist* perpetuates advantages
> - *The Integrationist* merges people of different cultures
> - *The Metritocratist* believes that with ability and hard work you can compete to realize your dream
> - *The Multiculturalist* celebrates the diversity of cultures
> - *The Seclusionist* considers that different groups should live and work apart
> - *The Transcendent* feels that race, ethnicity and nationality contribute to the richness of humanity
> - *The Victim/caretaker* sees liberation as a crucial goal

You may be skeptical about such tests, but this one helps create a practical awareness of the views of others; for example, by understanding other people's views, you can recognize strengths in colleagues and identify ways to help their professional development. The lens approach helps in communicating with, and responding to, users needs.

Drawing upon the ideas of Hofstede and Williams, managers can develop frameworks to come to grips with the concept of diversity, map out the way it impacts the operation of their service, and build services that meet the needs of the diverse workplace.

> ## Rᴇᴍᴇᴍʙᴇʀ
>
> The second chapter stressed the importance of understanding yourself; think about the ten lenses and take the lens test at www.diversitychannel.com to extend this self-awareness.

THE AIM OF DIVERSITY MANAGEMENT

One of the tasks of managers is to create a climate of trust which supports individuals and where individuals take a genuine interest in other people and their ideas, are willing to listen, explore differences in a positive way, and clarify what is said and done. The aim is to help people to work together as a team and be productive and efficient—but turning the aim into reality is not always easy.

> Diversity management involves:
>
> - leadership commitment and involvement;
> - direction-setting;
> - a strategic action plan;
> - accountability and responsibility;
> - a system of measurement; and
> - an assessment process which will answer the following:
>
> Are the strategies delivering the right results?
> Are the goals of the diversity-management process being reached?
> Are the organization's results showing the expected improvement?
> Do employees recognize the change?
> What is working?
> Are prejudice and discrimination being addressed?
> How do employees feel about the organization's diversity culture?
> (Hankins, 2000)

For managers, achieving the reality starts by examining current policies and practices within the service and the parent organization. One approach is to use the framework developed by Hankins (2000) outlined above.

Managing diversity is not only valuable to teamwork; there are legal implications as well. Equal opportunity legislation has grown from its original focus on gender and race to include discrimination against age and disability, for example.

Policies and practices must also extend to the meeting the needs of diverse users of services by providing leaflets or Web pages in a range of languages and checking that facilities are suitable for the disabled—including the visually impaired.

We stress the need for sensitivity—don't patronize, but don't ignore.

Managing Diversity in the Information Sector

The professional associations in the service sector paid early attention to the issues of inequality emerging in society at large. More recently, discussion has centered on issues of social inclusion and social justice. Partly prompted by the dilemmas emerging from increased immigration, European services have been debating cultural diversity versus integration (Skot-Hansen, 2002).

WORTH CHECKING OUT

Diversity and the information sector

Several journals have published themed issues focusing on diversity and multiculturalism. They include:

American Libraries ("Diversity," 1999)

Journal of Library Administration (Neely and Lee-Smeltzer, 2001a and 2001b)

Library Management (Layzell Ward, 2002)

Library Trends (de la Peña McCook, 2000)

New Managers and the Responsibility for Diversity Management

Newly appointed managers need to find out and, more importantly, clearly understand their personal responsibilities and accountability for diversity management. What expectations do senior management and bosses hold? Where does the topic appear in the strategic plans? What do you have to do, and what must others see you do? If this isn't clear, raise questions with the next manager up the hierarchy.

DIVERSITY AND STRATEGIC PLANNING

The extent to which strategic planning is required to encompass diversity issues depends on:

- what legislation is currently in force
- how much has been done to ensure that staff reflect the diversity of the community

You need to be aware that there are different approaches to diversity management in the public and in the private sectors. The public sector provides just and equitable services to meet the changing demographics. The private sector relates diversity to its organizational success. Interestingly, research carried out in U.S. academic libraries indicates that the latter relationship also holds in the academic sector (Winston, 2001).

Organizations are about people, which is why strategic planning, implementation, and monitoring are vital, and diversity management needs to be at the core of strategic planning. It is important that the topmost layer of management demonstrates a strong commitment to diversity and does not see it only as an add-on to its strategic plan.

Top Management and Commitment

Sometimes resistance comes from top management. It may be related to age—senior management may not have had firsthand experience of the issues or experienced discrimination themselves. They may find it difficult to understand the feelings and viewpoints of newcomers or minorities. These feelings might be the result of fear if managers are anxious to maintain their position, but find it difficult to accept the changing nature of the community.

Two attitudes can emerge—the manager may become obstructive, or perhaps worse, apathetic. Obstruction is usually evident to those around them and it can be handled. Apathy is more difficult to diagnose and overcome.

Senior management needs to show a visible and active commitment to diversity management by setting the direction and indicating demonstrating a concern that extends beyond the need to meet legal requirements. As in any aspect of strategic planning, people within the organization need to be consulted so that everyone has a sense of ownership and an involvement in preparing objectives, goals, timetables and agreeing upon the ways in which the outcomes will be evaluated.

When agreement is reached, a vision statement on diversity can be integrated into the core of the organization's strategic plan, becoming a key focus rather than a separate, or subsidiary, plan. Training about diversity issues should be at the core of the training program for all new employees to make sure that they are clearly aware of the organization's commitment to diversity management and that they have a responsibility to ensure that the goals are met.

As with any aspect of the strategic plan, there must be a clear link between the rhetoric and the reality. Policies require a commitment of funding if they are to be successful, and management must have the authority to ensure that policies are turned into practice. No organization is likely to be successful if it pays lip service to policies at a time when accountability and quality procedures are part of the management process.

Progress Must Be Audited

Progress is measured through the collection, publication, and scrutiny of data and information and should be demonstrated in the outcomes. But sometimes practice does not always follow policy.

If it is clear that the expected changes have not taken place, take action to find out why this has not happened. Is there a need for more effective training programs? Is one group finding it difficult to achieve promotion?

Since change cannot happen overnight, it may be that any achievements made will not yet be visible. Auditing progress may confirm that some gains have been made which, in turn, will motivate everyone to make more gains.

Qualitative information gathered through user feedback, exit interviews with staff, and focus groups with both staff and users can help to judge the effectiveness of policies and practices and demonstrates that management is committed to good practice. The informal nature of exit interviews and focus groups can feed into the planning process.

Diversity Committee

Progress reviews are generally overseen by a committee that is representative of the organization, may have external members, and disseminates its findings. Some large information services may have a committee that has oversight of diversity issues, or it may form part of the responsibilities of the Human Resources Department of the wider parent organization such as a city or county.

Arguments can be made for a narrow committee that is departmentally based, or for the committee to have a broader role across the organization. The final decision will be made bearing in mind the organizational culture of the service and its parent body. In any case, there must be a committee to monitor progress that is accountable to senior management, to all staff and to all users.

DIG DEEPER

Drawing on current research, Weiss gives extensive coverage to cross-cultural diversity, ethics, and the impact of change on an organization and its people.

Weiss, Joseph W. 2001. *Organizational Behavior and Change: Managing Diversity, Cross-Cultural Dynamics and Ethics.* Cincinnati, Ohio: South-Western College Publishing.

POLICIES THAT PROMOTE DIVERSITY

Developing Goals for Multicultural Diversity

As with any aspect of strategic planning, the information service prepares its own goals within the context of those set by the parent organization. Ensuring staff awareness of diversity issues through training and involving them in setting goals will produce policies that will more easily become practices.

The end goals need to be realistic and achievable, communicated to both staff and users, supported by earmarked funding, and include a system for monitoring and evaluation. While the involvement of staff is essential, in some services it will also be vital to involve representatives of users.

The context and an overview of this process are summed up in the steps needed to create a multicultural environment described by Kendall (1994):

- Assess the climate using both formal and informal measures.
- Create a long-term plan and establishing goals.

- Select a group of employees to work on diversity, and prepare them to work as models and facilitators.
- Organize training sessions for staff.
- Build diversity into the structure of the service.

Making a successful transition to a hospitable work environment is as essential for information services as it is for organizations in general:

1   The service must believe in the goals it sets and that people can change.
2   The service must address diversity at the personal and institutional level.
3   Management must genuinely and seriously commit to an ongoing examination of its own attitudes as well as its policies and procedures.
4   The service must view diversity as a long-term multifaceted, continual process, not as an event or a quick fix.
5   The service must expect and be willing to deal with discomfort and resistance.
6   The service must not avoid discussions on institutional racism when addressing diversity and multicultural environments.
7   The service must develop a long-term plan for creating diversity.
8   The service must develop a core staff willing to commit time and energy to bringing about a hospitable work environment for all people.
9   The service must know that its diversity activities will mirror its other activities.

The following factors can cause complications that make it difficult to evaluate the outcomes of diversity management:

- the difficulty of measuring attitude change
- a lack of a discrete beginning and ending of the task
- the isolation of the information/library experience from the outside world
- stress caused by other events in the service manifesting itself as resistance to diversity (Kendall, 1994)

The final point is very important. All information organizations are continually going through rapid technological change and many are facing challenges to operate more efficiently with less resources. In the background are the pressures of the work/life balance. Sometimes staff can see a new policy as being the last straw and they might take out their frustration on the new diversity practices rather than address the underlying cause.

Much of the success of the program will depend upon the leadership skills of senior management and the work of the middle manager in leading and implementing change. Complications can emerge if managers are recruited from outside the community in which the service is located, for the culture can vary even between geographic areas within a country—consider the contrast between a capital city and a rural area. There may also be more than one official language used within a country, as in Canada. Managerial and professional posts are sometimes advertised internationally and a person is appointed from overseas.

Regardless of cultural differences, managers are expected to perform from their first day in the way anticipated by their new colleagues. Leadership styles can be culture-dependent, ranging from the autocratic, to the quasi-autocratic, to the democratic or participative. There is a body of literature that draws on the experiences of international organizations, for example, the volume edited by Rahim and Blum (1994).

WORTH CHECKING OUT

The gurus write about managing diversity

Harvard Business Review on Managing Diversity. 2001. Boston: Harvard Business School Press

---

The Legal Framework

The framework of anti-discrimination laws vary between countries. In some, several aspects of discrimination are grouped in one overarching piece of legislation; more commonly, separate legislation covers such aspects as sex discrimination, racial discrimination, sexual preference, ageism, and disability.

Relevant legislation may also have been enacted at several levels of jurisdiction. Within the U.S. and Australia, there can be legislation at both a state and at a federal level. Within the European Union, legislation is enacted at a national level, but the Union issues separate directives to member countries on employment matters. However, the European Court of Justice is responsible for cases that fall into the category of human rights legislation.

Managers must keeping abreast of this complex and fast-changing situation as it relates to the workplace. Consult with colleagues in the organization's Human Resources Department or search the Web for official government publications and guides to the specific areas of legislation. Although the individual manager must be aware of the legal framework within which they are working, it is ultimately the responsibility of the parent organization to put policies in place and to ensure that they are carried out according to the law.

Staffing Policies

In reviewing staffing matters, we are drawing attention to issues that managers should be aware of—we could call them tiger traps. Implementing change in policies and practices may not be a responsibility for middle managers, but managers need to be aware of good practices. Staffing and hiring policies vary between organizations, and the degree of responsibilities held by managers will also differ.

The organizational policies that need special attention are:

- hiring,
- working conditions,
- working practices and their flexibility,
- training and career development, and
- promotion.

Each policy should be clearly stated in the documentation made available to staff, and policies must be regularly reviewed to ensure they reflect best practice. This is an area where regular changes occur in legislation.

At a general level, those in charge of nondiscriminatory selection policies for hiring, promotion, training, and career development should:

1. make sure documents are free of bias regarding personal characteristics e.g. race, gender, etc.;
2. ensure the person selected satisfies criteria which are job-related;
3. document the selection process making it available to applicants in clearly stated terms;
4. take care that those carrying out the selection process are capable of implementing the selection policies effectively;
5. record decisions together with the reasons why the decision was made;
6. convey decisions, in writing, to the successful and unsuccessful candidates;
7. indicate the reasons for the decisions in writing to the successful—and on request to unsuccessful candidates;
8. file the documentation so that it is capable of being retrieved if required at a future date.

In essence, the process must be transparent to everyone involved.

Policies regarding work conditions are governed by health and safety regulations, which vary from country to country; for example, Australia introduced requirements for ergonomic desks and other equipment for people using computers way back in the 1980s. In archives and records management services, policies are needed to ensure the safe handling of heavy objects and boxes. In libraries, there is the question of how books are shelved—sometimes shelves can be high, or there may be moveable stacks. Policy statements relating to health and safety will need to be checked if a person joins the team who has a physical disability, or if their height or size differs markedly from the norm in that country. This ensures that they are not required to carry out tasks that might lead to injury.

Flexible working practices may help solve some policy problems for managers. Many information organizations divide work into shifts, which means that special requirements relating to religious practices and holy days, national holidays or family commitments may be more easily accommodated.

There are two aspects of training that should be covered by policy statements. First, all staff should receive training about diversity issues. Second, new recruits from minority groups should be assessed to check whether they have special training needs. In Wales, for example, the introduction of bilingual language policies have resulted in employers offering Welsh language lessons to their English-speaking staff.

The question of promotion policies is very sensitive, and reverse discrimination may be a concern in the workplace. People from minority groups may feel they are overlooked for promotion; for example, women may find it difficult to break through the "glass ceiling" into top management. But reverse discrimination may cause those from minority groups to feel uncomfortable when they do gain promotion.

Patricia Layzell Ward recalls an uncomfortable situation when a new Australian university introduced the title of Professor. Top management wanted to uphold high standards for appointment to chairs in higher education, so rigorous requirements were set down and a searching selection process employed. Of seven successful candidates, two were women. Male colleagues at their former level who were unsuccessful made comments—publicly and privately—about the "token women." For a time, working relationships within a peer group were strained. The situation might have been avoided if the documentation provided by the candidates had been made public.

PRACTICES THAT PROMOTE DIVERSITY

As strategic planning leads to the development of policies, those policies need to be transformed into practices.

WORTH CHECKING OUT

Achieving success

Two writers offer practical advice on achieving success and best practice:

Carr-Ruffino, Norma. 1999. *Diversity Success Strategies.* Boston: Butterworth-Heinemann.

Loden, Marilyn. 1996. *Implementing Diversity: Best Practices for Making Diversity Work in Your Organization.* Chicago: Irwin Professional.

Communication

Effective communication underpins all good practices. In a culturally diverse situation, it is essential that managers ensure that staff members fully understand messages.

In some ways, communication is easier between people who have different mother tongues—you know there can easily be a misunderstanding. The greater danger occurs when two people come from countries which use the same language, but which have subtle, or not so subtle, differences of meaning. This frequently occurs in the idiomatic use of language or regional accents.

Colleagues can help a newcomer by being sensitive to their predicament. Do not continually correct their use of the language, but listen to understand why a word or phrase is presenting a problem and then offer an explanation and advice to build self-confidence. Go gently when helping newcomers to speak or write the language of the workplace. They will learn much more quickly.

Recruiting Staff

When you become the person who has responsibilities for hiring, the complexity of the hiring process becomes clear. There is much to think about, including the issues of diversity that lie at the core of the process. If you have been recruited, you can use your positive and negative experiences to help develop good practice.

The first step is to reflect on the diverse backgrounds of the staff, and to check how much they match those of the users served. Given the problems of attracting applicants from ethnic minorities to professional programs, there is likely to be an imbalance. The service may need to consider whether recruitment from minority groups should be a hiring goal.

A review of hiring practices should focus on:

- the composition of the staff;
- their levels of attainment;
- the number of years they have been in their current post; and
- the attrition rates.

Quantitative information should be gathered about the past and present patterns of recruitment and retention, but qualitative information about the reasons why people have left the service should be added to that data. Bear in mind that the reasons may be difficult for a person from a minority group to articulate, except within a sensitive exit interview.

An analysis of the information collected may indicate that those in the minority may not have received promotion at the rate for staff as a whole. Perhaps there has been recruitment from minority groups, but people have not stayed for any length of time. They might have felt that the organizational climate was not hospitable to them. Perhaps there is a shortage of trained staff from their ethnic background, and they move on because they are in high demand in the labor marketplace. This has been the experience in a number of countries where programs have been introduced to encourage minority recruitment. Remember that creating an organizational climate that supports diversity will aid in the retention of staff in general.

Job descriptions may discriminate in a way that is not immediately obvious, so it is essential that they be reviewed for bias. For example, there is regular comment and criticism from minority groups, and particularly from women, that job descriptions and hiring criteria have been prepared by white males. It helps to state the requirements in terms of desired outcomes. To ensure everyone competes on a level playing field, requirements should be clearly stated regarding:

- academic achievements,
- previous experience,
- behavioral attributes, and
- technical skills.

Good diversity practice within the organization achieves alliances within the local community, and these networks can be used to publicize staff vacancies. The organization's Web site should state its policies and practices concerning diversity to further encourages people from minority groups to apply.

The way in which the recruitment process is carried out varies within the different sectors of the information professions. In the field of local government, it may involve a process of competition. The private sector often uses a recruiting agency to prepare an advertisement and carry out the process to the point of selection, working closely with the client organization. The manager will be required to follow whichever process the organization employs, but will expect to be consulted on specific points, such as the job requirements and the likely state of the labor market.

Advertisements need to be written and placed to attract the widest attention. To attract minority candidates, they may need to be placed in a wide range of sources, such as in the professional and the local press. Local media, particularly newspapers and radio, can be helpful by carrying features that draw attention to the positive work on cultural diversity that is taking place within the service.

Many organizations in the public sector organize the placement of advertisements centrally and have a standard layout. But if there can be any influence over the content and design, ensure they are attractive and eye catching but also accurate and clear about diversity policies. The aim is to gather a wide pool of potential applicants.

In long-established and larger organizations, there may be less movement at the higher level, which will present problems for increasing diversity at those levels. At the entry level, maintain contact with centers of professional education and training that may identify potential applicants who can contribute to the diverse profile of the service. Another approach is to make contacts by attending professional conferences that organize job fairs.

A job description should be sent to applicants together with some basic information about the organization and the department in which the vacancy has occurred. The organization will generally have a standard application form, and a short curriculum vita may be requested from applicants, together with a letter of application.

At the closing date, the manager with the vacancy and the Human Resource Department generally sift through the applications. The decision to progress an application must depend on an objective view of how the person fits the selection criteria for the post. No discrimination should take place, and there may be a legal requirement with established guidelines.

It is good practice to immediately contact those not selected at this stage and thank them for their application.

In the case of those moving to the next stage, a packet of additional information should be provided. Arrangements for the selection process should be put in place, including time to visit the department, to look at what the job involves, to witness the working conditions, and to talk with staff. Try to ensure that candidates meet up with someone from their own ethnic group—this will encourage them to gather information informally.

If technical skills are to be tested, applicants will need to be informed about the nature of the test and how long it will last. Make sure that bias does not enter into the administration of the test or the scoring of the results.

This is the stage of the process when references are generally taken up in order to provide more detailed information for those who will make the decision. Ask permission to contact references; sometimes applicants withdraw when they receive additional information, or perhaps they have already secured another job. Requests for information about candidates should be made in good time if some referees are based at a distance, and e-mail speeds up the process

The letter to referees should clearly indicate the nature and level of detail of the required information. Make it easy for referees to respond—and always send a letter of thanks when the reference is received.

Now it is time to make a hiring decision. The manager who will be responsible for the new recruit should take part, but there is also merit in having the experience of a manager from a higher level. They will be aware of the organization's overall standing with regard to diversity and of its needs and their objectivity, experience, support and advice will also be of benefit if difficult decisions have to be made. In some organizations, the staff of a department nominate a person to sit on interview panels. The selection process can also be assisted by the appointment of representatives from the minority groups to be interviewed.

The interview process requires careful planning. The essential points to consider are:

1   What type of interview will be given—formal, informal?
2   How long should it last?
3   How many people should be involved?
4   Who should be involved—both management and non-management?
5   Are all participants trained in the skills of interviewing and aware of legal considerations, e.g. the unlawful questions and bias that can be introduced into the process?

Legislation generally indicates that decisions to hire staff must be based on the requirements set out in the job description, and not irrelevant or subjective criteria.

The role of the chair of the hiring committee is to ensure that legal requirements are met, that courtesy and consideration is shown to applicants, that members of the panel listen, and that the applicant has some open ended questions to put them at ease. The chair should take action if a member acts inappropriately or interferes with the goal of reaching an objective decision.

> **TIP**
>
> Think carefully about the timing of the interviews. Ensure that applicants can arrive in time or have them accommodated overnight. Starting later gives members of the hiring committee time to check their mail and attend to urgent matters that could distract them during the interview.
>
> If interviews are held after lunch, don't feed the panel too well—they may start to doze.

At the end of the interviews, all members of the committee should review the issues, including the salary and benefit expectations of the candidates. Some candidates may have ruled themselves out by overoptimistic expectations that will not fit into the salary practices of the organization or the department.

When a decision has been made, the chair collects the comments of the individual members of the committee and puts the decision in writing, noting the reasons for the decision.

The Human Resources Department generally makes the job offer, and when it has been accepted, notifies the unsuccessful candidates. If those not appointed ask for the reason, have the answer ready—usually it is because the person appointed matches the criteria more closely. Next, the manager and staff are informed of the decision, and the newcomer's induction program is organized.

Cohen (1994) provides good advice for reviewing recruitment policies:

- Review position descriptions.
- Review selection criteria.
- Review current outreach techniques and incorporate new ones in order to broaden the pool of applicants.
- Assess the pool and interview candidates.
- Review the search file and recommendations.
- Examine the additional considerations.
  - Target funding opportunities.
  - Provide training support.
  - Provide individual job counseling to minority candidates.
  - Utilize internship programs.
  - Recruit minority librarians and administrators who can serve as leaders and mentors.
  - Recruit minority support staff.
  - Recruit minority student assistants for temporary support staff positions.
  - Travel to recruit.

Drawing on the experiences of the University of Michigan, Cohen comments that the issues surrounding retention are a bit more difficult to describe. She makes two good points that we endorse: 1) create the climate that supports diversity, and 2) educate staff (Cohen, 1994).

Appointment of staff who come from a range of backgrounds and who can speak the languages spoken within the community is one of the ways to provide an effective service. Multilingual countries may require that services are provided in several languages; for example, services in Canada must take into account both English and French; in Wales, they must provide service in English and Welsh. The service may need to have multilingual policy documents, staff members, publications, Web sites, inquiry services, and other materials.

FOR FURTHER THOUGHT

Some organizational practices that focus on staffing in a culturally diverse workgroup have been outlined.

List three of the most important characteristics of these practices.

Training for Everyone

At the basic level, there must be an understanding between staff members that differences exist in the attitudes and patterns of behavior by different groups within society. Newcomers to a society experience a level of culture shock, which can be difficult for colleagues to imagine. There may be a different use of jargon or new sets of acronyms, and they may need to learn new ways of doing the job, since different systems may be used. Plus there will be a new work group to get to know. Recall your feelings when joining an organization as a new employee, and think about the mild culture shock you probably experienced. This can provide clues as to how a newcomer from another country might feel.

We carry natural values that may differ from those of people we meet. Some of the differences are obvious; for example, the day devoted to religious activities. Others are subtler, for example, relaxed or rigid attitudes toward time. The rituals when meeting another person will vary from the warm smile, friendly handshake and use of first names to greater formality and distance, use of formal names, and the presentation of gifts. Eye contact can be seen as reassuring and listening may be accompanied by nods, or eye contact may be avoided entirely.

The pattern of the working day varies in different parts of the world—there may be a long break midday, with work resuming late in the afternoon or into the evening. Rituals and symbols may be difficult to grasp for the newcomer, as the problems really lie in identifying and understanding the unstated values of the society.

The experience of culture shock lies at the heart of a paper written by a consultant on preservation from the United States who went to Malaysia on a three-month fellowship (Child, 1997).

WORTH CHECKING OUT

Culture shock

Child, Margaret. 1997. "Taking Preservation Across Cultural Frontiers." *Libri* 47 (3): 139-146.

During the learning process, the newcomer can experience frustration, helplessness, and perhaps hostility to the new environment as they compare it to the life they have left. The first reaction is a short period of euphoria—the time when everything is new and thrilling. The second is the period of culture shock, as the differences become more obvious. A sense of isolation from the new community emerges, as it seems to be impossible to grasp the subtleties of the new situation. In time, they move to a third stage of acculturation as they learn to operate in the new society, learn the norms of behavior, and gain self-confidence. These reactions can equally apply to someone moving within a country.

A number of training programs are provided by external training bodies to assist the newcomer, but these are generally short courses that cannot deal with the subject in depth. This is where the organization's staff can assist by making them feel welcome and helping them to adjust.

The worst experience for the newcomer is to find that the employer ignores the question of culture shock. Then there is a greater expectation of the new staff member than they can hope to achieve, and/or they are faced with hostility within the work team.

Wynn's (1992) steps in building cultural bridges can assist in working through the process of understanding:

1. Become aware of the commonalties and differences among and between various cultures: Take a look.
2. Recognize that your way may not be the "right or only" way: Take a perspective.
3. Invest yourself: Take a part
4. Develop positive relationships with people of different cultures: Take a hand.
5. Get assertive to confront the prejudice in others and ourselves: Take a stand.
6. Evolve bridge-building projects: Take a step.
7. Share the cultural bridge's vision: Share the Dream.

Training programs for staff in culturally diverse organizations need to focus on a number of issues. First, consider the impact of tradition and the expectations of the family by working in small groups. Family customs and traditions, stereotypical beliefs about other cultural groups, and your family's view of the culturally different shaped your own views. Has anything happened to change your traditional views, and what are the family customs or traditions that can create barriers between people? These issues can stimulate discussion and an exchange of experiences.

Second, consider stereotypical thinking. Pinkney (1984) has described the North American perspective in which conformity is valued and rewarded, while diversity is feared and discouraged. Stereotypes, prejudice discrimination and racism, draw attention to the differences between people.

Stereotypes emerge from our need for coherence, simplicity and predictability in an increasingly complex world. Without using stereotypes, we would have to interpret each new social situation as if we had never encountered anything like it. Stereotypes are a way of organizing information and observations, and prejudice occurs when negative feelings are attached to a stereotype. Similarly, prejudicial attitudes do not automatically result in discriminatory behavior toward minority groups, but it is a danger.

Discrimination is the denial of power, privilege, and status to members of a minority group whose qualifications are equal to that of the majority group. The belief that some races are inherently superior to others is dehumanizing and violates the dignity and self-respect of the individual to whom it is directed.

Third, examine communication styles and learn to recognize and understand different modes of interaction and communication. Reference points will vary, with many Western countries focusing on the individual, while those from Asia may focus on the group or family. The authority base may be different, as, for example, between men and women; men tend to rely on facts in arguing a point, while women tend to trust their intuition. The degree of self-disclosure will vary; some will find acknowledgement of personal information an asset, but others may see it as an intrusion into their personal lives.

Provide understanding, assistance, and support to the newcomer—whether they are part of the work team or the user community—so that they may live and work comfortably in their new society.

The American Library Association has developed training programs to create cultural diversity, and their documents and training materials provide a useful starting point as the content is applicable not only to libraries, but also to other information organizations. While they are designed to be used in a North American situation, they can help managers and trainers in other countries to recognize the issues to be considered in the development of culturally based materials and programs.

WORTH CHECKING OUT

Diversity issues and resources

ALA Action no. 4, Diversity, indicates what you can do and lists a sample of ALA resources:

www.ala.org/work/diversitybrochure.html

Remember that the ultimate goal of the manager in a culturally diverse service is to ensure that all staff are aware of their personal responsibilities to be sensitive to the cultural differences of colleagues and users and that this goal should be reflected in training and development programs.

Some of the ways in which staff can operate in a sensitive manner are:

- by learning to understand what others actually believe and value, and letting them express this in their own way;
- by respecting the convictions of others about dress, food and social etiquette and not behaving in such as way as to cause offence;
- by avoiding the habit of imposing their views on colleagues and users;
- by respecting the right of others to disagree with them;
- by asking how people would like to be addressed, how their name should be pronounced and how to spell it;
- by treating everyone with dignity and respect;
- by avoiding the assumption that treating everyone in the same way is treating everyone fairly;
- by being aware of the different value systems applied by people of different genders, faiths and cultures; and
- by recognizing that everyone falls short, at times, from the ideals of their own traditions and that they should never compare their own ideals with the practices of other people.

TRY THIS

The points above do not form a complete list of the way that people can value different cultures, so see how many more you can add.

IN-SERVICE PROGRAMS FOR MINORITY GROUPS

Now that you have ensured that existing staff members are receptive to cultural diversity, equal attention should be given to in-service programs for those from minority groups. In larger organizations, it may be seen as the responsibility of the corporation to prepare such a program at a general level.

The content of the programs will include the goals of the organization, its values, operating policies and practices, and expectations of new members of staff. Within the service, a special training program may need to be developed for staff recruited from overseas. Although many of the operating practices are similar around the world, some may differ—for example, the cataloguing and listing practices or software used within the service. You may need to design a custom training program after consultation with the new colleague and evaluate if it meets their needs, as well as the needs of the service.

But training should extend beyond the stages of assimilation, and there have been concerns expressed on both sides of the Atlantic about the problems of recruitment and career development of staff from ethnic minority groups. The American Library Association offers Spectrum scholarships to provide funding for students on first qualification courses. A number of U.S. University libraries have established internships that provide varied work experience programs (Cogell and Gruwell, 2001). Action is also taking place in other parts of the world; for example, in the U.K., the various library associations for minority ethnic groups have come together under the banner of a Diversity Council to promote equal opportunity for staff and users. The Quality Leaders Project is developing leadership skills in ethnic minority public library staff based on action learning principles (Durrani, 2002).

Mentoring

An appointed mentor—preferably someone with similar experiences—can aid in a new employee's adaptation to the working situation. This enables newcomers to raise points and ask questions that will help them "fit in."

TRY THIS

Patricia Layzell Ward moved to Australia and found one of the pitfalls, when being offered home hospitality, is to be asked to "bring a plate." Newcomers may interpret this as meaning that the host does not have enough crockery for the numbers expected, and may dutifully take along a plate. On arrival the real meaning is clear—they were expected to bring food as a contribution to the meal.

Can you think of similar social pitfalls for a person moving to the U.S.?

Dress codes are generally not stated within organizations, but there can be unwritten customs which are best be conveyed through mentoring. Having someone to assist in the learning and adaptation process and can speed up assimilation and help overcome feelings of isolation.

WORTH CHECKING OUT

Diversity Committees

The work of the University of Tennessee Libraries Diversity Committee can be seen at www.lib.utk.edu/~training/Diversity. The site provides definitions, a mission statement, plans, programs and links to other resources on diversity.

SUPERVISING A DIVERSE STAFF

Supervisors or managers working in a multicultural setting must be aware of the needs of colleagues, and colleagues must understand the needs of users who have different cultural backgrounds.

Bearing in mind that the process of communication differs between cultures, managers need to take care that their own listening and observation skills have been developed so that they can assess the comfort level of their staff and users.

EXAMPLE

Communication styles

One example of the differences in communication is the contrast between Japanese and Americans. Japanese communicate by not stating things directly, while Americans communicate in a very direct way.

Employees from different cultures may have different expectations of their supervisors or managers. They may not be comfortable offering advice or criticism to a person viewed as being "superior," so mistakes can occur which are unfortunate for both the supervisor and the staff member. Avoid making any assumptions about the level of awareness of local practices and customs, as this leads to problems that affect the operation of the service and its effectiveness to users.

The manager needs to be aware of the observance of religious holidays and the days and hours of religious abeyance. Most organizations find they should allow staff some flexibility in what holidays they celebrate, rather than enforcing a set of national and dominant religious holidays. In fact, it can be a win-win situation if the organization allows people from other cultures to "trade" time off for holidays with others. The service may have the staff resources to remain open on some popular holidays.

Overall, the manager has to take care that there is reasonable give and take by all members of the team and that one is not advantaged to the disadvantage of another. The person with few ties may not like to make a fuss if they are frequently asked to adjust holidays or days/hours on duty. The manager has to be sensitive to his or her needs.

WORTH CHECKING OUT

Religious issues and conflicts

Montgomery, Jack. 2002. "A Most Delicate Matter: Religious Issues and Conflict in the U.S. Library Workplace," *Library Management* 23 (8/9): 422-434.

Sensitivity

Issues such as holidays need to be handled with sensitivity. Making someone *aware* of the differences may increase his or her *feeling* of being different. MacAdam (1994) suggests the following advice to assist communication on the job:

- Organize on-the-job training and staff development.
- Provide direction and feedback.
- Keep expectations realistic and clear.
- Evaluate performance and contribution.
- Foster relations among staff members.
- Define professionalism.

In addition, it is essential to clarify any non-negotiable priorities concerning the family, religious matters, and social support.

The experiences of minority librarians in the U.S. are described in essays which challenge the view that the information professions are inclusive and offer equal opportunity (Pinkney, 1984). A survey carried out by *Library Journal* in 1997 indicated that two-thirds of the white respondents felt that racism was less prevalent and that their career opportunities were not any better than those of their minority colleagues. By contrast, the minority librarians, while not denying that there was much discussion, believed that it "amount[ed] to lip-service and hand-wringing, with a more fervent interest in diversifying collections than ranks." The article points to unequal opportunities, with race being a critical factor (St. Lifer and Nelson, 1997). Minority librarians in the U.K. have expressed similar views.

The process of achieving diversity is slower than anyone would like; it is complex and requires time and the attention of senior management.

Given the issues of sensitivity, one of the easiest mistakes for managers is to make token appointments, as noted earlier.

FOR FURTHER THOUGHT

List four or five factors that supervisors must be sensitive to in a culturally diverse workgroup.

SERVICE TO DIVERSE USERS

When developing policies, remember that the expectations of users who have used information services in other parts of the world will vary. Some users will have experienced highly developed services like those in Singapore. For others, information organizations may not have been a natural part of everyday life. Not all users will have a good command of the indigenous language or languages. This presents a challenge to the manager, but a greater challenge to the new user. Users from different cultures or countries are not a homogenous group—they need to be identified as individuals and their needs and expectations should be reviewed.

A number of studies examine the information-seeking behavior of U.S. multicultural students. One example is a survey carried out among students at San Jose State University where the "so-called minorities" accounted for 51 percent of the total student population. The findings indicated that for 60 percent, English was their second language, and over half said that their country of origin was an Asian country. In general, they reported that they used the library quite often, and the majority found that using the library was easy. Statistical analyses found that the student's level of success in using the library was related to English proficiency, frequency of library use, and the frequency of making inquiries at the reference desk.

Those who were less successful or rarely asked reference questions had several reasons that contributed to their avoidance of the reference desk:

- fear of asking stupid questions
- fear that their English was not good enough
- fear of not understanding the answers well enough
- not thinking of asking questions
- not knowing the role of the reference librarian (Liu and Redfern, 1997)

These findings are likely to be reflected in other culturally diverse communities and information organizations.

Users of services provided by the organization where they are working or studying must overcome difficulties if they are to succeed, and hence they are likely to be highly motivated to use services efficiently and effectively. However, the barriers to success will be greater in services provided for the community at large—for example, record offices and public libraries—where the degree of motivation for use may be less. Services provided for the public may seem forbidding to those who do not speak the language of the community and are unfamiliar with the rituals of use.

There is evidence to support the existence of unexpressed information needs that could be met by a public service. A study of the health information-seeking behavior of older African American women in Pittsburgh indicated that the women wanted health information and used a range of sources—their personal physician, print and nonprint media, family members, and close friends. When asked whether the public library had a role, nearly all responded positively; 38 percent thought it "likely" and 60 percent "very likely" that it could help them if they were to visit. However, their patterns of use were very different; only 11 percent visited the library "more than once a month" and 76 percent "hardly ever" (Gollop, 1997).

WORTH CHECKING OUT

Communities and their libraries addressing diversity

Two excellent articles on how communities and their libraries address the challenge of diversity are:

Hoxeng, Holly. 2000. "Addressing Diversity in the Public Library Community with Diversity on the Library Staff." *Colorado Libraries* 26 (2): 15.

Sannwald, William W. 1999. "Managing Diversity; the City of San Diego Experience." *Library Administration and Management* 13 (1): 18-22.

Collection Development

The majority of services have a collection policy, but not all services have addressed the question of developing the cultural diversity of the collection. Guidelines for building and strengthening the collections in academic libraries can be adapted to meet the needs of a wider range of services; for example, archives can:

- lobby for support from management;
- assess the demographic make-up of the community to be served;
- review current collection development policies;
- evaluate current holdings decide how to acquire these materials;
- assess the needs of the community served in relation to the strategic plan of the service;
- identify a subject to be addressed in the first instance;
- determine the scope and depth of the project;
- develop guidelines for evaluating documents;
- look for sources that list major sources;
- keep track of the materials that the service does not already own, and identify sources for these materials; and
- acquire the documents (Diaz, 1994).

Changing a collections policy may meet with resistance from those who have been well served by the former policy, and it may not be accompanied by additional funding. Providing an enhanced service to one group may mean reductions elsewhere.

EXAMPLE

Reaction to a policy change

The National Library of Australia determined as part of its strategic planning that the library would have to substantially reduce its acquisition of overseas materials, knowing that some would be available electronically. The collection policy shifted to emphasize national identity, multiculturalism and the Asia-Pacific region. The dissenters in this instance were the academics who had looked to the National Library of Australia to augment the collections held in their universities, principally the universities in Canberra where the National Library is situated (Macintyre, 1997). Few libraries can make changes without making some cuts.

One way to augment the document collection can be to set up exchange agreements with organizations serving similar ethnic groups. Cooperative acquisitions policies can build a shared collection that can circulate between services. This can be helpful, for example, to public and school library services where the collection can easily be "read out" by enthusiastic readers.

SPECIALIST DOCUMENT SUPPLY

Library services find that identifying appropriate titles is not always easy, and acquiring them can present further problems. There are specialist suppliers of documents in particular languages, but the identification of titles and the ordering and payment of invoices from foreign suppliers can present problems for smaller services.

Some ethnic groups and national libraries have produced listings of materials, particularly for children; publishers of materials in minority languages can provide catalogues of publications and assist with the selection of appropriate titles. Specialist suppliers can also provide foreign language audio recordings, films, videos and DVDs.

Accessing the Collections

The multicultural service needs to be sensitive to the ways in which it provides access to its collections. Moorcroft, in her discussion of the field of Australian Aboriginal Studies, has drawn attention to ethnocentrism in subject headings, and similar examples can be found in other countries that use Library of Congress Subject Headings. Headings can be long and convoluted; Moorcroft quotes as an example "Aborigines, Australian-Australia, Northern-History-Congresses." Some of the headings are value-laden, such as "Mixed Blood." Other headings show that Aborigines are seen as the "other." Aboriginal adolescence cannot be found under the general heading of "Adolescence;" one must look under "Aborigines, Australian—Social Life and Customs and Aborigines," or "Australian—Northern Territory—

Arnhem Land—Social Life and Customs." She makes the point that "Librarians have a social responsibility to ensure that information is easily accessible to all groups regardless of whether the content is politically uncomfortable to the dominant paradigm" (Moorcroft, 1992).

Multilingual Signage and OPACS

The accessibility should also extend to examining the need for signage in several languages. It is helpful to provide multilingual OPACS and Web sites, allowing the user to work in the language with which they are most comfortable. The simple use of different languages to describe how to search the catalogue or Web site can help users to increase their skills in retrieving references and information.

Displays and Exhibitions

Exhibitions and displays are useful tools in making users aware of the resources that can be accessed through the service. Giannini has provided a list of the benefits:

- It makes a powerful visual statement about the content and scope of a collection.
- It brings the user's attention to the service.
- New users are attracted by services that promote information of interest and relevance to a range of ethnic and racial backgrounds.
- Doors can be opened to new areas of interest—different cultures, beliefs and points of view.
- The community can see that information professionals have access to collections of great depth and scope.
- Staff can be sensitized to multicultural issues. (after Giannini, 1994)

Organizing and preparing displays and exhibitions can be an effective way to draw community groups to archives and library services. Offering the facility to minority groups in a public place will bring out community pride, provide information to the community at large, and increase the awareness of members of the minority groups to services available to them.

FOR FURTHER THOUGHT

Reflect on the difficulties that someone might face in using a service that has lived in another part of the world.

Identify six ways in which the service can take action to help them.

IS THE ORGANIZATION A DIVERSE ORGANIZATION?

As we have stressed, it takes time for change to be implemented, so a new manager needs to work out how much the organization has achieved and what still needs to be done. Although change takes time, this should not be an excuse for a lack of action. Many organizations have yet to achieve what we might call "total diversity" beyond the necessary legal requirements.

Jackson and Holvino (1994) developed a model to help organizations move from being monocultural to multicultural. The model has three levels:

LEVEL I: The monocultural organization "seeks to maintain the status quo by enhancing the dominance, privilege, and access of those in power."

Stage 1

The Exclusionary Organization is primarily interested in the dominance of one group over the other oppressed groups on the basis of sex, race, gender, or cultural identity.

Stage 2

The *Club* does not outwardly espouse white male supremacy "but does act out views in an attempt to maintain control and [the] privileges of those who have traditionally held power."

LEVEL II: The non-discriminating organization consists of "non discrimination in a monocultural context," i.e., it admits people of different cultures into the organization without changing fundamentally.

Stage 3

The Compliance Organization is committed to removing some of the discrimination found in the earlier stage of the Club by allowing minorities and women to enter, but avoids tampering with the actual structure, mission, and culture of the organization in the process. The organization's method for changing the racial and gender profile is often to recruit actively and to hire more racial minorities and women at the bottom of the system. If they are hired or promoted into management positions, they are generally seen as "tokens," and must be "qualified team players." They must be exceptional and not openly challenge the organization's mission and practices.

Stage 4

The Affirmative Action Organization actively recruits and promotes women, racial minorities, and members of other social groups that are generally denied access. Moreover, support of the growth and development of these minority employees is demonstrated through programs that increase their chances of success and mobility in the organization. The Affirmative Action Organization has evolved and now addresses employee attitudes toward oppression, conducts workshops on racial and sexual discrimination, and broadens its perception of diversity to include all socially oppressed groups. "Regardless of this, the organization members remain committed to confirming to the norms and practices of the majority group's world view."

LEVEL III: the multicultural organization "emphasizes: a) diverse cultural representation; b) equitable distribution of power and influence; c) the elimination of oppression; and d) multicultural perspectives in the larger society.

Stage 5

The Redefining Organization is no longer content with just being anti-racist or anti-sexist; a commitment is made to examine the organization's activities for their impact on all of its members' ability to participate in and contribute to the organization's growth and success. The limitations of the prevailing cultural perspective are questioned as to their influences on the organization's mission, structure, management, technology, psychosocial dynamics, and product or service. New approaches and alternative methods of organizing are explored which guarantee the inclusion, participation, and empowerment of all of the organization's members.

Stage 6

The Multicultural Organization will take a long time to be realized. There is no overnight fix. Change efforts must be systematic, comprehensive, multi-faceted, multi-interventionist, and multi-year. There is no checklist of right things to do or series of events, which once held, will lead to success. It is more difficult to manage a diversified workforce, because it includes different people with legitimately different wants and ideas on what and how work should be done. The path will not be smooth and mistakes will be made; however, progress can be made in the short run if mistakes are acknowledged and learned from and it is regularly stressed that managing diversity is challenging new work. The key element for creating a multicultural organization is accepting that it is a *process*, not a product. New issues will constantly emerge, as old ones are resolved. The work is never done (Jackson and Holvino, 1994: 17-21).

FOR FURTHER THOUGHT

Which stage has your organization reached?

And which stage has the service achieved?

Sketch out a plan for your area of responsibility to reach Stage 6.

What will help the achievement of this level?

Can you identify any roadblocks?

Although it has focused on diversity management, the principles, policies and practices discussed in this chapter also form the basis for good personnel management and user-centered services in general.

AFTER READING THIS CHAPTER YOU SHOULD BE AWARE:

- of what is meant by diversity, and why it is important in managing in the information sector;
- of the Ten Lens test;
- that the manager has responsibility for diversity and that it should be at the core of strategic planning;
- that organizational policies and practices developed for staff and users that promote diversity should be reviewed; and
- of how to assess your organization's progression toward becoming a diverse organization.

REFERENCES

Carr-Ruffino, Norma. 1999. *Diversity Success Strategies*. Boston: Butterworth-Heinemann.

Child, Margaret. 1997. "Taking Preservation Across Cultural Frontiers." *Libri* 47 (3): 139-146.

Cogell, Raquel V., and Cindy A. Gruwell. eds. 2001. *Diversity in Libraries: Academic Residency Programs*. Westport, Conn.: Greenwood Press.

Cohen, Lucy. 1994. "Employment Practices." In *Cultural Diversity in Libraries*, edited by Donald E. Riggs and Patricia A. Tarin. New York: Neal-Schuman.

Conger, Jay A., and Beth Benjamin. 1999. *Building Leaders: How Successful Companies Develop the Next Generation*. San Francisco: Jossey-Bass.

de la Peña McCook, Kathleen, ed. 2000. "Ethnic Diversity in Library and Information Science." *Library Trends* 49 (1): 1-219.

Diaz, Joseph R. 1994. "Collection Development in Multicultural Studies." In *Cultural Diversity in Libraries*, edited by Donald E. Riggs and Patricia A. Tarin. New York: Neal-Schuman.

"Diversity." *American Libraries* 30 (7): 44-64.

Durrani, Shiraz. 2002. "Combating Racial Discrimination in British Public Libraries: The Role of the Quality Leaders Project." *Library Management* 23 (1/2): 23-52.

Fulmer, William E. 2000. *Shaping the Adaptive Organization: Landscapes, Learning, and Leadership in Volatile Times*. New York: AMACOM.

Giannini, Janis A. 1994. "Exhibits." In *Cultural Diversity in Libraries*, edited by Donald E. Riggs and Patricia A. Tarin. New York: Neal-Schuman.

Gollop, Claudia J. 1997. "Health Information-Seeking Behavior and Older African American Women." *Bulletin of the Medical Library Association* 85 (2): 141-146.

Hankins, Gladys Gossett. 2000. *Diversity Blues: How to Shake 'Em*. Cincinnati, Ohio: Telvic Press.

Harvard Business Review on Managing Diversity 2001. Boston: Harvard Business School Press.

Hofstede, Geert. 1997. *Culture and Organizations: Software of the Mind.* New York: McGraw-Hill.

Hoxeng, Holly. 2000. "Addressing Diversity in the Public Library Community With Diversity on the Library Staff." *Colorado Libraries* 26 (2): 15.

Jackson, Bailey, and Evangelina Holvino. 1994. "Multicultural Organization Development." Quoted in *Cultural Diversity in Libraries*, edited by Donald E. Riggs and Patricia A. Tarin. New York: Neal-Schuman.

Kendall, Frances E. 1994. "Creating a Multicultural Environment in the Library." In *Cultural Diversity in Libraries*, edited by Donald Riggs and Patricia A. Tarin. New York: Neal-Schuman.

Layzell Ward, Patricia, ed. 2002. "Aspects of Diversity." *Library Management* 23 (1/2): 10-100.

Loden, Marilyn. 1996. *Implementing Diversity: Best Practices for Making Diversity Work in Your Organization.* Chicago: Irwin Professional.

Lui, Mengxiong, and Bernice Redfern. 1997. "Information-Seeking Behavior of Multicultural Students: A Case Study at San Jose State University." *College and Research Libraries* 58 (4): 348-354.

MacAdam, Barbara. 1994. "Supervising a Diverse Staff." In *Cultural Diversity in Libraries*, edited by Donald E. Riggs and Patricia A. Tarin. New York: Neal-Schuman.

Macintyre, Stuart. 1997. "Whose Library? What Culture? The Library as Cultural Custodian." *Australian Library Journal* 46 (2): 118-124.

Montgomery, Jack. 2002. "A Most Delicate Matter: Religious Issues and Conflict in the U.S. Library Workplace." *Library Management* 23 (8/9): 422-434.

Moorcroft, Heather. 1992. "Ethnocentrism in Subject Headings." *Australian Library Journal* 46 (1): 40-45.

Moore, Sarah. 1999. "Understanding and Managing Diversity Among Groups at Work: Key Issues for Organizational Training and Development." *Journal of European Industrial Training* 23 (4/5): 208-218.

Neely, Teresa Y., and Kuang-Hwei Lee-Smeltzer, eds. 2001. "Diversity Now: People, Collections, and Services in Academic Libraries." Parts 1 and 2. *Journal of Library Administration* 33 (1/2): 1-164; (3/4): 165-292.

Pinkney, Alphonso. 1984. *The Myth of Black Progress.* New York: Cambridge University Press.

Rahim, M. Azahur, and Albert A. Blum, eds. 1994. *Global Perspectives on Organizational Conflict.* Westport, Conn.: Praeger Publishing.

Sannwald, William W. 1999. "Managing Diversity: The City of San Diego Experience." *Library Administration and Management* 13 (1): 18-22.

Skot-Hansen, Dorte. 2002. "The Public Library Between Integration and Cultural Diversity." *Scandinavian Public Library Quarterly* 35 (1): 12-13.

St. Lifer, Evan, and Corinne Nelson. 1997. "Unequal Opportunities: Race Does Matter." *Library Journal* 122 (November 1): 42-46.

Weiss, Joseph W. 2001. *Organizational Behavior and Change: Managing Diversity, Cross-Cultural Dynamics, and Ethics.* Cincinnati, Ohio: South-Western College Publishing.

Williams, Mark A. 2001. *The Ten Lenses: Your Guide to Living and Working in a Multicultural World.* Sterling, Va.: Capital Books Ltd.

Winston, Mark D. 2001. "The Importance of Diversity: The Relationship Between Diversity and Organizational Success in the Academic Environment." *College and Research Libraries* 62 (6): 517-526.

Wynn, Michael. 1992. *Don't Quit.* South Pasadena, Calif.: Rising Sun Publishing.

Launching Pad

Agosto, Denise E. 2001. "Bridging the Culture Gap: Ten Steps Towards a More Multicultural Youth Library." *Journal of Youth Services in Libraries* 14 (3): 38-41.

Arredono, Patricia. 1996. *Successful Diversity Management Initiatives.* Thousand Oaks, Calif.: Sage Publications.

Avery, Elizabeth Fuseler, Terry Dahlin, and Deborah A. Carver. 2001. *Staff Development: A Practical Guide.* 3rd ed. Chicago: American Library Association.

Caver, Keith A., and Ancella B. Livers. 2002. "'Dear White Boss...'" *Harvard Business Review* 80 (11): 76-81.

Coats, Reed, Jane Goodwin, and Patricia Bangs. 2000. "Seeking the Best Path: Assessing a Library's Diversity Climate." *Library Administration and Management,* 14 (3): 148-154.

de la Peña McCook, Kathleen. 2000. *A Place at the Table: Participating in Community Building.* Chicago: American Library Association.

Edwards, Heather M. 2000. "Managing Multicultural Staff in a South African University Library." *IFLA Journal* 26 (1): 25-27.

Erera, Pauline I. 2001. *Family Diversity: Continuity and Change in the Contemporary Family.* Thousand Oaks, Calif.: Sage Publications.

Farmer, Helen S. 1997. *Diversity and Women's Career Development: From Adolescence to Adulthood.* Thousand Oaks, Calif.: Sage Publications.

Howland, Joan S. 2001. "Challenges of Working in a Multicultural Environment." *Journal of Library Administration* 33 (1/2): 105-123.

Jordan, Peter, and Caroline Lloyd. 2002. *Staff Management in Library and Information Work.* 4th ed. Aldershot, England: Ashgate Publishing.

Love, Johnnieque B. 2001. "The Assessment of Diversity Initiatives in Academic Libraries." *Journal of Library Administration* 33 (1/2): 73-103.

McCray Pearson, Joyce A. 2001. "Affirmative Action and Diversity: A Selected and Annotated Bibliography." *Legal Reference Service Quarterly* 18 (4): 67-81.

Maxwell, Gillian, Sharon Blair, and Marilyn McDougall. 2001. "Edging Towards Managing Diversity in Practice." *Employee Relations,* 23 (5): 468-483.

Murray, Janet. 2001. "Training School Library Staff to Cater for Diversity." *Education for Information*, 18 (4): 313-323.

Musser, Linda R. 2001. "Effective Retention Strategies for Diverse Employees." *Journal of Library Administration* 33 (1/2): 63-72.

Nichols, Nancy A., ed. 1994. *Reach For the Top: Women and the Changing Facts of Work Life.* Boston: Harvard Business School Press.

Owens, Irene. 2000. "A Managerial/Leadership Approach to Maintaining Diversity in Libraries." *Texas Library Journal*, 76 (1): 20-1, 24, 26-7.

Prasad, Pushkala, Albert Mills, Michael Elmes, and Anshuman Prasad. 1997. *Managing the Organizational Melting Pot: Dilemmas of Workplace Diversity.* Thousand Oaks, Calif.: Sage Publications.

Simmons-Welburn, Janice. 1991. "Using Culture as a Construct for Achieving Diversity in Human Relations Management." *Library Administration and Management* 13 (4): 205-209.

Thomas, David A. 2002. "The Truth About Mentoring Minorities: Race Matters." *Harvard Business Review* 79 (4): 98-111.

Warner, J. N. 2001. "Moving Beyond Whiteness in North American Academic Libraries." *Libri* 51 (3): 167-172.

Wey Smola, Karen, and Charlotte D. Sutton. 2002. "Generational Differences: Revisiting Generational Work Values for the New Millennium." *Journal of Organizational Behavior* 23 (4): 363-382.

Whiteside, Andrew. 2002. "Enhancing Provision of Archive Services for the Visually Impaired." *Journal of the Society of Archivists* 23 (1): 73-86.

Winston, Mark D., ed. 1999. "Managing Multiculturalism and Diversity in the Library." *Journal of Library Administration* 27 (1/2): 1-202.

Winston, Mark D., and Jennifer Dunne. 2001. "Children's Librarians: A Research Study of Diversity and Leadership." *Public Library Quarterly* 19 (1): 23-38.

Winston, Mark D., and Haipeng Li. 2000. "Managing Diversity in Liberal Arts Colleges." *College and Research Libraries* 61 (3): 205-215.

8: PROVIDING EFFECTIVE SERVICE TO USER COMMUNITIES

"If you keep your head down, you may not be shot at—but you may be trampled on."

IN THIS CHAPTER YOU'LL DISCOVER:

- the importance of knowing the characteristics and needs of the community served
- how to carry out a community assessment project
- what data needs to be collected
- how to collect the data
- what marketing is
- what promotion is
- key strategies for marketing success
- the elements of a tactical framework for an integrated promotional project

KNOW THE COMMUNITY SERVED

Providers of products and services have increasingly focused on their customers and how to provide them with what they need, when they need it, and the form that best suits their needs. The importance of this approach is emphasized in the use of terms such as "customer service excellence." Library, information, and archives services have always placed a high priority on the service element of their work—meeting users' needs. In recent years, texts written for practitioners have taken the important concepts from the expanding management literature on the subject and applied them to the information sector.

WORTH CHECKING OUT

Customer service excellence in the information sector

Melling, Maxine, and Joyce Little, eds. 2002. *Building a Successful Customer-Service Culture: A Guide for Library and Information Managers.* London: Facet Publishing.

Weingand, Darlene. 1997. *Customer Service Excellence: A Concise Guide for Librarians.* Chicago: American Library Association.

The middle manager has a pivotal role in ensuring an important aspect of quality—anticipating user needs and providing them with the information they require. Middle managers are the link between the front-line staff and senior managers. They receive feedback from the front desk and enquiry staff, enter it into the planning process, and communicate the results to senior management.

Let's run over some basics.

Services are provided for a defined population. Successful service depends on:

- accurately determining and understanding the characteristics of that population (e.g., educational level, age, subject field(s) of interest, etc.);
- assessing their information wants and needs; and
- studying the way they use information.

Knowing the characteristics and needs of the population ultimately has an impact on financial support. The greater the degree of user satisfaction, the greater the likelihood that funding authorities will grant additional funds for new or expanded services.

Therefore, data must be collected about users' information needs and wants, including:

- why they need information,
- what type of information they need,
- how they go about seeking and securing it, and
- how they *use* it.

Gathering and interpreting these data help in:

- shaping collections and services
- determining service hours
- deciding on locations and means of access (both physical services and electronic access)
- providing assessment and evaluation

Although information professionals have a broad understanding of user needs and wants and the latest developments in the field, they need more precise data about the local service community.

> DIG DEEPER
>
> One can see how the needs, wants, and demands issues play out in the "real world" in:
>
> Shearer, Kenneth. 1993. "Confusing What Is Most Wanted with What Is Most Used." *Public Libraries* 32 (4): 193-197.
>
> Another informative article that explores needs and wants is:
>
> O'Hanlon, Sean, and Ann Phillips. 1999. "Benchmarks for the Future." *Illinois Libraries* 81 (2): 99-103.

Definitions

Westbrook (2000: 26) defines a "community user needs analysis" in a library service as "a structured, planned, formal study that identifies the information requirements of a library's patrons," carefully noting that the term "user" should include both actual and potential users. This definition can be applied to other types of service in the information sector—for example, in archives and information services.

Before undertaking any study of needs—a community analysis or marketing program—define what you want to know: information needs, information wants, expressed demand, satisfied demand, or even information behavior. Each phrase has a slightly different connotation and requires a different approach to data collection. Need, want, and demand are different.

> DEFINITION
>
> **Need, want, and demand**
>
> A **need** is something that requires a solution; it does not necessarily follow that a community need is something the community wants.
>
> A **want** is something a person/community is willing to devote time, energy, or money to acquiring; it is not necessarily true that the person/community needs what it wants.
>
> A **demand** is something a person/community wants and is willing to act in concert to obtain (by letter writing, telephoning, testifying, etc.).

Clearly, the ideal outcome of a study is the identification of one or more *needs* that the community served *wants* and is ready to *demand*. In most cases, the best outcome is a set of needs that the community wants.

> TIP
>
> When implementing a plan, start with needs that users want and demand. These are the easiest to get funded. Then move on to wanted needs, and only then, if funds allow, look at needs alone.
>
> A service is not an identified need unless there are individual members of the community who do need and would like the service. It is not enough to justify its classification as a general "community" wanted need.

USER NEEDS AND THE OPERATING ENVIRONMENT

Each environment differs, and studying the differences is vital for success.

> WORTH CHECKING OUT
>
> **Organizational environments**
>
> Emery, Fred, and Eric Trist. 1965. "The Causal Texture of Organizational Environments." *Human Relations* 18 (1): 21-32.

Way back in the 1960s Emery and Trist (1965) published a seminal paper about environments that is still of value today. They wrote about organizational environments in general, but their work has clear implications for information professionals in terms of understanding their service community and its institutional environment.

Four types of organizational environment were identified: *placid-randomized*, *placid-clustered*, *disturbed-reactive*, and *turbulent*.

A *placid-random* environment is one in which organizational goals and activities are relatively unchanging and any dangers (threats to stability) are random in character and therefore unpredictable. Archives and specialized humanities libraries (for example, the Huntington Library) would be organizations that have, in the past, operated in this type of environment. Although changes in economic conditions have had some impact on such organizations, they still remain in this category, at least in comparison to other types of services. Operating in a placid-random environment can lead to a sense of complacency about the service community and its needs that can be detrimental in the long run. There is less pressure to assess user needs as frequently as other services should; there is also less emphasis on marketing the organization, which can be useful in the fund-raising activities that are increasingly essential for nonprofit organizations.

Some services—especially archives and larger research libraries—are in the *placid-clustered* environment, where long-term mission and goals are reasonably constant but adjustments are fairly common. The changes arise from the dangers in the environment, which are often clustered—high taxes lead to unhappy taxpayers, who may, during economic downturns, decide that less money should go into social service/educational endeavors. Changing community demographics bring a number of dangers for organizations that fail to respond to changing attitudes and needs.

A *disturbed-reactive* environment is one in which there are competitors present and the organization must respond and react to what they are doing in order to survive. Some information professionals, and a surprising number of the general public, would say that this is today's environment for all services. This view is based on the widespread availability, both commercial and cost-free, of electronic information resources and technology. That, in turn, raises questions about the long-term viability of information services. This is not the case for service providers who develop strategies for incorporating these technologies into their service programs. Corporate services fall into this category, because their parent organizations respond to competitive environments. If you keep your head down in this or the next environment, you *will* be trampled on.

Turbulent environments are the most competitive, and organizational survival depends on rapid and effective changes in goals. Information, knowledge management, and records management services that operate in, for example, the financial, legal and research and development sectors, face a turbulent environment. The parent organization's goals can change overnight as new market opportunities emerge.

FOR FURTHER THOUGHT

In what type of environment does your service operate?
What implications does that environment have for your unit?

All but the turbulent environment require managers to spend time, money, and effort in learning about their service community. This requires data collecting in a variety of ways, including:

- community analysis
- needs assessment
- needs analysis
- user studies
- information audits

Marketing is becoming an important activity for the information organization. Essentially, a marketing program is broader in scope; it has the data collecting and analysis aspects of a needs assessment, but then builds the analysis into an implementation plan, which includes specialized communication activities to publicize the changes resulting from the assessment activity.

LEARNING ABOUT THE SERVICE POPULATION

Market analysis and methods for needs assessment employ similar techniques; the data provides vital information about topics such as:

- who uses the services, and when and how they use them
- who does not use the services, and not why not
- what new services users desire
- what information is desired
- what formats are desired
- how much time, effort, or money the user is willing to "pay" for a new service
- what image of the service the community has

These data feed into decision-making and planning for such matters as staffing, budgeting, technology, and service points.

One basic difference between traditional community assessment studies and marketing is that marketing always looks at the total community. Often, as the name suggests, assessment projects in the information sector focus on the user. But remember that there can be more than one class of users—for example, regular, infrequent, one-time, and even non-users.

Before turning to marketing, let's examine a traditional community needs assessment project.

Elements of an Assessment Project

The planning of an assessment project starts by answering several questions:

- What specific information will be gathered?
- How will it be collected?
- Who will be involved in the data-collecting?
- How will the information gathered be analyzed and used?

Clearly the first and last questions are interrelated—what you plan to do with the data determines which data you attempt to collect. As obvious as that may seem, in the reality of the workplace, that relationship is often overlooked as time pressures and other duties impinge on planning time.

It is critical to decide at the outset:

- whether or not non-users are part of the study
- whether non-users are the target group for the study
- whether the data collection is to provide the basis for a marketing program

That decision may impact who does the collecting, as well as how it is done and what data is collected.

> TIP
>
> Don't start with a comprehensive program. Pick a relatively modest-sized project to learn the ropes.

For almost any study of significance, it will be necessary to allocate funds for consultants, unless there are members of the team who have research and statistical skills. Westbrook (2000) strongly advocates involving the staff as much as possible. Staff involvement provides learning opportunities, and the staff will have insights into community needs that may not be apparent to senior, or even middle, management. But there is a need for research, methodological, and statistical knowledge that the staff of information services does not always possess. Therefore, it may be necessary to hire a consultant who has training in these areas. Engaging in a needs study without having such input/assistance is not likely to produce useful data.

Having a mix of staff and outside assistance is usually the most successful and cost-effective method. If outside consultants are hired, establish a steering committee of staff members who will oversee the consultants' activities. No matter what the staffing decision is, it must be stressed that such projects are *not* minor undertakings.

The service must be willing and able to commit a substantial number of staff to the project, even when a consulting team is hired. Staff may be involved in collecting survey data, conducting community forums, and interpreting data and developing proposals; holding any community meetings to present findings and proposals based on the collected data demands still more time from the service's staff.

Over time, benefits will accrue as a cadre of staff capable of carrying out projects emerges, but this will not reduce the time commitments required for the work. The plan of incorporating this work into normal staff duties and adding it to job expectations and descriptions is the best long-term approach. A number of U.S. public libraries have established a pattern of annual assessments, usually for one or two branch locations, which keeps the projects at a reasonable size.

Determining what data to collect is clearly a function of the study goals and the type of service, as well as the community's characteristics. There are some broad categories that apply to all types of service; these categories require further thought to see how they could apply to different information environments. Not all categories apply equally across all types. The categories are:

- Historical data
- Economic data
- Demographic data
- Legal issues
- Social/educational issues
- Cultural/recreation issues
- Transportation issues

- Geographic information
- Political information
- Communication systems
- Community information services

FOR FURTHER THOUGHT

Using your present service, or one you know well, think how each of the above categories does or does not apply to its service community.

Consider how you might collect data about the categories that you believe do apply.

Here are some examples taken from a number of issues that may be relevant to each of the categories listed above.

Understanding how the community developed over time and its relationship to the service is helpful in knowing how to present proposals for new developments.

The nature and location of service points influence how often people will use services. As in real estate, "location, location, location" is a key factor in the use of a physical service point, while the content, design, and site map influence the use of Web-based services. Related to this is the factor of service hours in an age when both goods and information are often available 24/7.

REMEMBER

Information-seeking behavior tends to follow the "law of least effort." That is, a person will seek information in the closest, most easily accessible source available, even if they know there is little likelihood that the information will be available from that source.

Transportation and geographical issues are interrelated. For example, many school libraries serve students who must take buses to and from school. This creates service hour issues, since students' library access times are limited by the bus schedules. For a corporate records management service that must provide service to several company locations in a large metropolitan area, the availability and cost of transportation becomes a significant concern.

Legal/proprietary issues may also impact what services you may offer a certain class of user. Within a corporate information service, access to certain types of information may be related to the status of the user within the organization.

Political issues come into play when the results of the survey will be incorporated into proposals for new services and funding. Understanding the level of support you are likely to get from users (based on their needs, wants, and demands) and their level of influence with funding authorities will be useful in the analysis and proposal-formulation stage of the project.

Demographic data is often the core of the project. National census data can supply vast amounts of information. In the U.S., it is possible to secure census data at county, city/town, census tract, and block levels. For public records offices and school and public libraries, using this already-available information saves a great deal of data collection time. Community organizations and local government agencies also collect a variety of demographic, economic, educational, and political data that are often available for the asking. In the corporate sector, human relations managers or personnel offices will be a source of data.

Economic data about the service community are of great value for a variety of planning purposes, as is knowledge of the community communication systems and their policies regarding public service announcements and programming. Information about cultural, educational, recreational, and social organizations can be useful in expanding a service's constituency and even in increasing overall support.

Data Collecting Methods

There are two sets of methods for collecting needs information, one primarily for the private sector, the other for the public sector. Public services may occasionally find the private sector methods to be of value, although the private sector rarely needs to employ methods from the public sector. For information and knowledge management services, the data collected must answer questions of use and value to the parent organization.

- What information resources are currently in use?
- How are those resources used?
- What are the outcomes of those uses, if any?
- What, if any, technology and software are required to use the resources?
- What is the cost of accessing the information?
- What is the value or cost-benefit of the outcomes to the organization?

DATA COLLECTING METHODS FOR AN INFORMATION AUDIT

In order to respond to questions about use and value, five methods have been developed for collecting data for an information audit—activities, data analysis, decision-making, problem solving, and empirical studies.

The first three methods require a high degree of user participation, so these studies usually are small-scale projects involving fewer than twenty people. The fifth approach (*empirical studies*) employs direct observation of customer behavior (expressed needs)—what they use, when and how long they use it, and, to some degree, what they use the information for. For example, most electronic resources provide usage data that can assist in demonstrating usage levels. If the network can trace usage to a static IP address, you can also determine which computer was used, which can provide clues about who used the resource.

> **TIP**
>
> When acquiring a new database, be certain to ask for management reports. These are very useful for a variety of evaluation/assessment activities. If the vendor cannot supply such reports, look for software to add to your server that will provide management data.

Activities studies, as the name implies, examine why and how a person seeks and uses information. An in-depth interview is conducted with each user who has agreed to participate. Normally, the focus is on getting the individual to describe a typical day's work—for example, decisions made, actions taken, topics discussed, forms processed, and reports, letters, memos, and e-mails sent and received. The activities are analyzed in terms of the information used and the source of that information.

There are two cautions about this method. First, individuals tend to forget highly repetitive activities, or view them as too routine to mention. Second, there is a tendency for the informant to overemphasize a current project that, while important, may not represent typical information usage.

Data analysis studies shift the focus to the documents produced and determine the source of the information they contain. Typical documents examined are reports, memos, forms, and letters. Clearly, you must obtain permission to examine such materials.

After conducting the analysis, there must be an in-depth interview with the person(s) who produced the materials in order to determine which information sources were actually used. This approach has two key advantages. First, it is less affected by user forgetfulness, because it is based on the actual documents produced. Second, the materials that it examines are those that the organization deemed worth keeping for some time, suggesting that the information is of value to the organization.

Decision-making studies narrow the scope of the assessment. The data analysis is limited to documents in which decisions are recorded. The idea behind this approach is that decision-making is one of the most critical ongoing activities in the organization, requiring timely, accurate, and up-to-date information. This information is likely to be highly valued by the organization.

As in data analysis studies, the document examination is followed by interviews with the person(s) who produced the materials, and, if possible, with the decision-maker(s). The success of this method depends upon the informant(s) accurately remembering what information was collected, whether or not it was used, for making the decision.

Problem solving studies also focus on one aspect of organizational activities. Effective problem solving is requires timely access to sound information in order to achieve a speedy resolution. Looking at what information was collected—used and unused—is the focus of this type of study.

One of the advantages of this method is that, very often, problems cut across unit and departmental boundaries. This can result in a more comprehensive picture of information usage throughout the organization.

Traditional community analysis studies also make use of *key informants*, but in a different manner. Rather than looking at the individual's personal information usage and needs, these studies select informants who are in a position to understand the information needs and wants of a segment of the community, or perhaps even the entire community.

Key informants are especially valuable for understanding the needs of cultural and ethnic groups or people working in narrow, specialized fields, who are only a small portion of the total community and who may not use the service. Even large groups may have special issues that the service would be unable to discover without the assistance of key informants. Another term sometimes employed instead of informant is *gatekeeper*.

WORTH CHECKING OUT

Gatekeepers/key informants

Metoyer-Duran, Cheryl. 1991. "Information-Seeking Behavior of Gatekeepers in Ethnolinguistic Communities: Overview of a Taxonomy." *Library and Information Science Research* 13 (4): 319-346.

Collecting Data from Groups

Another technique for gaining community involvement in an assessment study is the *community forum*. There are several variants of this process of obtaining group feedback—town meetings, community forums, and focus groups. While the methods differ in structure and procedure, they share the basic goal of gaining insight into multiple users' views, needs, concerns, and satisfaction. They will work in any information environment.

Town meetings and community forums are good methods for gaining a broad sense of the issues, concerns, and needs of community members who are willing to speak up. Focus groups are more like a group interview in which everyone is expected to participate.

This group of techniques is not as highly structured as a questionnaire/survey. There is normally a set of general issues or open-ended questions to help direct the discussion. All of the group techniques require careful preparation; however, focus groups are the most complex and will be emphasized in this section, as many of the issues apply to the other techniques.

Any group data-collecting method requires someone who functions as moderator. In the case of focus groups, the moderator should have some training as a facilitator. The factors that contribute to good facilitator outcomes include the personal characteristics of the moderator, which vary with the composition of the target population from which the focus group members are drawn. Obvious examples include age, sex, ethnicity, language skills, educational background, and subject expertise. One essential skill is the ability to balance sensitivity and empathy with objectivity and detachment. Therefore, the selection of a moderator should be based on the particular circumstances or situation, but it is important to recognize that the ideal moderator may not be available.

USE OF GROUP TECHNIQUES

Focus groups, and other group methods, are particularly effective for:

- obtaining general background information about a topic or issue;
- stimulating creative thinking and new concepts;
- identifying potential or real problems with new programs and services;
- determining areas of interest or satisfaction with a program, service, or the overall organization; and
- discovering how the target population thinks and talks about the product, service, or program. This, in turn, facilitates the development of questionnaires or survey instruments for use with a larger sample of the target population.

Group methods have some important limitations. Individuals who attend a community forum or agree to take part in a focus group are usually more motivated than the average person in the target population, and are likely to have a greater interest in the product or service. Their opinions may not typify those of the target population as a whole. Sometimes one or two individuals will dominate the session, making the data generated even less reflective of the target population. The open-ended nature of the questions and the unrestricted interaction make summarization and interpretation difficult at best. There is also always the risk that the moderator may bias the results, knowingly or unknowingly, by providing verbal or nonverbal clues as to the type of responses that are expected or desired.

Most of the group methods call for an eight-step process:

1. Start with a clear definition of the research topic and goal for the sessions.
2. Determine the sampling parameters.
3. Select an appropriate moderator.
4. Generate and test the interview guide. If the target group has a second language, especially one that they generally use among themselves, translate the guide into that language, and have it vetted by a native speaker in order to avoid unexpected results.
5. Recruit the group members. Depending upon the goal of the project, any volunteers may be acceptable or you may have to

develop incentives to get the desired cross section of the target population.

6. Conduct the group sessions.
7. Analyze and interpret the data. This can be time-consuming and occasionally frustrating, especially if an issue of interest to the target population arose in the group sessions but was not followed up on.
8. Write the final report and determine the recommendations that should be put forward.

FOR FURTHER THOUGHT

Think about the population(s) that use your service. What type of group interview do you think would be most effective in gaining a sense of service quality, desired new services, and services no longer needed?

THE USE OF THE COMMUNITY FORUM/TOWN MEETING APPROACH

The community forum/town meeting approach avoids selection bias by the researcher, as anyone in the community can express his or her opinion at one or more public meetings. The key to success lies in extensive publicity. There are several ways to encourage attendance, such as letters to individuals and selected organizations, notices in mass media, and posters in the community and the service.

In a large community, a number of meetings may be necessary in order to keep the groups small enough for people to feel comfortable expressing their opinions. Smaller, more numerous meetings also allow adequate time to fully hear all points of view.

Two advantages of the community forum are that it is inexpensive and easy to arrange. Forums also help identify individuals who have an interest in improving the quality of service. When it comes time to implement new programs, these people can be called upon to assist.

One significant disadvantage of the community forum is that people who do not use the service will probably not attend the meetings. If they feel they have no need for the service, they are unlikely to feel the need to talk about it. This means that there will be little or no feedback on why the service is not used and how it could attract these non-users.

Another major disadvantage is that the data obtained are impressionistic and subjective. These data are extremely difficult to categorize and are not readily amenable to systematic analysis.

SOCIAL INDICATORS AND STATISTICS

Social scientists sometimes employ social indicators to determine the needs of various segments of the community. According to Warheit, "The notion of the city as a constellation of 'natural areas' has...proven useful as a method of describing social subdivisions within communities" (Warheit et al., n.d.: 48).

A natural area is a unit within a community that can be set apart from other units or areas by certain characteristics. Those characteristics, or social indicators, may be:

- geographical features, such as rivers or transportation patterns
- sociodemographic characteristics, such as age, sex, income, education, and ethnicity
- population factors, including distribution, density, mobility, and migration
- health and social well-being indicators, such as housing conditions and suicide rates
- institutional layout features, including location and accessibility of services

By using the statistics in public records and reports, a public records office or library conducting community analysis can deduce certain information needs of the community's population. By selecting factors that researchers think are highly correlated with those groups in need of information, surveyors may be able to extrapolate the information needs of the entire community. However, what these social indicators (also called factors, variables, or characteristics) may be is a point of much disagreement among researchers.

What are the implications of these indicators for managers? Library research provides some broad generalizations:

- Senior faculty, researchers, and organization officials tend to use services less as they advance in status and age. (They still use information; however, the actual gathering is done by junior or support staff, who tend to be younger.)
- Women make greater use of services than men do, regardless of the institutional environment (public, academic, or corporate).
- As the number of years of education increases, so does use of libraries, up to about sixteen years of formal education. For individuals who have attained a bachelor's degree, library use curves downward.
- Income level and use of formal information systems also show a J-shaped curve. That is, low income usually translates into low use; use rises through middle and upper-middle income levels; and use sharply decreases at high income, perhaps because persons with high incomes can purchase most of the information they require.
- Generally, as health declines, there is a decrease in the use of formal information systems. However, with proper equipment and special services, this tendency can be reversed.
- Persons employed in manual labor tend not to use formal information systems. Information use tends to increase in direct rela-

tionship to increased skill levels required for their work.

- The law of least effort is clearly evident in the finding that, as the distance of the residence or workstation from the information increases, there is a corresponding drop in use.
- Single persons and married couples with no children tend to use formal information systems less than couples with children, and as the number of children rises, so does use.
- People will often turn to another person for information before attempting to use a formal service.

USING FIELD SURVEYS

The *field survey* approach to needs analysis collects data from people living within a given area, either a sample or the total population. The most common means are interview schedules or questionnaires. The methods most frequently used are telephone interviews, person-to-person interviews, and mailed questionnaires.

When formulating questions, researchers must take care not to violate an individual's right to privacy. If the person or group designing the questionnaire is not certain of the legality of the questions, seek legal counsel.

Questions should be directly related to the objectives of the survey. Questions that elicit peripheral information lengthen the questionnaire, raise the cost of the survey, overburden the respondent, and create unrealistic expectations. These factors may decrease the response rate and reduce the validity of the findings.

It is important to decide between a structured or unstructured questionnaire format. Open-ended questions (unstructured format) take more time to answer than fixed-alternative, or closed, questions (structured format). The type of question can affect both the response rate and data analysis. Open-ended questions are much more difficult to code and analyze.

With the structured format, data are homogenous and are more easily coded and analyzed. This format is much easier to use, especially when volunteers are conducting interviews or working with the data. However, even when using the structured format, the researcher must prepare careful instructions for volunteers and provide some training to ensure accurate results.

The next step in the field survey is to select a sample. According to Warheit, "The selection of the sample depends largely upon the information needed: the unit for analysis, i.e., individuals, household, etc.; the type of data-gathering techniques used; and the size it must be to adequately represent the population from which it is drawn" (Warheit et al., n.d.: 48).

REMEMBER

Sampling techniques were discussed in chapter 6.

Cost must be taken into account when selecting a sample. A large sample may call for complex selection methods, and more time will be required to complete the survey. The use of volunteers can keep the cost down, but the survey method is not a simple procedure. This is an area where the services of a paid consultant may be valuable.

A popular method of obtaining information from respondents is the personal interview. This permits face-to-face contact, stimulates a free exchange of ideas, and usually produces a high response rate. The telephone interview, though popular, has the disadvantage of a limited amount of time in which the interviewer can hold the respondent's interest. Twenty minutes is about the maximum length for telephone interviews that provide a good response rate. Whatever the method, with a highly structured interview schedule and a well-trained interviewer, the research team can gather the necessary data efficiently.

Mail surveys require less staffing and training than surveys that depend on personal or telephone interviews. These two advantages can significantly reduce the cost, in both time and money, of conducting a survey. However, there are two significant disadvantages to the mailed survey. Firstly, most have a low response rate, sometimes as low as 15 percent, which seriously affects the validity and reliability of the survey, and the cost of keeping track of who has or has not responded is high. Secondly, some persons in the community are unable to respond to anything but the simplest questions. This may be especially true in bilingual or multilingual communities. The problem of language can be overcome by printing the questionnaire in all the appropriate languages, but the problem of literacy level will remain, regardless of the language used.

Another consideration is that, in an interview, a trained interviewer can detect, from the respondent's verbal and nonverbal signals, when there is something not quite right about a question and answer. Because it does not include this feedback, the mailed questionnaire data requires additional analysis.

Because of these disadvantages, the questionnaire must be carefully designed and use the simplest and most succinct language possible, while still meeting the established objectives. The researchers should also attempt to determine what response rate will be acceptable before expending the time and money for a survey that could be of questionable value.

In general, the survey approach, like other needs assessment approaches, has certain advantages and disadvantages. The primary disadvantage is its cost. Designing a survey of a large sample, extensive interviewing, and advanced statistical analysis, for example, tend to cost more than other methods. Another disadvantage is that many individuals refuse to supply information about themselves or their family members. In many communities, the refusal or non-return rate may be high enough to make the data of questionable value.

Data analysis is, in many ways, the most critical step in the procedure, as it is the basis for developing recommendations. Analyzing the data is a multistep process that takes time and skill.

The first step is tabulating the data. The method selected depends on how the team collected the data and the capabilities of the agency or group performing the analysis. After tabulating the data, elementary statistical analysis can be performed, such as the calculation of averages and standard deviation.

One simple and inexpensive method for analysis is to prepare maps indicating the study units (such as census tracts) and the variables or responses analyzed. Adding map overlays improves this method, as they can illustrate distributions of, and relationships among, the selected variables. This produces the most useful results when there is a small number of variables.

Analysis involving a large number of variables requires more sophisticated techniques. However, the team must have sound reasons for using each type of analysis. The ability to do something is not reason enough to do it. It can be just as difficult to draw conclusions from a multitude of statistical test results as it is from raw data, if you have not planned for each test.

TIP

A combined approach allows the team to compare results from the different methods. It is especially valuable to compare the data from a user study with that gathered by a field survey.

The Interpretation of Data

Most assessment projects yield large quantities of data that can be manipulated statistically. However, this will only provide a level of statistical significance, which is related to the probability, not the importance, of the results. The main question—how to interpret the data—remains. One way to interpret data is in terms of social needs: normative, felt, expressed, and comparative.

Normative needs usually arise from expert opinion. One commonly cited normative need is the need to increase the literacy level. Teachers, librarians, and others, in their professional roles, express this normative need. To some degree, the general public accepts this need, but little funding is available to meet it.

Felt needs arise from the population or community, based on its insight into its problems. How appropriate or realistic felt needs may be is not the issue; they are important as a reflection of a problem. However, just as normative needs are not always what the community wants, felt needs do not always reflect what is good for the community. When normative and felt needs conflict, interpretation and compromise are required.

Expressed needs reflect behavior. Individuals often say that they really want or need something, but behave in a way that shows that they actually want or need something else. Information organizations respond well to expressed needs—that is, they are likely to meet a greater percentage of the needs of active users than of infrequent users. Libraries react to expressed needs for information by adding more material about the subject to the collection. While this is not wrong, it does risk unbalanced spending or failure to respond to real, but unexpressed, information needs. The needs assessment project can reveal whether the service is overresponding to active users' needs.

Comparative needs are determined by comparing the target population to other populations. One such comparison might be the number of items consulted or checked out, per capita, by the target group versus the overall usage by registered users. When making such comparisons, the services for the two groups need to be the same. One advantage of focusing on comparative needs is that they usually provide some quantitative measures that can be useful in setting goals for any new services or programs resulting from the assessment project.

The project team and an advisory board can begin their analysis and interpretation by considering a series of questions. The answers to these questions can provide the basis for a draft report. Each project generates its own set of question; here is a sample of the types that might be used.

- What are the most important felt needs within a community?
- What are the most important normative needs, as identified by the experts?
- Which needs are the most relevant to the mission and experience of the service?
- How can multiple and conflicting needs be reconciled?
- What is the realistic expectation for resources to respond to needs?
- What are the clients' costs for each alternative?
- What are the direct and indirect costs to the institution or parent organization for each option?
- What impact or outcome is likely for each alternative? Are they measurable?
- What is an appropriate timeline for setting up an effective program?
- What documents and resources are required? Are they available?
- How will the option(s) fit into the existing service structure?

After the team has analyzed the results of the study, they must select the most suitable format for presenting the findings to the community. The factors for the selection relate to the character of the community, the type of survey, and the intended audience.

Advanced statistical analysis may be a suitable format for audiences that can understand the assumptions and implications of such tests (e.g., academic and corporate environments).

For services provided for the community at large, the target audience is more varied, from highly literate to illiterate. The team must present the results in a way that allows individuals in the community, the service, and public office to easily understand the implications. One way is to use visual aids, such as descriptive summaries, charts, and diagrams.

The most important questions to ask following a needs assessment are:

- Do the present objectives of the service coincide with its new knowledge of the community?
- Are the objectives in line with the current needs of the community?
- Do they reflect a past need, or are they merely self-serving?

The findings of the study should answer these questions. If the objectives of the service do not reflect the needs and interests of its community, the staff must make recommendations to ensure that the proper changes will occur.

DIG DEEPER

The material presented above is somewhat abstract and theoretical in nature, as well as generic in approach. Examples of the application of needs-assessment methods can be found in:

Welch, Alicia, and Christine Donohue. 1994. "Awareness, Use, and Satisfaction with Public Libraries: A Summary of Connecticut Community Surveys." *Public Libraries* 33 (3): 149-152.

Data collected in three large metropolitan library systems—Philadelphia, Minneapolis, and Atlanta-Fulton County—are described in:

D'Elia, George, and Eleanor Rodger. 1994. "Public Library Roles and Patron Use: Why Patrons Use the Library." *Public Libraries* 33 (3): 135-144.

The last article illustrates how one might tailor an assessment project for a special user group:

Holt, Cynthia, and Wanda Clements Hole. 1995. "Assessing Needs of Library Users with Disabilities." *Public Libraries* 34 (2): 90-93.

WHAT IS MARKETING?

> ### DEFINITIONS
>
> **Marketing**
>
> Marketing is "the management process for identifying, antici-
> pating, and satisfying customer requirements for profitability"
> (Institute of Marketing, 1991).
>
> "The marketing concept holds that the key to achieving orga-
> nizational goals consists of determining the needs and wants
> of target markets and delivering the desired satisfactions more
> effectively and efficiently than competitors" (Kotler, 1994: 18).
>
> Marketing for libraries is "a process of exchange and a way to
> foster the partnership between the library and its community"
> (Weingand, 1995: 296).

Another approach is strategic marketing, which draws on the methods of
both strategic planning and marketing. This is an excellent example of the
integration of management activities that is a crucial ability for a successful
manager.

Over the past thirty years, Kotler has created and developed the field of
nonprofit marketing. In his *Strategic Marketing for Nonprofit Organizations*
(Kotler and Andreasen, 1996), he extends the strategic planning aspects to
include social marketing and a strong international element. What follows
has been influenced by his writings.

There are some important similarities in the definitions of marketing
given above. All mention the customer as a key element in the process and
suggest that customer needs are the focal point of marketing. However, services in the information sector can emphasize at least four different aspects of
their programs:

- product,
- service,
- sales, and
- users.

Social marketing developed as a tool for nonprofit groups with a relatively
narrow focus or cause—such as health care and environmental or consumer
protection—that they want to "sell" to the general public. This approach uses
sales-oriented marketing techniques to generate support for social causes or
agendas. Public libraries often have social programs and activities—adult literacy programs, after-school storytelling, and programs for latchkey children—that can benefit from this kind of marketing.

Social marketing is sometimes difficult to differentiate from public relations activities, but Kotler makes this distinction: "social marketing seeks to
influence social behavior not to benefit the marketer but *to benefit the target*

audience and the general society" (Kotler and Andreasen, 1996: 43; emphasis in the original).

Earlier it was noted that there are several types of users, including the non-user. One question to consider when creating a marketing program is "why is a non-user a non-user?" Below are some general statements about non-users that apply both information and commercial organizations.

- **The person does not know your product.** This is evident in non–library-focused surveys that ask, "Does your community or organization have a library?" Many respondents say "no" when a library does in fact exist.
- **The person cannot find your product, or the product is not available when needed.** Service location and hours are always an issue. Among the factors governing them is the cost to the user, even if there is no monetary exchange. Fine (1990) identified four types of social price for the use of nonprofit service organizations: time, effort, lifestyle, and psyche. The first two are the ones normally considered when planning, but the others should also be noted. The lifestyle price is partly related to effort—in order to reach the location during service hours, people may need to adjust their activities and schedules. Too much adjustment usually turns a potential user into a non-user. This is important for corporate services in which working hours extend beyond nine-to-five, and public services in communities with work-life balance issues. The psyche price involves self-esteem and emotions—fears of losing face, losing privacy, or losing control. These concerns may discourage people who are unfamiliar with information services or uncomfortable with modern information technology, such as online catalogs and databases, as well as those who are self-conscious about their level of education or literacy.
- **The person does not need your product.** This factor is less likely to affect services in the information sector, as everyone needs some information to carry out necessary activities. However, a particular service may not have the type of information that the person needs.
- **The person prefers a different brand of product.** This is probably the most rapidly growing factor. In this case, the competing "brand" is the Internet. The law of least effort comes into effect—a person with Internet access can obtain information 24/7 without leaving the home or office. Also, the psyche price is very low—no one else will know if the person could not spell a certain word or did not know a particular fact. Control, self-esteem, and privacy are no longer an issue.
- **The person does not understand what your product can do.** This is frequently the case for services in the information sector. For example, many people perceive archives or libraries as

offering, at best, a limited range of print information resources. The idea that an archive or library is a comprehensive information service is only beginning to be recognized by individuals outside the field. This is an area where marketing and public relations can help convert non-users into users.

- **The person believes the cost of your product is too high or the value for the cost is too low.** For this to be a factor, the person must have used your product at least once in order to form an opinion. Many people generalize about all services on the basis of one or two experiences in the past, rather than a recent experience with a specific service.
- **The person has had difficulty using your product.** In the days of card catalogs and complex filing rules, it could be very difficult to gain access to documents in the collection. Many former users do not know how things have changed. Again, effective marketing and public relations programs can address this issue.
- **The person does not expect good service.** While it is impossible to please everyone all the time, displeasing too many people can lead to disaster. Service quality studies can help determine how often, for how many people, and in what situations problems developed and whether similar problems exist for other brands. Reducing the problems for existing users, and not creating a cadre of dissatisfied former users, can make potential users think well of your service and lead them to become users.

FOR FURTHER THOUGHT

How many types of non-user do you think are in your service community?

Do you know of any existing studies that could provide useful data?

A sound marketing assessment program will provide market intelligence that can be used to address the user issues described above and to develop a plan for increasing both the number of users and the market share.

Market intelligence considers data from four broad areas: environmental, activity type, customers (users), and competitors (Fine, 1990).

Environmental data is essential in planning and goal setting. Much of this data will have already been collected for use in other management activities. All of the environmental factors noted earlier (e.g. social, political, and economic) also apply to any marketing program.

Activity data are really subsets of environmental information; they include supplier/vendor activities, technological developments, and competitors.

Users are a logical source of data, such as level of use, age, and major responsibilities (e.g. research, teaching, or administration).

Competitor data is most useful when considered in terms of subsets such as market share, distribution methods, and price range.

Some of the marketing data must be collected directly from the source. Direct collecting can be expensive and time-consuming. However, when it is incorporated into the normal operational routine, data collecting becomes almost cost-free. For instance, an organization often has a wealth of data already collected about existing users via user registration data and collection usage reports, which may be divided into subsets by user type and document delivery services.

Existing user data provides the staff with profiles of what are, at the very least, semi-satisfied users. This information is useful in deciding whether it is more cost-effective to seek out people with similar profiles or to reach out to a very different segment of the population. No matter how much data is accumulated, however, the information is of no value without a sound marketing plan.

TIP

It can be expensive and time-consuming to collect the data needed for a marketing plan. Services are not always good at estimating the internal costs—principally staff time—of carrying out projects. It is worthwhile to get a quote from a market research organization such as Gallup or National Opinion Polls. They piggyback small surveys onto general data-collection exercises, which greatly reduces costs. The charges will be much smaller than expected, especially if the cost of the alternative—an in-house survey—is fully evaluated.

The Marketing Process

Porter (1979: 137) suggests that strategic planners need to locate a potentially profitable niche, develop products to meet the needs of customers in that niche, and create a defensive plan for dealing with possible competitors. Kotler's strategic marketing process has three major elements: analysis, strategy, and implementation (Kotler and Andreason, 1996). Here is a nine-step model for strategic planning:

STEP ONE: GENERIC PRODUCT DEFINITION

Any organization seeking long-term success must be able to answer the question, "What is our business?" Every organization produces at least one of the following: physical products (tangible), services (intangible), persons (press agents), the organization itself (political parties or professional organizations), or ideas (population control or human rights).

Too often, the answer to the question is product- rather than customer-oriented. Thinking about the organization in terms of the user broadens the scope of possible activities. For example, rather than focusing on records management, think in terms of providing information to the user. Increasing the user base is key for long-term survival.

STEP TWO: TARGET GROUP DEFINITION

The generic or user-based product definition usually results in the identification of a very wide market. But the danger of developing a broad marketing program is that it often fails to produce the desired results. One way to make the process more manageable is to segment the large market into smaller, more homogenous units. For this purpose, a unit is a group that:

- has similar or related characteristics
- shares common needs and wants
- has similar responses to like motivations
- accepts a service/product that fulfills these needs at a reasonable price

Some examples of a unit and the broader market are: family genealogists and archives, secretaries and a records management service, senior management and a knowledge management service, new undergraduates and a university, and preschool children and a public library. Segmenting a market takes time and effort, but it will pay off in a better response to efforts targeted to a particular segment.

Considering smaller units also helps managers make the difficult decision of where to allocate the available marketing funds. For each segment, ask the following questions:

- What are the common needs/wants of this group?
- Which, if any, of those needs do we now serve?
- What do we know about this group's behavior patterns?
- How much benefit do they currently receive from our services?
- What do we know about their perceptions of the service?
- What is our potential gain from meeting more of this group's needs and wants?
- What is the most effective means of reaching this group?
- Compared to other market segments, how important is this group?
- Who is our competition for this group?

The last question should provide the information for ranking the various market segments. (These will vary over time as the situation and environment change.) Some of the other questions may show that it is necessary to collect more data before a final decision is made. All of the answers will help determine which group(s) to target.

STEP THREE: DIFFERENTIAL MARKETING ANALYSIS

Different segments require different approaches; hence, differentiated marketing. While most services have three basic product lines—collections, services, and programs—the emphasis or importance may vary for a particular segment.

Using the terminology of for-profit organizations, each product line consists of several different, specific products. For a university library, specific collection products might be defined by dividing the collection into instructional, secondary, and primary research materials. Services might be document delivery and online searching. Program products might be electronic search instruction and dissertation format assistance. By looking at the specific products, you can see how different packages would have greater or lesser interest to various market segments.

For-profit organizations learned long ago that, when serving more than one target population, the best results are gained by differentiating the products and communications about the products for each target population.

Considering the costs and benefits a user accrues in using the package provides marketing planners with two useful perspectives. First, it offers a complete picture of what the package consists of and the relationships between the component parts. Second, it gives planners a sense of how the user will perceive the package. This element is especially important for non-profit organizations, because they tend to believe their service or package is much more vital than does the end user.

STEP FOUR: CUSTOMER BEHAVIOR ANALYSIS

For many years, information professionals have known that it is vital to have an understanding of users' work- and lifestyles. Knowing what topics users are interested in, how they use the product, when and where they use the product, and when and where they would *prefer* to use the product, allows managers to more effectively structure services, products, and programs. This information also assists in determining the most effective approaches to marketing existing services and promoting new services.

STEP FIVE: DIFFERENTIAL ADVANTAGES ANALYSIS

Once a manager understands the behaviors and needs of the various customer segments, it is possible to seek out differential advantages for each segment. A differential advantage is one that exploits the reputation of services or programs by creating or enhancing a special value in the minds of potential users.

For example, a hospital library might have a special document delivery service for medical staff that would provide papers not locally available within one hour. By meeting urgent information needs, the library would reinforce the value the medical staff places on delivering effective healthcare. It is essential for service organizations to reinforce the values and reflect the needs of the users and the parent organization.

STEP SIX: MULTIPLE MARKETING APPROACHES

A marketing effort should employ several different marketing tools; those available include Web sites, Intranets, newsletters, flyers, advertisements, and annual reports. The tools selected should be those that best fit the work/lifestyle of the target segment.

Receptions or open houses can be effective promotional tools, especially when there is a new service or product to demonstrate. For a public library attempting to reach new immigrants, presenting materials in the native language of the target population is essential. But be sure that the material is reviewed by a native speaker who understands both formal and slang usage of terms and phrases.

STEP SEVEN: INTEGRATED MARKET PLANNING AND STEP EIGHT: CONTINUOUS FEEDBACK

An integrated program is the best insurance against the ineffective use of marketing funds. The best way to achieve this is to have one person responsible for coordinating all marketing and promotional activities.

Only the largest services can employ people to work solely on marketing. However, even when the service cannot afford a full-time marketing position, there should be only one person—or, if this is not possible, a committee—responsible for coordinating all marketing and promotional activities.

STEP NINE: MARKETING AUDIT

A marketing audit essentially consists of monitoring activities. It also draws on feedback from users, front-line staff, and governing boards. An audit provides information on what worked and why, what did not work and why not, how the environment and user base have or have not changed, and what changes have taken place within the organization in terms of staff, services, and resources. These are all important aspects to consider in adjusting and maintaining a viable marketing program.

Other elements include assessing the resources available to carry out the program, evaluating how well the people responsible for carrying out the program have performed, and determining how successful the program is in achieving long-term organizational mission, goals, and objectives.

Weingand suggests that:

> the audit should also develop a 'futures screen' that identifies trends and projections in both external and internal environments in order to develop contingency plans that will relate to alternative future scenarios. The futures screen places considerable emphasis on securing data on what "may be" in the next five years (and beyond); objectives can then be developed to reflect that informed projection. This typically will mandate three parallel sets of objectives for each goal: 1) an extended set, which assumes an economic climate similar to the present year; 2) a worst case set, in which objectives are written to respond to a worsening economic picture;

and 3) a blue sky set, in which possible windfalls and economic upturns are spent in advance. (1995: 303)

Other points to consider include how different factors have or have not changed since the program's inception.

- Have staff members changed?
- Are there slight differences in services that are not reflected in the marketing program?
- Might small increases or decreases in organizational resources in any one year, in totality, be significant?
- Are there new, different, and or perhaps fewer competitors for the service?

WORTH CHECKING OUT

Lifestyle marketing analysis

Hazel Davis provides a fine example of how one can employ lifestyle marketing analysis as an element in developing a service program.

Davis, Hazel. 1993. "Lifestyles, Local Community, and Libraries: A Partnership for the Future." *Public Libraries* 32 (6): 323-328.

All changes that could be relevant, both internal and external, should be examined. Then consider whether an appropriate marketing effort can help to gain the support, and perhaps the financing, that would make the project viable.

FOR FURTHER THOUGHT

Apply the marketing model to a service you use regularly.

Work through each step to see how it can be applied to the selected service.

WHAT IS PROMOTION?

Kotler (1980: 89) defined the marketing mix as consisting of price, promotion, and product. "Promotion" refers to a cluster of techniques to communicate, inform, persuade, stimulate, and remind the user of the merits of a variety of programs offered within a particular service. The goal is to modify or reinforce existing behavior, and a successful approach will blend selective activities to reach and recruit potential users.

The basic forms of promotion are advertising, personal selling, sales promotion, and publicity (McDaniel, 1996: 8). Relatively few information services employ a comprehensive advertising approach, partly for reasons of cost, but also because, traditionally, advertising was considered somewhat inappropriate and too impersonal, and it was thought to be unnecessary. Today this is not so.

The purpose of promotional activities is to communicate, inform, persuade, and remind. A manager should monitor the design process with a particular goal in mind, never leaving the outcome to chance and never delegating it without determining accountability and responsibility.

News as Promotion

Publicity is a form of indirect promotion and is, in many ways, the most powerful. However, it is also the least controllable of all the techniques from the promotion or marketing communications point of view.

To paraphrase Kotler, publicity is non-paid communication about a company or its products appearing in the media as news. As a result, "the seller pays nothing for the news coverage" (Kotler, 1980: 469).

Information about staff, services, or a special category of user appearing in the media can be legitimate news, but also serves as a form of promotion—at least if the news is good.

Unfortunately, negative publicity is often easier to get, and the results can be highly disruptive. Positive publicity requires patient cultivation and strenuous efforts to package information for the media, and this costs money. Publicity may be unpaid media, but it's not free, and large public relations budgets do not always produce better results.

Ideally, everyone on the staff acts, in a way, as a salesperson or a press agent. They can contribute to the public image of the service by being positive and highlighting the many worthwhile and fascinating activities that, after all, are characteristic of service operations.

FOR FURTHER THOUGHT

Think about an information service with which you are familiar.

What forms of promotion does it use?

Does it target its promotional activities to the community at large or to specific segments?

How effective is its current program?

How effective is it for different groups of users?

How do users react to it program(s)? Try to get feedback from the users themselves.

Could you suggest improvements to its promotional activities?

FOUR KEY STRATEGIES FOR MARKETING SUCCESS

When the principle of strategic imperative has been accepted, the next question is, "What kinds of strategies lend themselves to institutional marketing and promotion?" Four strategic platforms have a particularly good fit to the typical needs of a library. These are positioning, segmentation, targeting, and the TQM (Total Quality Management) approach.

Positioning is defined by Kotler and Andreasen as "the act of designing the organization's image and value offer so that…customers understand and appreciate what the organization stands for in relation to its competitors" (Kotler and Andreasen, 1996: 205). From an ethical standpoint, the most desirable image is also the most authentic. These are values to which good marketers subscribe, but on which marketing itself has little to say. From the purely utilitarian perspective of marketing, it "is not important whether your product is the best of its kind. What is important is whether people think it is best" (Nash, 1986: 216).

When the general positioning principle is applied to services in the information sector, the product's position is the image it projects in the minds of potential customers in relation to competitive institutions. In concentrating on the perceptions of the prospective user, a positioning strategy looks for windows in the mind (Wright, 1973: 63). It is then simply a matter of "determining what someone is really buying when they buy your product or service and then conveying those impressions and motivations to the buyer" (Ries and Trout, 1986: 12).

Segmentation is the process of identifying discrete divisions of potential customers according to demographic, geographic, psychographic, and psychometric characteristics (McCormack, 1980: 123). This allows you to better use limited resources (to concentrate your forces) by applying them only to potential users.

Targeting is closely related to segmentation. In this strategic method, an organization sets out to tailor its message so well and deliver it so close to the prospect's interest and sphere of attention that the message cannot be missed.

Target markets consist of those customers whom the service can attract effectively (via strategy) and efficiently (via tactics). Kotler and Andreasen view this as "a style of marketing appropriate to a customer-oriented organization. In it the organization distinguishes between the different segments making up the market" (Kotler and Andreasen, 1996: 167).

The key to targeting is found not only in the unique characteristics of the segment, but in the organization's ability to evaluate it. As Drucker noted, "only if targets are defined can resources be allocated to their attainment, priorities and deadlines set and somebody be held accountable for results" (Drucker, 1974: 140).

Total Quality Management (TQM) remains an important process. Research in progress at Arizona State University's First Interstate Center for Services Marketing indicates how this strategy addresses the issues organizations face as they move to create a more service-oriented culture. It is not enough for the organization to simply meet the expectations of prospective users; it ought to *exceed* those expectations.

Services must make a commitment to quality service and customer satisfaction, and this commitment must begin at the top. It must manifest itself in the actions of those in the highest positions and those with the greater visibility. Following this TQM strategy will result in a decentralization of authority within an organizationally developed strategic plan, a factor required for success today.

A TACTICAL FRAMEWORK

Once the institution has a strategy—a sense of the direction it wants to follow —and has decided to mount an integrated promotional effort, managers will have a proper frame of reference for the selection of tactics.

When strategies are relatively few, tactics are bountiful and can be extremely creative, as well as superbly executed. These highly-focused efforts can concentrate resources on doing the key things well, rather than dissipating available time, energy, and money over a wide range of activities—which, in some institutions, is simply the years' accumulation of everybody's "pet projects" related to goals that have long been superseded.

The service's Web site is a powerful tool that can convey not only basic information about the services offered, but also the image and culture of the organization. The Web site may belong exclusively to the service, or may consist of pages within the site of the broader organization. Careful consideration of the information to be included, indexing of the pages and links to other relevant sites, and a good design and layout will make it easy for the visitor to navigate the site and find the information they are seeking.

The information provided needs to be updated regularly—an out-of-date site creates a bad impression of the library. Graphics, video, and sound can heighten the impact of the site, but these can be expensive, and may actually be frustrating for the visitor. There must be a balance between ease and speed of access and enhancement through images and sound.

Preprinted advertising inserts and circulars can be used to publish service offerings, schedules, or a calendar of events. These can be inserted into weekly community newspapers or in bulk mailings to home and work addresses. Although this is a somewhat broad approach for the strategies of segmenting and targeting, such inserts have a self-screening property: the person attracted to a listing of events is likely to be a serious prospect, while non-prospects disqualify themselves by not reading or not acting upon the information.

"Canvassing" is the marketing label for techniques more commonly known in public libraries as outreach activities. If used with discrimination—by choosing events and locations where real prospects are likely to be concentrated—this tactic has can be effective for most strategies. If overused, it will drain resources from more cost-efficient alternatives.

Distributing well-designed brochures at the right time in the cycle and to carefully targeted populations can be the keystone of a well-orchestrated sequence of varied communications efforts.

Print advertising and billboards are mass media options that can reach thousands of non-customers, but they are typically a highly expensive option. In some circumstances, however, these tactics can lend key tactical support. For example, they can be used to promote a special event by identifying the time and place and its specific benefit to the target population.

Signs are often considered too mundane a subject for creative marketers. For prospective customers, however, effective signs and clear directions can make the difference between a positive experience with the library or extreme frustration. Libraries, especially public libraries, are often surprised when a survey of community members reveals how many people do not know that there is a library in their region or cannot identify the nearest branch.

Newspaper, magazine, TV, and radio are all mass media outlets well suited to targeting or segmentation, but not all media are equally effective. Certain sections of newspapers in targeted zip codes and certain radio or television programs may best fit the profile of the targeted population. If so, these media should be evaluated on the basis of cost per contact. This may be one of the few ways to effectively reach non-users. In the end, regardless of which tactics are chosen, the institution must "decide what it wants to say and how (by what media) it wants the message delivered" (McDaniel, 1996: 377).

Assessment became a buzzword in the 1990s, and is receiving increasing attention in the information sector. If five percent of revenue or more is going to be invested in marketing and promotional programs, there must be careful assessment and ongoing evaluation of the effort.

If services use appropriate research and resources, the battle for the minds—and support—of future users will be an integrated process of communication through which users will be well-matched to the services—a win-win situation.

FOR FURTHER THOUGHT

Think about your local public library.

Which tactics could it employ?

Rank them according to their likely costs and effectiveness.

Whether we are consumers or service providers, we all recognize the need to gain in-depth insight about ways of assessing customer needs and satisfaction; the following two titles are recommended.

WORTH CHECKING OUT

Assessing customer needs

An excellent work on focus groups is:

Bloor, Michael, Jane Frankland, Michelle Thomas, and Kate Robson. 2001. *Focus Groups in Social Research*. Newbury Park, Calif.: Sage.

Developing an effective marketing program

Highly recommended:

Weingand, Darlene. 1998. *Future-Driven Library Marketing*. Chicago: American Library Association.

AFTER READING THIS CHAPTER YOU SHOULD BE AWARE:

- that effective service relies on knowing the characteristics and needs of users and potential users
- how to plan an assessment project
- what information you need to collect and how to select an appropriate method
- why marketing is important and how to plan a marketing program
- the difference between marketing and promotion
- the value of promotional activities and the range of options
- the key strategies for marketing success
- how to develop a tactical framework for an integrated promotional project

REFERENCES

Bloor, Michael, Jane Frankland, Michelle Thomas, and Kate Robson. 2001. *Focus Groups in Social Research*. Newbury Park, Calif.: Sage.

Davis, Hazel. 1993. "Lifestyles, Local Community and Libraries: A Partnership for the Future." *Public Libraries* 32 (6): 323-328.

D'Elia, George, and Eleanor Rodger. 1994. "Public Library Roles and Patron Use: Why Patrons Use the Library." *Public Libraries* 33 (3): 135-144.

Drucker, Peter. 1974. *Management Responsibilities: Practices*. New York: Harper & Row.

Emery, Fred, and Eric Trist. 1965. "The Causal Texture of Organizational Environments." *Human Relations* 18 (1): 21-31.

Fine, Seymour. 1990. *Social Marketing: Promoting the Causes of Public and Nonprofit Agencies*. Needham Heights, Mass.: Allyn and Bacon.

Holt, Cynthia, and Wanda Clements Hole. 1995. "Assessing Needs of Library Users with Disabilities." *Public Libraries* 34 (2): 90-93.

Institute of Marketing. 1991. *"What Is Marketing"* brochure. London: Institute of Marketing.

Kotler, Philip. 1994. *Marketing Management Analysis: Planning and Control.* 8th ed. Englewood Cliffs, N.J.: Prentice-Hall.

Kotler, Philip. 1980. *Marketing Management Analysis: Planning and Control.* 4th ed. Englewood Cliffs, N.J.: Prentice-Hall.

Kotler, Philip, and Allen Andreasen. 1996. *Strategic Marketing for Nonprofit Organizations.* 5th ed. Englewood Cliffs, N.J.: Prentice-Hall.

McCormack, Mary J. 1980. *Marketing of Public Issues as Private Troubles.* Ann Arbor, Mich.: University Microfilms.

McDaniel, Carl D. 1996. *Contemporary Marketing Research.* 3rd ed. St. Paul, Minn.: West Publishing.

Melling, Maxine, and Joyce Little, eds. 2002. *Building a Successful Customer-Service Relationship: A Guide for Library and Information Managers.* London: Facet Publishing.

Metoyer-Duran, Cheryl. 1991. "Information-Seeking Behavior of Gatekeepers in Ethnolinguistic Communities: Overview of a Taxonomy." *Library and Information Science Research* 13 (4): 319-346.

Nash, Edward L. 1986. *Direct Marketing: Strategy, Planning, and Execution.* 2d ed. New York: McGraw-Hill.

O'Hanlon, Sean, and Ann Phillips. 1999. "Benchmarks for the Future." *Illinois Libraries* 81 (2): 99-103.

Porter, Michael. 1979. "How Competitive Forces Shape Strategy." *Harvard Business Review* 57 (2): 137.

Ries, Al, and Jack Trout. 1986. *Marketing Warfare.* New York: McGraw-Hill.

Shearer, Kenneth. 1993. "Confusing What Is Most Wanted with What Is Most Used." *Public Libraries* 32 (4): 193-197.

Warheit, George J., et al. n.d. *Planning for Change: Needs Assessment Approaches.* Rockville, Md.: Alcohol, Drug Abuse, and Mental Health Administration.

Weingand, Darlene. 1995. "Preparing for the New Millennium: The Case for Using Market Strategies." *Library Trends* 43 (3): 296.

Weingand, Darlene. 1997. *Customer Service Excellence: A Concise Guide for Librarians.* Chicago: American Library Association.

Weingand, Darlene. 1998. *Future-Driven Library Marketing.* Chicago: American Library Association.

Welch, Alicia, and Christine Donohue. 1994. "Awareness, Use, and Satisfaction with Public Libraries: A Summary of Connecticut Community Surveys." *Public Libraries* 33 (3): 149-152.

Westbrook, Lynn. 2000. "Analyzing Community Information Needs: A Holistic Approach." *Library Administration and Management* 14 (1): 26-30.

Wright, Peter L. 1973. *Analyzing Consumer Judgment Strategies.* Urbana, Ill.: College of Commerce and Business Administration.

Launching Pad

Alexander, Ralph S. 1961. *Marketing Definitions.* Chicago: American Marketing Association.

Ansoff, Igor. 1988. *New Corporate Strategy.* New York: John Wiley & Sons.

Broady-Preston, Judy, and Lucy Steel. 2002. "Internal Marketing Strategies in LIS: A Management Perspective." *Library Management* 23 (6/7): 294-301.

Broady-Preston, Judy, and Lucy Steel. 2002. "Employees, Customers and Internal Marketing Strategies in LIS." *Library Management* 23 (8/9): 384-393.

Bruce, Andy, and Ken Langdon. 2002. *Putting Customers First.* London: Dorling Kindersley.

Cope, Robert. 1987. *Opportunity from Strength.* Washington, D.C.: American Association of Higher Education.

Cronin, Blaise, ed. 1992. *Marketing of Library and Information Services.* 2d ed. London: Aslib.

Curtis, Donnelyn. 2002. *Attracting, Educating, and Serving Remote Users Through the Web.* New York: Neal-Schuman.

de Sáez, Eileen Elliott. 2002. *Marketing Concepts for Library and Information Services.* 2d ed. New York: Neal-Schuman.

Debowski, Shelda. 2000. "The Hidden User: Providing an Effective Service to Users of Electronic Information Services." *OCLC Systems and Services* 17 (4): 175-180.

Elam, Houston, and Norton Paley. 1992. *Marketing for Nonmarketers.* New York: American Management Association.

Evans, Joel, and Barry Berman. 1985. *Marketing.* New York: Macmillan.

Feber, Robert. 1980. "What Do We Know About Consumer Behavior?" In *Marketing Management and Strategy: A Reader,* edited by Philip Kotler. Englewood Cliffs, N.J.: Prentice-Hall.

Fleming, Helen R. 1993. "Library CPR: Savvy Marketing Can Save Your Library." *Library Journal* 118 (September 15): 32-36.

Karp, Rashelle S. 2002. *Powerful Public Relations: A How-To Guide for Librarians.* Chicago: American Library Association.

Levinson, Jay C. 1989. *Guerilla Marketing Attack.* Boston, Mass.: Houghton Mifflin.

Lilley, Emma, and Bob Usherwood. 2000. "Wanting It All: The Relationship Between Expectations and the Public's Perception of Public Library Services." *Library Management* 21 (1): 13-24.

McNeal, James U. 1992. *Kids as Customers: A Handbook of Marketing to Children.* New York: Macmillan.

Pantry, Sheila, and Peter Griffiths. 2002. *Creating a Successful E-Information Service.* London: Facet Publishing.

Rapp, S., and T. L. Collins. 1994. *Beyond Maxi-Marketing: The New Power of Caring and Daring.* New York: McGraw Hill.

Reed, Sally Gardner. 2001. *Making the Case for Your Library: A How-To-Do-It Manual.* New York: Neal-Schuman.

Walters, Suzanne. 1992. *Marketing: A How-to-Do-It Manual for Librarians.* New York: Neal-Schuman.

Weingand, Darlene E. 1987. *Marketing/Manning Library and Information Services.* Englewood, Colo.: Libraries Unlimited.

Wolfe, Lisa A. 1997. *Library Public Relations, Promotions and Communications.* New York: Neal-Schuman.

Wood, Elizabeth J., and Victoria L. Young. 1988. *Strategic Marketing for Libraries*. New York: Greenwood Press.

Wright, Peter L. 1973. *Analyzing Consumer Judgment Strategies*. Urbana, Ill.: College of Commerce and Business Administration.

9: WORKING WITH COLLEAGUES

"You cannot turn geese into swans, but you can usually make them better geese...but some people may be frustrated swans who have been treated like geese."

IN THIS CHAPTER YOU'LL DISCOVER:

- how to create the right atmosphere
- the importance of motivating colleagues—and yourself
- ways of handling crises
- how to build effective teams
- the intergenerational differences in attitudes to work
- the significance of duty of care
- ways to organize flexible working
- the value of workplace learning and training

CREATE THE RIGHT ATMOSPHERE

At a time when recruiting and retaining staff is difficult, there is an increasing incentive to create a good atmosphere in the workplace. In many countries, demographics indicate that more people are retiring than are entering the labor market. Services in the public sector must face the additional staffing problems of low salaries and work hours that are often unsociable—nights and weekends.

Staff resignations are a major problem, because the quality of service to users must be consistently high regardless of staffing levels. Recruitment and training of new employees entails high costs. There is usually a gap between the time when a person quits and their replacement starts, and during this time the work has to be taken up by other members of the team.

Staffing problems can make organizations unstable. One way to prevent or minimize these problems is creating the right atmosphere. Determining what atmosphere is "right" involves studying what helps to recruit and retain staff.

Some information comes from surveys compiled about the best places to work that are based on questioning staff. These surveys indicate that today, employee satisfaction depends on more than salary increases.

Employees want to work on challenging projects in positive environments. The best organizations are rated highly by their staff on diversity, training, career development, benefits, cutting-edge services and projects, and good staff retention rates. In the information services field, OCLC, the bibliographic utility, was on *Computerworld*'s list of "Best Places to Work in IT U.S." in 2002, with a ranking of 36 out of 100 (www.computerworld.com /bestplaces2002).

Another important management factor is trust. Managers create a good atmosphere when they demonstrate that they have trust in their staff.

Focus on Trust

Building a climate of trust requires a foundation of well-developed interpersonal skills that demonstrates:

- excellent listening skills;
- the ability to withhold judgmental comments;
- expression of a sincere concern for individuals; and
- a display of empathy.

This creates a bond between the manager and their colleagues by encouraging the sharing of concerns, problems, aspirations, and information.

Building trust extends beyond the immediate work team. Trust must exist between managers and their superiors, other managers, and service staff within the organization. A lack of trust is one of the most significant wasters of time and resources, so gaining and holding trust is a critical success factor for managers.

One way to achieve trust is to delegate tasks. On a purely practical level, managers cannot do everything themselves without having a breakdown. Delegating tasks indicates trust in and regard for the abilities of staff members. A manager checking everything the staff does is the quickest way to demoralize the team, as well as a major drain on the manager's time and effort.

Delegation

THINKING AHEAD

Effective delegation involves:

- anticipating tasks and responsibilities that can be delegated—not leaving them to the last minute
- considering what the tasks consist of—it is usually better to delegate tasks requiring the gathering of information and evidence, rather than those with a people or political content—and avoiding the confidential and contentious
- determining what needs to be accomplished and who might be the best person to do it—not always selecting the same person

- delegating a little more than you are comfortable with—without overwhelming the person taking on the task
- working through the implications and making time available for the task to be accomplished

BRIEFING

For the person taking on the task, a careful and thorough briefing is vital.

- Allow sufficient time away from the person's workplace, preferably in your office.
- Ensure that they have the necessary skills, or can easily acquire them.
- Provide sufficient information, especially if they are new to the task.
- Don't overload them.
- Encourage them to come up with new ideas and approaches.
- Discuss and set down the objectives, agreed targets, timeline and deadlines, resources required, and expected outcomes.
- Make sure they understand what is required.
- Set down the expected outcomes in writing and exchange copies—this protects both the person undertaking the task and the manager.

INFORMING

Provide appropriate information to:

- the person who has a delegated task—so people they may need to contact will be informed
- those in the immediate work team—who may be approached for information and evidence
- other members of the team—who will need to know what information the person is gathering, and how the work will be covered
- your boss—so they know how the project is organized and how it is progressing
- other departmental managers—who may need to be consulted

FOLLOWING THROUGH

Seeing the task to completion requires that you:

- Delegate authority for the agreed task to the person to whom the task is delegated.
- Ensure the agreed resources are available when they are required—remember that the time to work on the task is also a resource.

- Monitor progress informally—don't make the person feel you are watching over them, let them know they should feel free to consult you.
- Review the outcomes after the person completes the task.
- Acknowledge their achievement to others—if a problem emerges, discuss it with the person concerned and use it as a learning situation.
- Be sure the delegation and successful outcomes are featured in the next performance appraisal.

MOTIVATING COLLEAGUES AND YOURSELF

Everyone needs to be motivated. This is especially true at times of rapid change. Managers at every level must create the right environment and motivation to ensure their staff can work as an efficient and effective team.

Managers have to understand what makes their colleagues tick, and this can take a little time. Managers do not have to be psychoanalysts; a study of personality types can help indicate what motivates individuals. You can also help understand yourself and your own temperament by taking Keirsey's test—are you an idealist, a guardian, a rationalist or an artisan?

RECALL

In chapter 2 it was suggested that you take the Keirsey test. If you have not yet done so, go to www.keirsey.com now.

FOR FURTHER THOUGHT

What is your personality type? What motivates you?

Now think about your team members and try and assess their personality types. How can you best motivate each member of the team?

Review your understanding of the theory about motivation. Much of the literature is based on the theories derived from the Hawthorne studies and the writings of Maslow (1954), Herzberg (1959), and Skinner (1953).

REMEMBER

We referred earlier to the Hawthorne studies and the finding that taking interest in the workers improved their performance. To put it more formally in management-speak, "worker self-esteem affects worker performance."

Today is practiced when managers leave their office and walk around the workplace to talk with staff and see what is happening.

Herzberg examined motivation in the late 1950s and, building on Maslow's hierarchy of needs, developed a two-factor theory that distinguished between *hygiene factors* and *motivation factors*. He found that managers need to provide the hygiene factors to remove sources of dissatisfaction, but once this has been settled, staff are only motivated by motivation factors (Herzberg, 1959).

The hygiene factors consist of:

- organizational policies and procedures—the rules, privileges, and grievance procedures
- supervision—methods to ensure that the tasks are performed well
- salary and benefits—pension plan, health insurance, vacation time, and study leave
- interpersonal relations—staff relationships with colleagues and bosses, and opportunities to mix at tea and coffee breaks
- working conditions—heating, air conditioning, ventilation, lighting, cleanliness, freedom from building hazards, privacy of workstations
- status and privileges related to the position held

The first five of these factors are the most important.

The motivation factors are:

- achievement—a feeling of accomplishment
- recognition of achievement by colleagues and managers
- the work itself—its degree of challenge and satisfaction
- responsibility—for the work allocated, especially increased responsibility
- advancement—opportunities for promotion
- access to information—about the job and the organization— being "in the know" or "in the loop"
- involvement–participation in decision-making

Again, the first five appear to be the most important. However, not everyone is motivated by the same factors, and people may be motivated by different factors at different stages in their career. For example, study or family leave time may be important at an early stage in a career, while a person close to retirement may be more interested in a salary rise to boost their pension or a reduction in working hours to avoid a sudden change in lifestyle.

Two theories help to explain why people behave the way they do—they are *Expectancy Theory* and *Reinforcement Theory* (Vroom, 1964; Skinner, 1953).

Expectancy Theory indicates that managers should:

- get to know what rewards are valued by employees, and provide them if possible
- link the rewards to specific behavior or tasks
- let staff know what is expected of them, and what the outcome will be when expectations are met

- ensure that staff are capable of performing the tasks that are required of them
- work to increase the skills and knowledge of staff so that their competencies can be extended

An appraisal system provides information about the capability of individual staff members and whether rewards are appropriate. However, the question of rewards can be sensitive, and monetary awards are expensive. However, a less tangible award, such as public recognition, can be highly prized.

Appraisal interviews provide a way for staff to raise issues that relate to motivation. It is often easier for staff to raise matters during an appraisal interview than to make a request at another time, and knowing when an appraisal is scheduled helps them plan ahead.

Reinforcement Theory, developed by Skinner, indicates that managers should recognize the reasons for good or poor performance. When performance quality is the result of an employee's behavior, rather than the work environment, the behavior needs to be reinforced. Performance that is desirable should be rewarded, or "positively reinforced." If performance is less than expected, it should be punished, or "negatively reinforced."

To be effective, the reinforcement should be provided as close as possible to the time that the behavior occurred. Don't wait for an appraisal interview; talk to and counsel the employee, and be specific so that they know what behaviors are performing well and what is not acceptable.

In writing about motivation, Levant (1998) identified 5 key steps to ensure desired performance.

- Define the expectations
- Make the work valuable to the organization
- Make the work achievable
- Give regular feedback
- Reward employees when they meet expectations (Levant, 1998: 261-262)

When times are difficult and monetary rewards are limited, remember that, above all, people want to be recognized and valued.

Recognition and Rewards

Many recognition programs operate across the organization. They may be of the "employee of the month" type, based on overall performance, or may focus on specific areas such as diversity, user service, and public service. But be aware that some people crave recognition, while others prefer to remain unidentified. A public award may motivate many people, but others might find it a source of self-consciousness or embarrassment.

Two different views of recognition and rewards programs

Musser, Linda. 2001. "What We Say and What We Reward: Valuing Employees Through Recognition Programs." *Library Administration and Management* 15 (2): 85-90. This article describes the recognition and reward programs in place at Penn State University.

Another article to consider is:

Lubans, John Jr. 1999a. "'She's Just Too Good to Be True, But She Is': Recognition Ceremonies and Other Motivational Rituals." *Library Administration and Management* 13 (4): 213-215.

Lubans (1999a) takes a critical look of recognition ceremonies and "other motivational rituals" and provides sound advice.

Be sure to clearly communicate:

- the purpose of the award
- the criteria for selection
- the nomination process
- the reason the team receiving the award was selected

For the recognition program, ensure that there is:

- frequent turnover on the recognition committee
- an assessment of the program from time to time
- a moratorium on an award when it begins to tire

These viewpoints are confirmed by experience of recognition programs—but there is another piece of advice:

- Think twice before naming the award in honor of someone (unless there is a large donation attached).

Appraising Team Members and Being Appraised

Appraisal is another way for staff to gain recognition. This is a major responsibility, and a new appraiser may find the process as worrying as the person being appraised does. Often an employee views the process in a negative way, a judgment about their performance. To some extent it is, but the results are not necessarily negative. People need to know what their bosses think of their work, in both quantitative and qualitative terms. We all need security.

DIG DEEPER

Managers are appraised and feel nervous too. Advice on how to recognize fears, counter them with adaptive techniques, and prepare for a review is provided by:

Jackman, Jay M., and Myra H. Strober. 2003. "Fear of Feedback." *Harvard Business Review* 81 (4): 101-107.

Appraisal must be seen as a developmental process, and, moreover, a two-way process. Find out if your organization has a standard process that must be followed, with the outcomes reported up the hierarchy.

The person being appraised should prepare for the interview in a way that will help them gain useful information from the feedback. They should reflect on and note down what they have achieved since their last review, consider their goals and development needs, and determine any areas of concern. Often appraisal interviews are opportunities for employees to call attention to service policies or practices that are in need of revision. This serves as a health check for the unit, and staff should be encouraged to view it in this light.

At the interview, the person being appraised draws upon the notes they have prepared. They are invited to give their view of what has taken place since the last interview, and what might have been difficult to achieve. This enables the setting of goals and plans that can be achieved within the allotted time span. The appraisal should be a focused discussion—a general gripe session will not help anyone. With careful handling, the appraisal will result in an honest self-assessment.

The manager should prepare a record of the meeting and share it with the person being appraised so that they can provide comments and check for accuracy and completeness. When the report is mutually agreed upon, both parties sign it. Copies may be sent to the appraiser's manager and to the personnel or human resource management office.

The report is reviewed after a period of six or twelve months, depending on local practice. If the report was unsatisfactory, the interview may be repeated after a shorter period—one or three months.

A more sophisticated approach is the use of 360-degree appraisal. This technique requires team members to appraise their team leader, in addition to the team leader appraising individual members of the team. This method is usually accomplished by using anonymous questionnaires. The team leader then discusses the outcomes with the manager. In turn, the team leader's manager is appraised by the team leader. In some organizations the appraisal cycle extends to other people with whom the individual has work contact, such as users, vendors, and colleagues from other departments. This approach requires a high degree of trust between everyone involved in the gathering of information. Some staff members may be reluctant to criticize their bosses, while bosses can find it hard to take critical comments in the spirit in which they are offered.

The essential point is that appraisal is a developmental process. It requires that both parties listen carefully to what is being said and remember that it is as much about functioning of the service and its parent organization as about the individual. Lubans (1999b) provides sound practical advice on how to make the process work and describes the tools that have provided positive results at Duke University.

TIPS

Listening skills are very important—both on the part of the person being appraised, and the person doing the appraising.

Often the appraiser doesn't give the person being appraised time to speak, and the person being appraised is so anxious that they don't really hear the words of the appraiser.

The appraisal requires a quiet room, no interruptions, and a specified time for the interview.

Reports should be quickly prepared and agreed upon.

Good preparation by both parties must take place before the next interview

---

Negotiating with the Team

The middle management role requires the manager to spend an increasing proportion of their working day on negotiation. For example, after conducting an appraisal, the manager may need to negotiate a change in an employee's behavior. A less stressful example is negotiating with staff members over how to cover service hours when someone is absent. Generally, a manager's most crucial negotiations involve the responsibilities and expectations of employees; after that come concerns about vacation time and work hours.

In chapter 4, negotiation skills were covered in greater detail. However, this chapter will provide five additional points about negotiation that can be specifically applied to working with teams.

1. Know yourself.

- Understand your temperament and how it will affect your negotiating abilities. Some people can handle tension better than others; don't try to fool yourself about your capabilities. If conflict makes you very uncomfortable, teach yourself how to handle it—through reading or, better still, counseling or training. You must also consider your experience of negotiation—in general and with team members—and what resources or benefits you feel you can offer to the other party.

2. Consider possible outcomes and options:

- Do your homework—think of the various ways that you could reach an agreed settlement and consider the impact of each.

3. Know the person with whom you will be negotiating:

- If you do not know the person well, try to assess their temperament, their negotiating experience—with yourself, if possible, and with other staff members—and what resources or benefits they can offer.

4. Determine your strategy and decide where you are willing to compromise.

- The goal is a win-win situation, which may require one or both parties to sacrifice some objectives. You must not get caught up in a win-at-all-costs mentality, refusing to reach an agreement if it does not meet all your terms. Sometimes it is better to take a small loss for the sake of a long-term gain. This judgment comes with experience of the situation and person.

5. Review each negotiation to build up your experience:

- What did I do well? What could be improved? What did I learn about the other party? What did the negotiation achieve?

Negotiations do not always run smoothly; people who usually work harmoniously can suddenly become opponents, and possibly even aggressive. When the negotiation is completed, make sure there is harmony again—have a coffee together and talk about something else. This is where company social events pay dividends—talking to a person about their interests outside work can make them feel at ease. Make sure neither of you is a loser.

HANDLING CRISES

Chapter 6 reviewed crisis control and disaster preparedness. But what happens when the crisis hits? You have the plan, but how do you implement it?

Crises come in all shapes and sizes: systems failures, natural disasters such as earthquakes and floods, problems of morale if funding takes a dive... The middle manager is often one of the first people involved. Knowing what action to take provides the manager—and the team—with confidence and enables people to work to overcome the problem.

The golden rules are:

- Define the problem—for example, it might not be immediately obvious why the power has failed.
- Take appropriate action, following the disaster preparedness plan.
- Stay calm.
- Prioritize.
- Make sure everyone knows what is happening and keep them informed of developments—spread the word through a planned communication chain.

Hold an emergency planning session with key members of the team to review the problem and prioritize actions. Be confident but don't domineer, indicate urgency without panic, and maintain a "can-do" approach. Make sure every member of the group understands the situation and how it is to be resolved.

Delegate and indicate the responsibilities involved. Allocate the right tasks to the right people. Knowing the talents and experience of each member of the team will make this easier—identify the "doers," the organizers, the persuaders, and the people who have been through the crisis before. Above all, keep the team positive and motivated.

Consider the effect on public relations. Some crises will attract attention from the media; this requires careful handling. If the organization has a public relations department, pass this responsibility on to them; keep them updated with progress reports and try to give them positive messages to pass out. If you have to handle the media yourself, do so with the utmost care—be positive, but avoid false optimism as well as pessimism.

When the crisis is over, revisit the emergency planning procedures with the team. Discuss what can be learned from the experience, what changes you think should be made, and pass on any recommendations to your boss.

Hold a celebration to release some of the tension that has accumulated and to show how much you appreciate everyone's work.

Disasters can be an emotional experience for everyone involved. Staff members who appear cool on the surface and function well during the crisis may suffer a reaction after it is over. Situations that can lead to emotional disturbance include accidents to colleagues, threat of personal danger, and damage or destruction of the workplace by fire, flood or earthquake.

> TIP
>
> **It may take time to recover**
>
> Some time ago a fire destroyed a large children's library in a major U.K. city. The manager of the service mentioned the event when presenting a conference paper that described the work of the service in general. Suddenly unexpected emotion was evident. The paper was set aside and a vivid picture was painted of the impact upon staff and users. And Brits are assumed to have "A stiff upper lip."

Crises are not always due to physical or external factors. They can also emerge if the service comes under great pressure—a sudden increase in workload without additional resources, the introduction of new software that fails to perform well, the hiring of new colleague who turns out to be disruptive. Even events outside the workplace can have an effect—a colleague experiencing stress in their personal life can bring their negative emotions into the office.

Some crises are the result of employee failure. If the mistake was yours, own up to it; but if it was an error by a member of the team, it is a time to be generous.

Another type of crisis that everyone faces from time to time is when relationships start to break down. Handling this crisis effectively starts with listening; make sure you recall the basics.

- Listen—don't talk. You can't hear what people are saying if you are talking. If you think of something while the other person is talking, don't interrupt; marshal your thoughts and wait till they are finished.
- Provide feedback to show that you are listening and understanding. Nod and say "uh huh" at appropriate points, and make a few notes when others are not talking.
- Be empathetic. Look at the total message—the words, the facial expression, and the body language. What emotions do they reveal?
- Take into account the effects of culture. There can be problems if the speaker or the listener does not receive the signals they expect.
- Try to identify the *real* problem, which may not be the one being presented. People generally prefer not to talk about personal problems, and try to assign the issues a work-related cause.
- Avoid giving feedback, negative or positive, until the person has finished. This is not easy—be sure to monitor your facial expressions and body language as well as your verbal responses.

- Ask questions to clarify and develop points. This indicates your involvement and interest in the communication process.
- Be patient and allow the other person to make their point. If you find yourself running late for another appointment, send a deputy or a message to explain that you are not available. If it is critical that you keep the appointment, make this clear to the speaker, and fix the earliest possible time to meet with them again.
- Indicate that you have to withdraw from the listening role with nonjudgmental signals, such as closing a file or putting a cap on a pen. Try not to keep glancing at a watch or clock—the speaker may think you do not believe they are worth your time.

Mini-Crises

Mini-crises do not involve the organization as a whole, and may not even affect the entire department or unit. They occur when an employee steps out of line—for example, being sharp with a user, publicly arguing with a colleague, or failing to follow guidelines. A manager cannot ignore these problems; on the other hand, it is important not to judge the person too harshly. Remember that everyone makes mistakes; the person may be under stress that is not obvious to colleagues, or may not have understood the impact of the behavior. Few people go out of their way to present problems.

The goal in handling a mini-crisis is to defuse the situation, help the person understand the implications of their action and how they can avoid it in the future, and let them retain a sense of being valued. Following the steps below should help you achieve that goal.

- Gather the facts or information discretely.
- Talk to the person face-to-face if possible; if they work a different shift, contact them by phone during their working time. Get their view of what happened and say you'll fix a time to talk further—this will give them time gather their thoughts.
- Identify a time when you will not be distracted and a quiet place to talk is available.
- Ensure the time is convenient to the person you need to talk with.
- Thank them for attending the interview or meeting.
- Choose your words with care—be friendly but make your position clear.
- Identify the causes of the problem.
- Determine if the organization can take action to avoid the problem in the future. For instance, an employee who did not follow guidelines may not have understood them, in which case rewriting the procedures could solve the problem.

- Ask how the staff member would like feedback—in person or in writing. If the employee's behavior was caused by a personal problem, they may prefer to read your response in private, rather than discuss it openly.
- Provide honest feedback. This is essential—being too soft may spare feelings at the moment, but does not help them employee or solve the problem in the long run.
- Remain courteous and professional, even if the employee becomes agitated; handle any anger carefully.
- End the conversation on a positive note.

If the problem persists after this discussion, it may be necessary to take disciplinary action. The organization should have set procedures that take into account the labor union issues and legal implications of employee discipline. Be sure to follow them carefully. Generally both parties will have a representative with them during a formal disciplinary meeting. Choose someone with experience in this area to advise you so that the problem will not keep escalating. Remember, at the middle management level you have the support and backup of your superiors in the organization.

BUILDING AND MANAGING TEAMS

Chapter 4 provided an overview of collaborative and team working conditions. This chapter will focus on different approaches to team building, the roles played by team members, and the ways to manage an effective team.

Teamworking, as an approach to management, emerged from the process of delayering organizations in the 1990s. In the information professions, teamwork vital for services that have hours beyond 9-to-5, involve a range of operations requiring varying levels of expertise, and belong to national or international organizations.

Building an effective team benefits the manager by freeing up some of his or her time; the employees benefit by gaining greater control over their jobs and using their experience to improve services.

Teamworking is a "win-win" situation, improving trust between managers and staff, increasing productivity, and raising morale. Teams can be drawn from individual departments, or involve employees across the organization. When teams work effectively, the organization functions more effectively as well.

A number of management consultants today make the interesting point that a team doesn't work for the manager—rather, the manager works for the team. Other consultants have commented that when a person joins a service, they are investing their talents in the organization.

The manager can take different approaches to team building. If they are perceived as a member of the team, they will be expected to take on the leadership role; if they want the team to function more independently, they may choose a different approach. Whatever the method, the manager must make five vital contributions if the team is to be successful.

1. Orientation—introducing team members to the task and gaining their commitment to work together and bring the project to completion.
2. Preparation—training the team members in group processes and problem solving techniques that will help them function effectively and efficiently.
3. Motivation—advising the team and keeping a discrete watch on progress.
4. Information—providing advice and experience when the team requests it. For a delegated task, the manager should waits until the team makes it report.
5. Recognition—promoting awareness and appreciation of the team output by colleagues in the organization.

When building the team, the manager must select an appropriate team leader. This person should demonstrate flexibility and comfort with authority, because the position involves many responsibilities. A leader must be able to:

- employ a range of communication skills
- recognize and tolerate differences
- ruse the appropriate leadership style in a given situation
- perceive the strengths of each team member and use them in the right place at the right time
- maintain a sense of humor and the ability to smile

Belbin (1993) found that all members of a team have a dual role. The first role is based on their special knowledge in relation to their job. The second, less obvious role arises from their personal characteristics. Through further research in a number of organizations, he identified nine roles that make up the ideal team.

The *coordinator* is the chairperson, delegator, and objective-setter—they may not be the leader in the group, but it is team leadership for which they are best suited. Their traits are stability, dominance, and extroversion. They often possess a high degree of charisma or authority. They focus on recognizing individual skills and using the team's combined resources as effectively as possible.

The *shaper* is the motivator and change agent; while the coordinator is the social leader, the shaper is the task leader. Their traits are anxiety, dominance, and extroversion. Full of nervous energy, they are emotional, impulsive, and impatient; easily frustrated; quick to challenge or respond to a challenge. They often have disagreements, but do not bear grudges, and are easily hurt. They want action, and want it now—their goal is to make things happen.

The *plant* scatters the seeds that the other team members bring to fruition. The plant is the idea person and the problem solver, the source of original ideas and suggestions for the team. Their traits are dominance, intelligence, and introversion. They may not like criticism and often go off onto tangents.

The *monitor-evaluator* examines the ideas of others and identifies and judges options. Their traits are intelligence, stability, and introversion. In temperament, they are serious; they are not very exciting, but can contribute measured and dispassionate analysis.

The *resource investigator* is an enthusiastic communicator who is excellent at exploring opportunities, since they have many contacts both inside and outside the service. Their traits are stability, dominance, and extroversion. They are often the most likable member of the team because of their relaxed and gregarious nature and their interest in other people.

The *teamworker* is the most sensitive member of the team. Their traits are stability, low dominance, and extroversion. They know the most about their colleagues in the team and are good internal communicators because they are likable, popular and unassertive. They avoid confrontation and counterbalance friction—valuable skills when the team is under pressure.

The *implementer* is the team member who turns ideas into action. Their traits are reliability, discipline, and efficiency. They tend to be conservative, even inflexible. Their strength is being able to make the project work.

The *completer* is compulsive about meeting deadlines. Their traits are anxiety, perfectionism, and introversion. They constantly worry about what might go wrong, and need to check every little detail to make sure that nothing has been overlooked.

The final member of the ideal team is the *specialist*, who provides the knowledge and skills necessary for the project. They occupy a more narrow role than other team members. Their traits are initiative, determination, and dedication to their specialty.

Tran (1998) drew attention to the importance of understanding the role of emotions in developing and managing organizations. Rosengarten (1995; quoted in Tran, 1998) identifies some of the key ideas associated with this concept:

- team working and team learning
- free vertical and horizontal flow of information
- workforce training
- systems for rewards and recognition
- continuous work improvement
- flexibile organizational strategy
- decentralized hierarchies and participative management
- constant experimentation at work
- a supportive corporate culture

It is worth stressing again that successful team building requires an investment in staff training. Providing a framework in which teams can operate helps them define their responsibilities, develop new skills, gain confidence, and use time efficiently and effectively. If teams are put to work without preparation, they may become frustrated and fail to achieve their goals.

Managers and team leaders can learn how efficiently and effectively the team is working by using performance measures. Hoevemeyer's (1993) team effectiveness survey measures improvement in five areas: team mission, goal achievement, empowerment, open and honest communication, and positive roles and norms. The team leader and members of the team each rate their work on a twenty-item inventory. The team members' answers are averaged and transferred to a scoring sheet, and numbers totaled for each of the five areas. The team leader's scores are first considered separately for comparison, and then transferred to the scoring sheet. A total of 100 points can be achieved if every aspect is perfect, but 95 percent means the team is doing well.

Many organizations now operate with virtual teams; in international organizations, it is a way of life. Some extra measures are required to maximize the effectiveness of the virtual team.

- Provide training for virtual team members.
- Support equal access to technology.
- Humanize virtual meetings with videoconferencing.
- Post photos of the team members on the organization's Intranet.
- Plan meeting times that will be convenient in several time zones.
- Bring the team together face-to-face at least once a year; combine it with a group training activity, and move the meeting location among the sites

In order to carry out their assigned tasks, work teams will need to meet together, record the meetings, plan actions to review their progress, and report the results to their managers.

GUIDELINES FOR TEAM MEETINGS

1. Agree upon a constitution and terms of reference.
2. Set objectives for each meeting.
3. Compile an agenda with items in order of importance, set a time and location, and circulate the information to the people who will attend the meeting.
4. Prepare the necessary materials and send them out in good time, whether on paper or electronically.
5. Start the meeting on time, indicate the expected length, and stick to the schedule.
6. Make sure each person fulfills their expected role. The chairperson reviews progress to date, guides the meeting according to the agenda and the allotted time, encourages participation, ensures there is a resolution for each agenda item, confirms that all participants understand the resolutions and the action required, and nominates a person to perform the action. The secretary keeps an accurate record of the meeting, including the items considered, the decisions made, and the person nominated for each action. Participants listen, contribute when appropriate, and report on the actions determined by previous meetings.

7. Ask those attending for feedback on how useful the meeting was.
8. Follow up—as soon as possible after the meeting, the chairperson and secretary must confirm the action list and send it to everyone who has been allocated a task, along with a date by which action should be taken.
9. Follow through—make sure the nominated people take action.
10. Prepare formal minutes and circulate them to the group and the responsible manager(s).

Some of the qualities of a team leader were mentioned above. Team leaders also have responsibilities—some are obvious, but others are easily overlooked.

YOUR RESPONSIBILITIES AS TEAM LEADER

- Identify everyone who should be in the team.
- Get to know each team member as an individual; recognize their strengths and weaknesses.
- Think of the benefits the team can provide to the individuals.
- Ensure everyone acquires the skills needed to work in the team.
- Develop and use good listening skills.
- Prepare thoroughly for meetings and discussions with team members.
- Recognize and praise accomplishments.
- Use encouragement, not criticism, when there are difficulties.
- Focus on the problem, not the person.
- Give thanks—and thanks again

Handling Conflict

Every person working in an organization is unique, and the closer they work with colleagues, the greater the potential for differences to arise. Working in a team may often involve dealing with conflict. Conflict can be destructive, but it can be also be harnessed to help the team perform better.

Two types of conflict can emerge in teams. In the first, feelings are so strong that discussion gives way to personal attacks. In the second, useful debate emerges, with criticism directed at the substance of the discussion, rather than individuals. Each can present problems for the team manager, because in both situations the team may divide into "winners" and "losers." In turn, this can prevent the task at hand from moving forward.

Five strategies can be used to handle conflict:

- Avoidance. Only use this for minor issues—don't ignore long-term problems that could explode at a later date.

- Accommodation. This can demonstrate goodwill to the other person, but can also be interpreted as reluctance or fear.
- Confrontation. Think carefully before attempting to force an issue. Are the benefits worth the cost? Will you lose goodwill?
- Compromise. Although decisions can be achieved, they may not be clear-cut—and neither party is likely to be happy with the outcome
- Collaboration. This requires more time and effort, but can overcome hard feelings and lead to a better solution

---

RESOLVING CONFLICTS BETWEEN COLLEAGUES

1 Summarize the situation; don't take sides.
2 Get the facts and confirm the information gathered.
3 Clarify points of view.
4 Get both parties to explain what they want.
5 Use a brainstorming session to generate ideas and identify the best solution.
6 Agree on a solution, how it can be implemented, and how its success can be evaluated.
7 Evaluate the outcomes with both parties after an agreed period of time.

AGE AND STATUS MATTERS

Age Matters

Attitudes toward work and careers undergo major shifts over time. Although every person working on the staff must be approached an individual, some generalizations that can be made about how different generations feel about their jobs. A number of management texts have addressed this issue in recent years.

Managers must be aware of the values held by successive generations and what, at a general level, motivates people in each cohort. Life experiences produce different responses in different members of the team. Understanding where people come from helps to anticipate reactions and attitudes. Chapter 1 reviewed the changes in management and services over the past forty years, which may be observed as the gap between the oldest and the youngest members of the workforce. This age gap represents a considerable difference in experiences and attitudes.

The older employees have experienced considerable changes in the workplace, including the introduction and successful implementation of new technologies. Their careers may have begun when information retrieval was not carried out by the computer, but by punched cards and knitting needles. They have experienced changes in the social, educational, and economic framework of society, and probably anticipate retirement on a safe pension if they work in the public sector. They may harbor a degree of resentment if they believe they might have attained a higher position had circumstances been different; this factor can loom large if retirement is close.

It can be easy to put an older colleague in the "difficult" category, but Hart (2002) has drawn up a "do" and "don't" list that provides good advice.

THE DO LIST

- DO enlist support from your manager, but if your manager is part of the problem, find a mentor.
- DO develop your assertiveness skills so that you can be fair but firm.
- DO set your own limits and standards.
- DO treat the employee as an equal.
- DO get to know them as a person. Meet the employee in an informal setting so that they can learn about you and develop respect.

THE DON'T LIST

- DON'T be authoritative—remember that you are trying to get the employee on your side, not alienate them further.
- DON'T behave as though you are superior. You may be higher up in the hierarchy, but the employee already knows that you have a different status and bigger paycheck. Treat them as a human being instead.
- DON'T act in a more aggressive way than the employee. This is very tempting, but will be hugely counter-productive.

Hart, 2002.

Generations X and Y have had the benefit of being brought up with information technology, and, in many parts of the world, in conditions of greater affluence than the preceding generation. Perhaps because they were raised in smaller families, they require more personal space than members of other generations—they don't like having colleagues and users in their face. They thrive on change and can laugh at times of stress—life is too short to be miserable.

According to Tulgan's study of generational attitudes towards work, the four features of corporate culture that matter most to Xers are:

1. Authority based on credibility—Gen Xers appreciate managers who stay well-informed about employees' work and remain engaged without imposing on the creative process.

2. Valuing employee input—When Xers' ideas, opinions, and work are regularly included in decision-making, Xers are more likely to go out of their way to support goals and implement decisions.
3. Supporting individual stars and champion teams—Xers thrive on the shared purpose and emotional and creative support of work teams driven by individual accomplishment.
4. A little care and feeding—Xers know that companies have to be lean and mean to survive, but a little fat provides insulation, allows the body to absorb critical nutrients, and prevents the burning of efficient muscle tissue under strain. Try to be generous with low cost/high return fringes like refreshments, exercise breaks, dress-down days, and "fun budgets." (Tulgan, 1997)

The Gen Yers are self-confident, optimistic, independent, goal-oriented, blunt, and savvy. Their approach to work may not appear to have the strong loyalties of the older colleagues, and managers may question their work ethic. They do put high priority on their careers, but they are mobile—they will readily shift jobs to ones they really want or take career breaks to explore other interests.

For many Gen Yers, travel is an important goal—the farther, the better. They are less tied down than other generations tend to be; they have a lower marriage rate, and in many countries having a family is not a high priority. In the private sector, salaries have been high, so it has been easy to set funds aside for career breaks. The public and nonprofit sectors have been unable to match the salary levels in the private sector, which causes problems for recruitment.

When seeking work, Gen Yers expect job advertisements to reflect the organizational culture so that they know what they might meet before they accept a position. They are attracted to job advertisements that are "playful" rather than formal, such as those that offer "lots of chocolate." Challenge areas need to be indicated at the interview and the salary needs to reflect the post that is open. The employer must have a commitment to staff development, including travel to conferences. Gen Yers prefer to work in an open-door atmosphere, but respect the privacy of a colleague's work diary. They appreciate a boss who takes time off to meet family commitments and ensures that employees are also given time for family responsibilities. They respect a boss who seeks their opinions, and are more likely to support a decision when they feel they have had some influence on it. They welcome frequent appraisal and feedback—hopefully weekly.

According to Tulgan and Martin (2001), Gen Yers expect their managers to:

1. provide challenging work that really matters
2. balance clearly delegated assignments with freedom and flexibility
3. offer increasing responsibility as a reward for accomplishments

4. spend time getting to know staff members and their capabilities
5. provide ongoing training and learning opportunities
6. establish mentoring relationships
7. create a comfortable, low-stress environment
8. allow some flexibility in scheduling
9. focus on work, but be personable and have a sense of humor
10. balance the roles of "boss" and "team players"
11. treat Yers as colleagues, not as interns or "teenagers"
12. respect Yers, and call forth respect in return
13. provide consistent constructive feedback
14. reward Yers when they've done a good job
    (Tulgan and Martin, 2001)

There are two notes to make about these observations. First, the findings are based on the corporate sector, whereas many information posts are located in the public sector. Often the public sector doesn't have the freedom to grant the rewards commonly found in the corporate sector, but some creative thinking could produce other rewards or benefits. One example might be flexible working hours in services that operate a shift schedule.

The second point is that, regardless of how well a department meets generational expectations, it will not necessarily be able to recruit and retain new staff. This is true of all generations, but is especially challenging in relation to the mobility of Gen X and Gen Y.

While it is dangerous to fit people into categories, keeping generational characteristics in mind can help to explain different attitudes and approaches to each individual's work and their contribution to the team. Managing a team composed of different generations is a challenge. Keep a copy of Tulgan and Martin's fourteen points close at hand.

DIG DEEPER

Intergenerational attitudes to the workplace

Meredith, Geoffrey, Charles D. Schewe, and Alex Hiam, with Janice Karlovich. 2002. *Managing by Defining Moments: America's 7 Generational Cohorts, Their Workplace Values, and Why Managers Should Care.* New York: Hungry Minds.

Zemke, Ron, Claire Raines, and Bob Filipczak. 2000. *Generations at Work: Managing the Clash of Veterans, Boomers, Xers, and Nexters in Your Workplace.* New York: AMACOM.

Status Matters—Working with Volunteers

Volunteers are making an increasing contribution to the operation of publicly funded services. People today are healthier and more active when they reach retirement age. They have a better education than their parents had, and many would like to pass on their experience and skills. Most want to give back something to the community.

Volunteers can be found in many situations in the information sector. Many have found a niche in local history collections and record offices, where they can offer advice to users with genealogical queries or index papers and documents. Retired people who have some computer skills can show other older people how to become "silver surfers" on the Web. Retired information professionals help run information services and special libraries in the voluntary and charitable sectors. They bring enthusiasm, willingness to help, and a scarce resource—time—but the situation must be managed with care and sensitivity.

The points made in the previous section about generational differences should be remembered when working with volunteers. Many volunteers are retired and fall into the veteran category. Some are even older—many people stay active and alert well into their nineties. Younger staff can feel threatened and find it difficult to supervise the work of someone old enough to be a grandparent or even great-grandparent.

When the labor market is tight and salaries are low, paid staff and unions may resent the volunteers who provide free work. There is also the question of where volunteers fit in the legal framework of the organization.

The U.S. has a long history of volunteers working alongside paid staff, and Driggers and Dumas (2002) have provided a toolkit that can be adapted for use in other parts of the world. It contains statements, forms and a host of good advice based on experience. They indicate that volunteers can provide benefits by:

- improving services;
- expanding support for routine tasks and special projects;
- enhancing the level and quality of customer services; and
- providing supplemental expertise.

WORTH CHECKING OUT

Working with volunteers

Driggers, Preston, and Eileen Dumas. 2002. *Managing Library Volunteers: A Practical Toolkit.* Chicago: American Library Association.

Volunteers need to fit into the management framework of the service. A staff member should be nominated to provide a volunteer job description, training, and orientation, ensure communication and feedback, evaluate volunteers' performance, and provide recognition.

Recognize that volunteers have rights and their contribution should be valued. The task(s) allocated should:

- have a job description
- have expectations and duties defined

- be meaningful to the functioning of the service
- contribute to the overall management plan
- be within the capabilities and expertise of the volunteer
- be achievable within a reasonable period of time

Driggers and Dumas stress the need for personal respect for volunteers. A contract should be prepared stating their responsibilities, a release form should be available, and timesheets should be completed. There should be an evaluation of volunteers to recognize their contribution, and, if necessary, counseling should be made available.

Our own experience in volunteering indicates that the volunteers often have to work in a much looser managerial framework, which can be difficult for both the volunteer and the paid staff. In some organizations, volunteers have the title of docent (from "I serve") and have a way to be easily recognized by users, such as a distinctive tie, scarf, polo shirt, or identification tag. This helps to clarify their role with users. With a graying community having special skills and expertise, volunteers are a valuable resource, particularly in the public sector.

DUTY OF CARE

Duty of care is one of the areas in which managers are assuming an increasing legal responsibility. Legal considerations are an important, but difficult, aspect of management, especially because legal requirements are subject to frequent changes. Managers need to have a basic understanding of how the law operates and must keep up with developments by scanning the legal columns of the daily press. But remember that your personnel or human resources office can provide information and advice, which in turn will be backed up by an in-house or consultant lawyer. If you encounter a problem, don't try to solve it on your own. Get a basic understanding of the law, learn the broad principles and some of the jargon—then go out for advice.

Although duty of care can involve legal considerations, there are ways to anticipate and handle problems before they reach this stage. The first sign of a potential problem is stress in a team member. Action should be taken as soon as it is clear that individuals are showing signs of stress. Don't expect people to just "pull themselves together," or wait until there are signs of an imminent breakdown.

Look for two factors that might have induced stress in the person.

1. Is the job particularly intellectually or emotionally demanding for this member of staff? Is the workload unreasonable? Are others doing this job also showing signs of stress? Is there a high level of absenteeism or sickness?
2. Is the team member particularly vulnerable? Have they suffered any stress-related illness in the past? Have they had long periods of absence that might have been caused by stress?

There are a number of ways to help colleagues under stress, directly and indirectly:

- Identify the cause of stress.
- Monitor their rate of absenteeism and when they last took leave.
- Remove the cause of stress when possible.
- Organize a training programs to assist in the recognition and handling of stress.
- Check that support systems, including confidential counseling, are in place and that the colleague is aware of them.
- Ensure that going to a counselor is not seen as a "failure."
- Create an atmosphere in which no stigma is attached to stress.

Stress and Burnout

Staff stress and burnout is a growing concern for managers, particularly with the increasing pressure to balance work and home life. Taking an overview of stress levels in the unit is a sensible precaution. This will partially depend on location. For example, U.S. workers have fewer weeks of annual leave than Europeans. In some countries, people are working longer hours, but not necessarily increasing their output.

Many people feel stress when faced with change. Change is an important factor in information services: users are more demanding in their needs and expect a fast response from staff; as the technological aspects of the work increase, staff need to spend more time updating their knowledge and skills. Whatever the cause of stress, people react in different ways. Some people may be sensitive to noise; others will not notice it. Some enjoy working under pressure and thrive in this environment; others find it very difficult.

Staff members who are stressed may not be working effectively. Work-related causes of stress include:

- poor working conditions—examine ergonomic issues, such as poor lighting, heating, and ventilation, noise, and uncomfortable desks and chairs.
- relationships in the department or team that may be strained
- a person's role in the organization—they may feel that they are at the bottom of the heap
- staff members feeling their career has is stuck in a rut
- team members feeling that they are not in the loop and do not know what is going on
- frequent changes of manager
- staff feeling that the organization that does not appreciate family and person issues
- changes in personnel within the organization, such as moving to a new post
- having to meet constantly changing targets for achievement and accountability

Burnout can result from:

- emotional exhaustion
- physical exhaustion, particularly if the person has a caregiver role in their family
- a sense of a lack of achievement and trying hard to compensate
- a sense of being isolated from colleagues and not sharing problems
- working more than one job if money is short
- working and carrying a heavy study load

Some aspects of the user-staff contact in an information setting can create stress; this can happen if:

- user contact is direct and staff have insufficient breaks
- user needs must be on a tight deadline and with high standards of quality
- satisfaction of user needs must also be cost-efficient
- staff must balance different forms of user contact—in person, on the telephone, and through e-mail.
- technology is frequently upgraded and may be unreliable

Another factor that can add to the stress in the information sector is shift working. Increasingly, shifts operate over seven days a week and start earlier and finish later in the working day. Working shifts can disturb sleep patterns and make it difficult to relax.

Warr (1987) has examined work characteristics and their impact on mental health, and has identified nine principal factors.

1. Opportunity for control: Low levels of personal control in a job are psychologically harmful; greater control is associated with better mental health.
2. Opportunity for skill use: The opportunity to use or extend skills is important for mental health.
3. Goals and task demands: Low demands give low opportunity for control and skills use. High levels of demand can cause job-related anxiety and exhaustion.
4. Variety: Repetitive work can be tedious and cause low job satisfaction
5. Environmental clarity: People need to understand their environment and predict what will happen to them. Lacking such clarity is detrimental to mental health.
6. Availability of money: Standard of living is an important factor in mental health
7. Physical security: Poor working conditions can lead to deterioration in physical health, which is often accompanied by a deterioration in mental health.
8. Opportunity for interpersonal contact: Friendship opportunities promote mental health. People undertaking repetitive

tasks that are deprived of opportunities for socializing and daydreaming are more likely to have a mental breakdown.

9. Valued social position: A person who sees social value in their work is likely to have mental health.

FOR FURTHER THOUGHT

Warr's nine factors in relation to the posts in your team

Take each factor in turn and consider its relationship to each position description.

Do you need to take action to improve the mental health factors of the positions?

What should the action be?

Resolving a problem that gets out of hand can be time-consuming and expensive, especially if it involves litigation.

The following factors are key points in legislation for stress-related claims:

- For an action to succeed, the "signs of stress in a worker must be plain enough for any reasonable employer to realize something must be done." If stress is not obvious, employees should warn employers of the problem.
- The onus is on the worker to decide whether to leave the job or to continue working and accept the risks. Employers may usually assume that the employee can withstand normal job pressures unless they are aware of a particular problem.
- An employer will not be in breach of his or her duty of care in letting a willing employee continue in a stressful job if the alternative is dismissal or demotion. The employer is in breach of duty of care only if he fails to take reasonable steps to identify and justify the risks, potential consequences, and the costs of prevention.
- Generally, no occupations are regarded as intrinsically dangerous to employees' mental health.
- Employers who offer confidential counseling services with access to treatment are unlikely to be found in breach of duty of care.

Most countries have introduced legislation covering workers' rights, and the number continues to rise. Details differ between countries, but the legislation usually covers several major situations.

Health and Safety at Work legislation requires managers to assess the risk involved in particular jobs. For example, injury can result from working at a computer terminal without adequate breaks, sitting at desks not designed for the job, working in close proximity to a photocopier, and lifting heavy weights.

Sexual and racial discrimination are among the grievances for which staff may seek redress. When matters deteriorate to the point of legal intervention, resolution requires a considerable amount of time and money—the organization will incur legal fees and may have to pay damages if the employee's suit is successful. There is also the cost of bad publicity and bad feelings among the colleagues of the aggrieved employee.

Cases of bullying have received wider attention in recent years, and more employees have entered into dispute with their employer. Bureaucratic styles of management, particularly in the public sector where there may be low pay and low morale, can sometimes be interpreted as bullying. A surge of new legislation on staffing matters may overwhelm the human resources manager and cause them to feel considerable pressure. A situation can develop slowly over a period of time…and then explode.

WORTH CHECKING OUT

Bullying

Douglas, Elaine. 2001. *Bullying in the Workplace.* Burlington, Vt.: Gower.

Restructuring—A Major Cause of Stress

In the private sector, there is a growing understanding of ways to handle restructuring—which in many cases means laying off staff. Experience of dismissals in the information and public sectors are limited, but does exist.

Middle managers should not have total responsibility for handling the process. It should lie in the province of the human resources or personnel office. However, middle managers can find themselves picking up the pieces and handling what can be a very unpleasant situation.

It is rare for a whole department to be cut. More often, restructuring involves staff cutbacks or reassignments to other positions. Even staff members who retain their posts will feel insecurity. To say restructuring produces turmoil in the workplace is an understatement.

Ideally, the organization will have a plan that considers each person who is likely to be laid off or reassigned, and strategies help them through the trauma.

In some circumstances, people may welcome the prospect of change. A person near retirement provided a suitable financial inducement could view a layoff as opportunity to spend time traveling or pursuing a hobby. A person who wants new challenges in their job may happily accept a reassignment.

But for other people, there is a period of transition to manage. Anyone being laid off needs information—both legal and financial—and counseling to help them come to terms with the situation. People being reassigned must be able to identify their training needs and have access to a program to help them acquire new skills. Both groups require monitoring of their progress. The middle manager can play a vital role at this stage.

The people retaining their positions they may feel angry or aggrieved and might lose trust in their immediate manager. They need to direct their feelings at someone, and it will be the person in authority who is nearest to them. Since action doesn't happen overnight, the middle manager can experience a great deal of hostility and stress, and it is painful. The middle manager needs to have:

- warning that decisions have been taken by senior management
- information about who is affected and why
- indication of what each person will be told, when, by whom, and how
- details of the support to be made available to them
- strong support from senior management

Senior management should meet with all members of the team at the workplace to inform them about the decision, why it has been taken, and how it will affect the team, and to answer broad-based questions

Restructuring involving layoffs is a difficult situation that is complicated by the need to preserve confidentiality and act sensitively. In the writer's experience, it is one of the most emotional issues to handle, particularly if senior management does not provide the support outlined above. If this support does not appear to be forthcoming, speak to your boss immediately and insist on getting the necessary information and advice. You shouldn't have to take all the responsibility for the decision and the criticism that will certainly follow.

FLEXIBLE WORKING

A flexible approach to working can help to reduce stress, and a view of the office of the future indicates how this may be achieved. According to Cooper and Jackson (1997), it is predicted that most organizations will have only a small core of full-time, permanent employees working from a conventional office. Most of the skills they need will be purchased from people telecommuting or hired on short-term contracts to do specific tasks. This will give organizations the flexibility required to cope with a rapidly changing world. While these predictions were made with the corporate sector and organizations in general in mind, the comments are also relevant to the public sector and to information services.

> FOR FURTHER THOUGHT
>
> Think about the nature of the service you are working in and identify tasks that do not necessarily have to be carried out on the premises if staff are equipped with appropriate technology.

Research indicates that managers and staff perform better in a flexible environment, as they have more control over their lifestyles (Holton and

Wilson, 2002). In the information sector, shift working has attracted some recruits. Where shifts operate, job sharing is easier to organize.

Flexibility can also help to lessen concerns about the balance between work and personal life. It can enable individuals to achieve more control over their lives. This is an issue of concern, since in many countries there is a falling birthrate and a need to create conditions where both partners in a relationship can work and raise a family. Maternity and paternity leave encourage parenting. Legislation enables employees to ask their employers to introduce flexible working arrangements.

Flexibility can take several forms:

- outsourcing work
- creating short-term contracts, rather than tenured or "permanent" posts
- job sharing
- flexible working locations and opportunities for telecommuting
- help for staff who want to take a sabbatical or unpaid leave to travel or pursue a special interest—at any stage in their working lives

---

FOR FURTHER THOUGHT

Anyone can feel that they are in a rut from time to time. They become bored and may loose interest in the job. Sometimes they recover quickly, but other times they get the itch to travel or do something else for a while. Resignation from the post may not be feasible, but a period of unpaid leave could be possible. This can result in benefits for the organization—the person returns feeling refreshed and is able to work better, or decides they really should resign. During their absence, the service can temporarily promote another staff member. It can be a great opportunity for the person in the temporary post and for the manager—both can see whether they are ready to move up the ladder.

Outsourcing is already practiced, and many services depend on it for such work as IT support, document supply, conservation, and digitization. Repetitive jobs that do not require user contact could be considered for outsourcing as a way to remove the jobs that provide lower levels of job satisfaction. It can also be a way to acquire the skills of specialists who are only needed for short periods of time, such as publicists, staff trainers and IT consultants. As the 24/7 service becomes the norm, outsourcing work to an external supplier can be essential.

Short-term contracts have been used in many information services as budgets have fluctuated, where funding is made available by grant or for special projects, and when organizational policies change.

Job sharing is an attractive option for people who also have a caring role, such as looking after young children or an elderly relative. They still have face-to-face contact with work colleagues, and many find this is a way to balance work and life while staying on the career ladder. Four factors are important in job sharing:

- those sharing the post must have a good rapport
- there must be a period of overlap in their work hours for adequate handoff and meticulous recording of events for the other person to work on
- the sharers must know that they can apply for benefits similar to those of other staff members
- the organization must accept that small additional costs will be incurred for the extra hours worked to cover the position

The writer set up a job share while working for the Equal Opportunities Commission in the U.K. at the request of a deputy librarian who was developing a career as a songwriter. It had been anticipated that applications for the other half of the job share would come from those with family responsibilities. But this was not so—the successful applicant was building up a new career as a yoga teacher. In this case, each person shared the week for just over 2.5 days with two hours of handoff.

With advances in technology making it easier to communicate with colleagues and users, telecommuting becomes possible for certain posts in the information environment. Telecommuting may not be the answer to caring for another person in the home while trying to work, because distractions will occur. Working in isolation removes the employee from office news and gossip—and politics. E-mail does not always substitute for informal communication. But for work that requires great concentration, telecommuting can be ideal, and in an age of call centers it may be that the answering of some types of enquiry can be effectively handled by telecommuters.

The most recent form of flexible working to be introduced in the workplace is the sabbatical or unpaid leave. From the younger person taking a year off between high school and college, the idea has spread to people established in their careers, but who feel that they want to take time off. People from any age group may want an opportunity to travel, focus on a hobby, learn new skills, or add to their qualifications. The break could last from three months to a year. Anecdotal evidence suggests that the person will gain benefits and return to work feeling invigorated.

Managers can be helpful in organizing a sabbatical or unpaid leave—there is no sense in losing a valuable trained member of staff forever. Someone who has wanted a break but who is refused leave could feel resentful. Organizational policies need to be in place to indicate the maximum and minimum length of a break, the amount of notice to be given, and the way in which benefits will be handled, e.g. if the person can continue to contribute to pension and healthcare benefits. A number of details need to be discussed and agreed upon with the employer. The first interview is probably best handled by the supervisor, who can direct the inquirer to sources of information and consider the likely impact on the department.

There are points about flexible arrangements that have to be discussed between managers and staff:

- how benefits may be retained
- the timing and length of the arrangement
- training and career development
- the impact on promotion and long-term career development

Preparing an agreement benefits both parties. There can be a downside to certain arrangements, but adequate and frank discussion and planning can give choice and control for the hard-pressed member of staff.

FOR FURTHER THOUGHT

Are there any posts in the department in which you are working that could have flexible arrangements?

What would be the options for the arrangement?

What can be done to help those with flexible arrangements work as a member of the team?

What benefits would accrue to the service?

What disadvantages might emerge?

What would be the costs to the individual and to the service?

Would you recommend flexible working?

Managing the Flexible Workplace

Staff working in the flexible workplace need to feel that they are functioning as a member of a team. As services move toward extended hours of access, it will be more difficult to get everyone together at the same time and place to meet and talk.

Yet those working flexibly shouldn't be left out of discussion, planning, and decision-making, which can make them feel like second-class citizens. One way to overcome this is to use simple technology such as an Intranet, e-mail message, or specialist software such as Lotus Notes or Quickplace. This is a simpler and cheaper alternative to videoconferencing. Sharing discussion, preparing documents, and commenting on plans can all be done offline to everyone's advantage.

There will be the need for everyone to get together from time to time, but the number of meetings and time spent can be minimized.

Managing a flexible workplace must ensure that the arrangement does not disadvantage employees who are not working in a flexible mode. Members of the team who are not in a caring role can be placed in a very difficult position if they feel that the caregivers get all of the advantages in selecting periods of leave or time off duty. For most people, it is natural to want to help parents to have vacation dates that coincide with school holidays, or to be able to pick up children from daycare. However, this may place demands on those who do not have children, and this must be recognized by the manager and every member of the team. Acknowledgement of the situation and a solicitation of preferred leave dates and shift patterns will often solve problems before they arise.

The question of providing a seamless service to users can normally be taken care of in the shift patterns drawn up to cover extended opening hours. However, special care should be taken by the employee working flexibly to ensure that a colleague takes on unfinished tasks, and the manager make sure this happens. We have all become frustrated by phoning with inquiries to an office where "the person handling your enquiry isn't here at present."

SUCCESS FACTORS FOR WORKING FLEXIBLY—WHAT TEAM MEMBERS NEED

- a clear understanding of the objectives of their team
- a definition of their role within the team
- a high degree of trust and autonomy by their manager
- some face-to-face contact to minimize isolation
- a statement about their career development
- regular appraisal
- ability to attend professional meetings and conferences
- effective technology support

WORKPLACE LEARNING AND TRAINING

Managerial responsibilities include staff development for all members of the team. Everyone benefits from education and training programs that assist personal and workplace development.

A supervisor or colleague can provide training in the workplace. Such training is of growing importance and has been practiced over time. However, it has not always received the recognition it deserves. Once called "sitting with Nelly," it is now called "workplace learning." This approach to learning produces a better outcome in many situations. It can relate more closely to local practices. Benefit can be gained by the person providing the learning experience, because they have to critically examine the way they do their job and be able to explain the process to another person. It also forces them to recognize their skills and abilities and can provide job satisfaction.

Short courses can be provided on-site by a trainer. These can be cost-effective for a group of staff members and also reinforce learning through later review and the sharing of experiences. The trainer comes in to cover topics that can benefit from an external viewpoint, such as diversity training and the development of interpersonal skills. The participants share the learning experience after the event. Courses offered across an organization can contribute to networking.

Short courses taken off-site have benefits, but some disadvantages. The benefits include separation from routine work and a lack of distraction from daily events. People feel "recognized" and valued. They will meet people doing similar jobs and can network and exchange experiences. The disadvantage may be that of cost, including the time taken from the job, travel, and accommodations and living expenses.

Formal educational programs may be appropriate if there is a need to upgrade qualifications. Increasingly, academic courses are offered in the distance learning mode and are Web-based. This may enable more people to participate. Paraprofessional staff in Australia and the U.K. has the opportunity to upgrade to a graduate level and hence achieve full professional status.

There is also coaching. Either the manager or a coach works with an individual in a one-on-one situation, developing a program that meets the needs of the individual. This is an expensive alternative, but may be considered in certain cases.

The final words in this chapter come from Bennis, and say it all.

"Stop trying to 'herd cats' and start building trust and mutual respect. Your 'cats' will respond. They will sense your purpose, keep your business purring, and even kill your rats."

Bennis, Warren. 1998. *Managing People Is Like Herding Cats.* London: Kogan Page.

AFTER READING THIS CHAPTER YOU SHOULD BE AWARE

- how to create the right atmosphere
- how to motivate the team
- how to handle crises
- how to build an effective team
- how to understand why age and status matters
- of your responsibilities for duty of care
- how to examine the options for, and organize, flexible working
- different approaches to workplace learning and training

REFERENCES

Belbin, Meredith. 1993. *Team Roles at Work*. London: Butterworth-Heinemann.

"The Best Places to Work in IT U.S." 2002. *Computerworld*. Available: www.computerworld.com/bestplaces2002.

Cooper, Cary, and Susan Jackson. 1997. *Creating Tomorrow's Organizations: A Handbook for Future Research in Organizational Behavior*. New York: John Wiley.

Douglas, Elaine. 2001. *Bullying in the Workplace*. Burlington, Vt.: Gower.

Driggers, Preston, and Eileen Dumas. 2002. *Managing Library Volunteers: A Practical Toolkit*. Chicago: American Library Association.

Herzberg, Frederick. 1959. *Motivation to Work*. 2d ed. New York: Wiley.

Hart, Justina. 2002. "Mind the Gap." *Professional Manager* 11 (6): 22-24.

Holton, Vicki, and Andrew Wilson. 2002. *Work/Life Balance: The Role of the Manager*. Berkhamstead: Roffey Park Institute, Ashridge Management College.

Hoevemeyer, Victoria A. 1993. "How Effective Is Your Team?" *Training and Development* 47 (9): 67-71.

Jackman, Jay M., and Myra H. Strober. 2003. "Fear of Feedback." *Harvard Business Review* 81 (4): 101-107.

Levant, Jessica. 1998. "Motivation." In *Gower Handbook of Management Skills*, edited by Dorothy M. Stewart. 3rd ed. Aldershot: Gower.

Lubans, John Jr. 1999a. "'She's Just Too Good to Be True, But She Is': Recognition Ceremonies and Other Motivational Rituals." *Library Administration and Management* 13 (4): 213-215.

Lubans, John Jr. 1999b. "'I've Closed My Eyes to the Cold Hard Truth I'm Seeing: Making Performance Appraisal Work." *Library Administration and Management* 13 (2): 87-89.

Maslow, Abraham H. 1954. *Motivation and Personality*. New York: Harper.

Meredith, Geoffrey, Charles D. Schewe, and Alex Hiam, with Janice Karlovich. 2002. *Managing by Defining Moments: America's 7 Generational Cohorts, Their Workplace Values, and Why Managers Should Care*. New York: Hungry Minds.

Musser, Linda. 2001. "What We Say and What We Reward: Valuing Employees Through Recognition Programs." *Library Administration and Management* 15 (2): 85-90.

Skinner, Burrhus Frederic. 1953. *Science and Human Behavior*. New York: Macmillan.

Tran, Véronique. 1998. "The Role of the Emotional Climate in Learning Organisations." *The Learning Organization* 5 (2): 99-103.

Tulgan, Bruce. 1997. *The Manager's Pocket Guide to Generation X*. Amherst, Mass.: HRD Press.

Tulgan, Bruce, and Carolyn A. Martin. 2001. *Managing Generation Y, Global Citizens Born in the Late Seventies and Early Eighties*. Amherst, Mass.: HRD Press.

Vroom, Victor H. 1964. *Work and Motivation*. New York: Wiley.

Warr, Peter. 1987. "Job Characteristics and Mental Health." In *Psychology at Work*, edited by Peter Warr. Harmondsworth, England: Penguin.

Zemke, Ron, Claire Raines, and Bob Filipczak. 2000. *Generations at Work: Managing the Clash of Veterans, Boomers, Xers, and Nexters in Your Workplace.* New York: AMACOM.

Launching Pad

Avery, Elizabeth F., Terry Dahlin, and Deborah A. Carver. 2001. *Staff Development: A Practical Guide.* 3rd ed. Chicago: American Library Association.

Bateson, Mark. 1999. "Social Club or Compulsory Experience: Reflections on the Proper Role of Volunteers in Record Offices." *Journal of the Society of Archivists* 20 (1): 75-84.

Bunker, Kerry A., Kathy E. Kram, and Sharon Ting. 2002. "The Young and the Clueless." *Harvard Business Review* 80 (12): 80-87.

Creagh, Mary, and Chris Brewster. 1998. "Identifying Good Practice in Flexible Working." *Employee Relations* 20 (5): 490-503.

Dale, Penny. 2002. "Using Worksheets to Encourage Independent Learning by Staff in an Academic Library: A Case Study." *Library Management* 23 (8/9): 394-402.

Dickinson, Gail K. 2002. "A New Look at Job Satisfaction." *Library Administration and Management* 16 (1): 28-33.

Gerlich, Bella K. 2002. "Rethinking the Contributions of Student Employees to Library Services." *Library Administration and Management* 16 (3): 146-150.

Jex, Steve. M. 1998. *Stress and Job Performance: Theory, Research, and Implications for Managerial Practice.* Thousand Oaks, Calif.: Sage Publications.

Jordan, Peter, and Catherine Lloyd. 2002. *Staff Management in Library and Information Work.* 4th ed. Aldershot, England: Gower.

Lubans, John Jr. 2000. "'I'm So Low, I Can't Get High': The Low Morale Syndrome and What To Do About It." *Library Administration and Management* 14 (4): 218-221.

Lubans, John Jr. 2001. "A Reason for Rain: Hoop Lessons for Library Leaders." *Library Administration and Management* 15 (1), 39-43.

Metz, Ruth F. 2002. *Coaching in the Library: A Management Strategy for Achieving Excellence.* Chicago: American Library Association.

Paterson, Alisdair. 1999. "Ahead of the Game: Developing Academic Library Staff for the Twenty-First Century." *Librarian Career Development* 7 (12): 143-149.

Picot, Anne. 2001. "The Story of the Australian Recordkeeping Competency Standards." *Records Management Journal* 11 (3): 143-153.

Salter, Brian, and Naomi Langford-Wood. 2001. *Successfully Dealing With Difficult People in a Week.* Corby: Institute of Management.

Todaro, Julie. 2000. "How Am *I* Doing?" *Library Administration and Management* 14 (1): 31-34.

Weeks, Holly. 2001. "Taking the Stress Out of Stressful Conversations." *Harvard Business Review* 79 (7): 112-119

Wilder, Stanley J., ed. 1999. *The Age Demographics of Academic Librarians: A Profession Apart.* New York: Haworth Press

10: PREPARING TO MOVE AHEAD

"When good bosses go, they leave behind organizations that can run without them."

IN THIS CHAPTER YOU'LL DISCOVER:

- the need to extend leadership skills
- how to be a mentor and be mentored
- the importance of continuing professional development
- the need to extend managerial skills
- features of career planning in an age of discontinuity
- what to do on leaving a managerial position
- factors that contribute to success

Earlier chapters have focused on role of managers in helping others achieve and operating an efficient and effective service. But now you need to reflect on your personal goals, so this chapter focuses on *your* management development.

If you report to a good senior manager they should have shared some thoughts with you on this matter.

EXTENDING LEADERSHIP SKILLS

By this point, you will have recognized that leadership is an elusive concept. It changes over time, and is easier to recognize than to describe in words. Around the globe, in all professions, there is a concern about how to identify potential leaders and provide the training and development they need to perform successfully.

Training and development for a leadership role is very important; we work at a time when the rewards for success can be very high, but being less than successful is not acceptable.

While managers should also be leaders, leaders need not be managers; even so, leaders should have experience in the managerial role.

Credit Suisse First Boston has been working with TSO Consulting to run leadership development programs to achieve serious culture change. As part of the program, the differences between managers and leaders have been defined. In this context, the difference lies between taking a reactive or a proactive approach.

MANAGERS AND LEADERS: SPOT THE DIFFERENCE

The Manager	The Leader
Is a copy	Is an original
Administers	Innovates
Maintains	Develops
Focuses on systems and structure	Focuses on people
Relies on control	Inspires trust
Has short-range view	Has long-term perspective
Asks how and when	Asks what and why
Has an eye on the bottom line	Has an eye on the horizon
Accepts the status quo	Challenges the status quo
Is the classic good soldier	Is his/her own person
Does things right	Does the right things
Eglin, 2001	

Many books and papers have been written about leadership; Warren Bennis has probably contributed more than any other writer, offering a consistent message that places an emphasis on human relations. Leaders are made, rather than born. Leadership is the exercise of control, manipulation, and direction by those at the top of the organization.

Recall the four abilities that leaders need to develop (Bennis and Nanus, 1985).

- The first is *attention*—creating a compelling vision.
- The second is *meaning*—communicating the vision through the use of analogy, metaphor, and vivid illustrations. In relation to this ability, it is not surprising that writers refer to storytelling as being a powerful means of communication.
- The third is *trust*—the emotional glue that binds followers and leaders together.
- The fourth is the "*deployment of self,*" which moves beyond time management to self-knowledge, persistence, risk-taking, commitment, challenge, and learning from failure.

Chowdhury (2000) brought together a number of management gurus to write about management at the start of a new century. The next breed of leaders are seen as being hard working, never satisfied, curious, and persistent. One paper paints the picture of the Janusian leader who has two faces— one looks back to the past, the other looks to the future and considers how to take the best of the past into the future. Other thoughts from this collection:

credibility is needed for leadership; leadership is everyone's business; challenge is the opportunity for greatness; a leader's focus should be on the future and on being a team player. Caring is at the heart of leadership, along with *believing* you can make a difference. Another important point is the need to see the world in shades of gray, not black and white.

WORTH CHECKING OUT

Thoughts about future approaches to management

Chowdhury, Subir, ed. 2000. *Management 21C: Someday We'll All Manage This Way*. London, Financial Times: Prentice-Hall

---

Experience plays a major part in developing leaders—no one can easily adopt a style that runs counter to their personality type.

Experience also provides clues to working out what makes a "leader" tick in a given situation. What is the organizational culture? What are the organizational goals and mission statement? What is the economic climate? How high does the government place the service on its list of priorities? What drives success in an organization?

Some of these factors emerge in articles that appeared in the *Harvard Business Review* of February 2002. This issue features an interview with Jack Welch, the archetypal U.S. organization man who ruled General Motors for many years, partly through the force of his personality and partly through his dedication to the job. Bennis (2002) discusses the interview, and feels that tomorrow's leaders will not have the monomaniacal passion that was a feature of Welch's style. They will be operating in less certain times and will need to have a broader perspective, be open to new ideas, and have a better balance in their lives. The latter need runs through many surveys of work attitudes carried out since the late '90s.

Sorcher and Brant (2002), writing in the same issue, examine the way that leaders are selected, concluding that what seems to be a good indicator of leadership potential may be the opposite. Team players may be better deputies; those who are good public speakers may be less successful at talking one-on-one; ambition may be a better indicator of ego than of leadership skills. These writers advocate the use of group techniques—an evaluation by those who have worked with the potential candidate over time and in a variety of circumstances. A wide set of criteria can be used. One implication of this approach is that organizations need to give more thought to succession leadership, or employ a longer and more searching process of evaluation for external candidates.

Two other papers in this issue are worth reading. Peter Drucker (2002) argues that organizations need to develop talent and give as much attention to managing contract and temporary workers as they do to "permanent" staff. This can be important in the information sector, where an increasing number of posts are offered on a short-term contract. Contract workers may have less access to training and lack fringe benefits. Bruch and Ghosal (2002) offer a warning: beware the busy manager. In research stretching over ten years, they found that 90 percent of managers squander their time on ineffective activities. Managers and leaders need to have energy and focus.

Kets de Vries (2001) focuses on the impact of "soft" psychological factors on how organizations work and what makes a good or bad leader. He argues for an understanding of the psychological rationale behind irrational behavior.

LEADERSHIP FAILURE FACTORS	EFFECTIVE LEADERSHIP QUALITIES
Conflict avoidance	Willingness to meet challenges
Oppression of subordinates	Sociability
Micromanagement	Receptiveness to new ideas
Inaccessibility	Agreeableness
Manic behavior	Dependability
Analytical intelligence	Emotional intelligence
Kets de Vries (2001)	

In the U.S., the concept of servant-leadership has been introduced into the corporate sector and a number of academic libraries. Servant-leadership helps individual stakeholders in an organization become healthier, wiser, freer, and more autonomous. The aim of servant-leadership is to build a better and more humane society. It is seen as being a practical approach which encourages collaboration, trust, foresight, listening, and the ethical use of power—supporting people who choose to serve first, and then lead. Robert Greenleaf (1977) founded the movement, and the Greenleaf Center for Servant-Leadership (www.greenleaf.org) supports the work.

A number of organizations plan leadership succession—choosing leaders from existing staff. One of the benefits is that people appointed to a leadership role already know the organizational culture and climate. A person coming in from outside needs a longer and steeper learning curve. The job interview process rarely gives either the employer or the candidate enough information to know whether there is likely to be a good fit.

LEADERS OF THE FUTURE WILL BE

- sensitive to the issues of diversity
- interpersonally competent
- skillful communicators and motivators
- community builders
- capable of building well-aligned organizational architectures
- developers of leaders

Conger and Benjamin (1999: 250)

BEING MENTORED

Mentoring is another term increasingly frequent in the management and professional literature. The term is derived from ancient Greek myth, in which Odysseus entrusted the goddess Athena, under the name of Mentor, with his son Telemachus. The role of the mentor—to provide guidance to another, less experienced person—has not changed since then.

A mentor takes care not to tell a person what to do, and does not necessarily give direct advice; they should serve as a sounding board, guiding the mentee to an appropriate decision.

There are three sources of mentors:

1 professional education—the person may approach a tutor with whom there has been a good relationship

2 within the organization—a more senior person who helps the new manager to find their way around the organization

3 mentoring programs—these should be developed and operated by a relevant professional body. Ritchie and Genoni (2002) describe a program developed by a professional association in Western Australia that has operated successfully for a number of years

The chemistry between the mentee and the mentor needs to allow a degree of trust and confidence from the outset. In some situations, a formal contract is prepared, but more often the arrangement is informal, perhaps organized on a regular basis or "as need arises" on the part of the mentee. Guidance might be sought when a change of job is considered or in the selection of a program for continuing professional development.

Mentoring has also been used in organizations to support staff from underrepresented groups, notably ethnic minorities and women. Mentors who have experienced and overcome the frustrations of the glass ceiling, discrimination, and the isolation of being seen as being "different" can support and share their experiences with others. Hearing about the unseen policies and practices of the organization can sensitize the newcomer and help them to develop strategies to handle situations before they are thrust into the center of them. The effectiveness of formal and informal mentoring programs for women in the U.S. workplace have been compared by Blake-Beard (2001).

After moving into a managerial role, a person gains an understanding that can help someone else to take this step, and so can become a mentor.

Walker (2002) describes the reaction of the new manager after the euphoria of attaining the position has worn off. About six months later they feel overwhelmed; they doubt their abilities, think their staff no longer respect them, must deal with small crises, are overworked, and find it difficult to delegate. Sounds familiar? It happens because managers are promoted for their technical competence, but are expected to acquire management skills by a process of osmosis. Among the good advice Walker offers is to clarify the role, indicate what the organization values in leaders, specify expectations, meet weekly to develop rapport, project confidence in the manager, get them to focus on the big picture, and provide constructive feedback. This understanding can be passed from the mentor to the mentee.

A variation on mentoring is life coaching. Life coaches find that, in handling career issues, the real questions may lie in personal relationships, self-presentation, lack of confidence, or a need to gain additional skills such as time management.

CONTINUING PROFESSIONAL DEVELOPMENT

There are many ways of extending knowledge and skills. The need grows for everyone in the workforce to extend their skills, adapt to change, and be actively involved in lifelong learning. There are a number of different modes of learning. It addition to formal courses for higher education, methods include short courses, learning on the job, attending meetings and conferences, and reading.

The Internet provides new methods: distance learning, gathering information from the Web, signing up for listservs, and e-mails with colleagues in other organizations and countries. Flexible modes of delivery widen opportunities. Moving up the career ladder involves a greater investment of time in learning. You have many choices.

Acquiring an MBA may be the choice for anyone aiming high on the professional ladder or for someone who has gained enough experience in a management role to want to manage in a wider setting. People who have headed up a professional unit, such as university librarians and directors of public libraries, have made the move into the higher levels of local government management, become vice-chancellors of universities, or taken positions as senior managers in the private sector. There is a wide variety of MBA programs, each with a slightly different content; you have a many choices.

Extending professional studies to the doctoral level doesn't necessarily involve pure research, but can help a professional develop research skills in an applied project—perhaps a study of an aspect of management in the information setting. In the U.S., certification will be introduced for public library administrators, and other countries have similar advanced certification.

In the U.K., there are second level master's degrees in ILS management that are offered in the distance learning mode and attract overseas enrollments.

Perhaps you've always wanted the opportunity to extend undergraduate studies—a second degree in your first discipline may be appealing. It could lead to a management role in a collection in your specific field. Academic and special library users would welcome a specialist managing their service, as would users of archives and knowledge management services.

Formal courses extend the general educational level, but shorter courses are also of value. A number of leadership programs are available, such as the ACRL/Harvard Leadership Institute, a one-week, well-tested program. LAMA, a division of the American Library Association, organizes an annual National Institute, and other institutes on topical issues are offered around the U.S.

Extensive programs of short one-to-three day courses are available in the U.K. In London, Aslib has organized courses with a focus on special libraries and information centers; the Chartered Institute of Information Professionals, TFPL Ltd., concentrates on knowledge management and related information issues; and other organizations, such as the Society of Archivists, offer similar programs. These programs are of a high standard and attract participants from outside the U.K.

Summer school programs offered overseas can combine study with the opportunity to exchange experience and ideas with other professional from around the globe. In the library sector, TICER (Tilburg Innovation Centre for Electronic Resources), based at Tilburg University in the Netherlands, organizes an International Summer School on the Digital Library. The University of Wales Aberystwyth, in partnership with the School of Information Sciences at the University of Pittsburgh, the Graduate School of Library and Information Studies at the University of Montreal, and the School of Librarianship the University of Cape Town offer an International Graduate Summer School. This has been provided for more than twenty-five years and has flexibility in the number of courses and study tours that can be taken. There are also study tours organized by a number of universities. Generally, the costs are kept low to encourage participation.

Workplace learning has replaced in-house training. In addition to skills-based courses directly concerned with the operations of a department, larger organizations provide a range of short courses that focus on topics such as communication skills, planning, and diversity. In addition to extending awareness, they have the advantage of being related to the workplace and allowing people from across the organization to meet. Many a useful collaboration has started during a coffee break. Internal courses will also be of a high standard, since the organization will evaluate the content, presentation, and outcomes and ensure they meet their requirements.

Another way to extend workplace learning is to organize an exchange with someone at the same level in a similar type of service. Some exchanges involve working overseas or in another part of the country. When this happens, the arrangement often includes swapping housing and cars. Seeing how another service operates can provide ideas about refinements to the "home" service and is refreshing. A number of organizations operate programs to help in the development of services overseas. In this case, qualified professionals, generally either at the start or the end of their careers, go overseas to work in a less developed country on a short-term assignment in return for housing and a small allowance.

Internships are available in the U.S. and have been particularly successful in encouraging new graduates of professional programs who come from ethnic minority groups. In the U.K. there is a Sharing Museum Skills project which includes archives and libraries. This scheme offers professional staff or volunteers the opportunity to work in a similar service for a period of up to six weeks to extend skills. The service that is supplying a staff member is reimbursed for their salary to allow for a temporary replacement, and the out-of-pocket costs are covered, including travel and living expenses. This is a comparatively inexpensive exercise that has brought benefits to participants.

Getting involved in the work of professional associations and attending conferences widens networks, provides a less formal learning experience, and helps the service to "be seen." The latter is important, because a future boss may first see you or hear you speak at a conference. In addition to local and regional conferences, the national conferences offer workshops, seminars, and exhibitions. At the international level, these conferences broaden horizons, help with thinking outside the box, and extend contacts. Conferences are useful for updating knowledge in your special field of practice, but also provide the chance to drop in at the presentation of papers to see what is happening in other areas of the profession. And the social aspect enhances social skills, which are much needed in career development.

If the cost or time of these options are prohibited, reading can be useful, whether it is print- or electronic-based. Membership in a professional and management organization will provide regular journals and access to a Web site. Don't put journals to one side to read "when I have time"—factor reading into your calendar. Identify Web sites of special value to you and visit them regularly. Keeping up to date with management issues can be done painlessly with the *Harvard Business Review*. Don't forget to check the lists of up and coming titles from publishers, and order copies for your staff library. Read the titles as they arrive. They can help you, and, more importantly, enable you spot titles that can help a member of the team. Encourage team members to read as part of their continuing professional development

EXTENDING MANAGEMENT SKILLS

Political Skills

Politics is a major part of organizational life—and it is ignored at the manager's peril. Some facets of politics are obvious. The one that we meet in daily life is that of the decisions made by governments at every level. Legislation, regulations, and accountability requirements—for example, the legal issues relating to the employment of staff—must be observed. Managers working in larger organizations in the information sector may well have their work backed up by specialists, or have sources of information readily available to them—on licensing and copyright issues, for example. They are unlikely to have a direct influence at this level.

The information professions and their international and national organizations develop their own political agendas and may lobby and influence international and national organizations. One example at an international level is the work of the Public Libraries Section of IFLA and the production of the public library guidelines.

At a national level, the professional associations lobby governments on such issues as copyright and freedom of information. Subsections come together to develop international standards and to form committees which produce the statements and submissions that allow politics to operate.

Individuals can get involved in politics at this level by first becoming active at a local level in their professional body, which can provide the standing to become a representative at national or international level. Involvement in the politics of the professional bodies can be an asset in gaining visibility and advancement in a career.

But the area of politics in which everyone may play a part is that of organizational politics. This is a game that is played out to gain resources and preferment. It is complex, often dirty, and rarely visible in its operation. One of the reasons why women and people from the ethnic minority groups have additional barriers to overcome is the invisibility of organizational politics. In the background, alliances are formed, information is traded and shared, opinions are sought, and chairs of influential committees are lobbied ahead of major decisions being made.

The difficulty is that people who play politics may well use the tactics employed in playing poker—no one shows all of their cards to other players. The political discussion that really matters doesn't take place in public places—it may be on the golf course, in the locker room, in the rest rooms, or at parties and social gatherings. Finding one's way into these circles is not easy. Universities can be hotbeds of political infighting, whereas business organizations may have politics that are more transparent.

How can one be successful?

- Get on the right committees—both internal and external.
- Listen carefully at meetings and look for alliances.
- Read all documents carefully.
- Keep in touch with the views of the labor unions and staff organizations.
- Obtain control of financial resources.
- Influence the decision process.
- Until you are sure of the stance of the person you are talking with, take care in sharing information.
- Don't make enemies.
- Work toward building alliances and coalitions with effective politicians in the organization and in the wider community served.

Networking

The further you advance up the career or organizational ladder, the more important it becomes to network—to develop a range of contacts with whom you can share ideas and information. There are several networks—in the organization, in the community served, in the broader community, and in the profession. Some may overlap; others are discrete.

A network is more than being a member of a group. It is involves active participation, contributing to discussion and events and taking action on behalf of the network. The Internet and e-mail provide a means to develop wide networks through discussion lists or by checking out ideas with someone you met at a conference or professional meeting in another city or country.

Networking is a familiar process in North America and Australia, where people tend to be open and comfortable; but other cultures may find it less easy. The British have a natural reserve—their social customs are different, and they need a little time to get to know others. This also holds true for some other cultures and is an important point to consider when working in a diverse team. Some members may need encouragement.

Presentations, Presentations, Presentations

Another aspect of a manager's work that grows in importance is giving presentations—to management, funding bodies, colleagues, professional groups, and the community. The most important will be the presentation you give when applying for the next job. It is often more stressful to make a presentation to an audience that knows you than to a group that doesn't know you. Practice and experience help to overcome the natural fears that most of us feel when we have to give a public presentation.

EXTENDING PRESENTATION SKILLS

Some people enjoy making presentations—it brings out the latent actor in them, and they can speak fluently with humor and appear relaxed. This does come with practice—but practice only emerges with experience. Along the way, the inexperienced speaker will feel uncomfortable, but can polish skills by watching others and learning from experience. It does get easier.

> ### RECALL
> Chapter 5 includes the basics of making presentations.

The basics were covered in chapter 5—let's consider the topic now that you will have had some experience.

Being asked to make a presentation is flattering, but ensure that you do know enough about the suggested topic to be able to talk with a degree of knowledge and the level of understanding to be able to field questions. Presentations get trickier as you gain more professional experience and people have greater expectations of you. That is where the real test lies. Don't agree to talk unless you know you have time to think about it and prepare, and really know the topic inside out.

People remember good speakers, but their memories of a poor speaker may be even better. Your reputation rests on it.

So what makes an effective presentation?

- Firstly—a clear purpose. You need to know who is likely to be in the audience, what should be communicated, and why it is important, and as the speaker you have to be committed to the message. This gives confidence to you—and the audience.

- Secondly—thorough preparation. You need to have a deep understanding of the entire topic, not just the material to be presented to the audience. You also need to know how much the audience understands the topic and their interest in it. Are they professional colleagues? Do you want to persuade them to part with funding? Do you need to inspire them? How large will the audience be? Where will the presentation be given, and when?

- Thirdly—be clear. Use words and phrases the audience will understand—you may need to avoid jargon. The presentation needs a structure—a beginning, a middle—the body of the content—and an end—a summary. Many speakers advise you to tell the audience what you are going to tell them, tell them again, and then tell them what you have just told them. Provide a clue that you are coming to the end, perhaps "in conclusion," as it alerts the audience. And talk, don't "speak"; use anecdotes, examples, and personal experiences to make the presentation "come alive." Don't talk too fast, vary the pitch and speed, and use hands and facial expressions. If you are speaking overseas or with people from overseas in the audience, slow down a little. If interpreters are being used, give them a copy of your presentation as far in advance as possible—or at the very least, before the presentation starts.

Tıp

One trick to help delivery is to decide where you need to take a pause—to change the topic, for effect, or for response to a joke. Some speakers develop their own style of stage directions and mark-up of the pages. It becomes less a paper to read than a script marked with their own hieroglyphics.

Even if you know the topic and the paper has been rehearsed, always have a script to fall back on—sometimes the mind does go blank.

- Fourthly—keep to the time allocated. Allow time for questions, but never run over. You can hold attention for about thirty minutes in total—after that, eyes glaze over. Remember that you will probably be introduced by a chairperson, which takes time. Rehearsals are vital, so ask someone you can trust to give an honest opinion. And although you know the script, keep it close at hand—just in case your mind goes blank.

Finally, give some thought to the management of the presentation. If PowerPoint, slides, or overheads are to be used, make sure you know how to operate the equipment, test it before the presentation, and have a backup if it fails. Some comments in the management press indicate that using PowerPoint with the intention to produce many "beautiful" and complex screens can confuse the audience. They audience may miss the total message and focus on the parts.

Look at the room or hall before the event to get some idea of its size and where you will be standing. Can you reach the lectern, can you see the slides, is the sound level OK?

Give some thought to how you want to present yourself—what is the audience likely to expect? If it's casual, make it smart casual—if formal, dress smartly, but comfortably. Breathe deeply, establish eye contact, bring on a big smile—and make the audience eat out of your hand!

TIP

A U.K. prime minister was giving a keynote at his party's annual conference. The message focused on critical political decisions and the speech was being televised. It was a hot day and he took his jacket off to reveal a deepish blue shirt. The heat, the television lighting, and stress produced more perspiration than usual. His deep blue shirt became an even deeper shade of blue at his armpits—which got in the way of his message. Use an effective antiperspirant, or don't take your jacket off!

The mind can go blank when questions come from the audience, so preparation should include thought about what may be asked by the audience. Have a pencil and paper handy to make notes on questions that have several parts. If you don't understand a question, don't be afraid to ask for clarification.

After the presentation, you'll need to return to earth and get your feet back on the ground. There will be an adrenaline low following the adrenaline high.

As experience grows and confidence emerges, then you can go for some humor, which is not easy to carry off if you are feeling stressed. The best speakers use stories to develop their arguments and laugh at themselves. But again—don't try this until you have some experience. Get the basics right and then build on them.

Remember, you will always feel somewhat nervous before speaking—actors will tell you they always have stage fright before going on stage. It makes the adrenaline flow.

BRIEFING MANAGEMENT OR THE TEAM

This is a different type of presentation. The outcomes will be critical for you and the team in either situation. Time will be much more limited, so you'll need to employ some tricks of the trade.

- Again, know the topic inside out.
- Break it up into a series of points.

- Deliver each point in one or two very short sentences—no digressions.
- Don't use long words or jargon (unless *everyone* will know what you mean).
- Don't repeat yourself.
- Pause briefly after each point.
- Avoid "hums" and "hahs."
- Use repetition for effect—"we must, must, must have the system up and running…"
- Use poetics—"it's got to be finished swiftly, surely, and certainly" rather than "it's got to be finished quickly."
- Use superlatives for effect: "we are absolutely nowhere with progress on the installation."
- Use visual effects to provide impact—"we are expecting 2,000 new books next week" could be enhanced by "that will take up 250 feet of shelving."
- Don't use clichés.
- Use humor sparingly. (after Clark, 1999)

Prepare a handout in the form of an executive summary for them to take away. Make sure it has an author and date.

Working with the Media

Moving up the career ladder means that you will be increasingly in demand to talk to the media, especially if you are based in the public sector. Publicly funded services have hit the limelight over funding or disasters, but are also known for good events such as the receipt of an award. Professional bodies such as the national library associations have awards for excellence in public relations and marketing. Campus, community, and local newspapers and radio and television stations are always looking for news stories, and if you can perform well, you may get a regular "spot." Good performance can also give you an edge in promotion if it appears on a résumé.

The types of interview that you might be asked to take part in are similar for both radio and television.

- *Face-to-face.* These are formidable, especially as the interviewer will be an expert. The best interviewers are helpful—but some stations are looking to expose the person interviewed, so if the interview follows a crisis, prepare with care.
- *Panel discussion.* Speak up and make sure you get "space"; don't let yourself be overlooked, but don't hog the interview. Watch the chair for cues.
- *Straight-to-microphone.* This is easier than straight-to-camera. Keep your voice warm and lively—don't go flat.

- *Telephone in a radio car or in the office.* This is convenient, but the sound quality can be poor. It may also go out live for a very short spot on the news. Beware!
- *Outside recording.* This has the advantage of having retakes if required, but there can be distractions. The writer recalls an interview with a local TV station outside a beautiful building. An automatic water system came on midway…the hair got wet and watermarks showed up on the dress. Thankfully, the day was warm, the hair and dress dried quickly, the water was turned off…and the retake went well!

The secret of successfully working with the media is quick thinking, preparation, and experience. The approach from the media comes by phone, and they will want a quick response. Ask why they want you, when, for how long, and where, and whether it be live or recorded.

Buy time for five minutes and phone back within that period saying whether or not you will do it. Saying "no" may get you crossed off their contact list. During the callback, ask why they are running the story or want to interview you, who have they lined up as the interviewer, whether anyone else will be involved, and what points they want to cover.

Sometimes the topic can be sensitive—a prominent member of the user community has made a complaint, there are major cutbacks in funding, a member of staff has committed a misdemeanor. Other times you can tell a success story—the service has received a major grant from a national body, for example (though in this case, you should have made the first move!).

Having agreed to the interview, close the office door, put up a "do not disturb" notice for the next hour, get someone to make you a coffee, and prepare a brief. Think out what you want to say, rather than what they may want to ask you. You have to get across a positive message—never go on the defensive. Consider the interview from their point of view and think up all the nasty questions that you might ask if you were the interviewer.

Draw up a list of three or four points, each having two or three subpoints, and develop some anecdotes. Set them out on one side of a sheet of paper in bold type and learn the brief. When your mouth dries up and your mind goes blank, you will have the brief to refer to.

Look in the mirror and check your appearance if it is a TV interview—white or checkered clothing doesn't go across well. Women should keep an attractive scarf in their desk, and men an appropriate tie. Arrive at the location in good time and take a good look around to become familiar with the setting.

In many ways, it is more difficult to be interviewed on the radio—there is no time for pauses, your voice becomes the focus, and you need to sound sincere, warm and enthusiastic.

Being interviewed away from the service may be easier than giving the interview on site. If you are in a public place within the service, people stop to watch, which increases nervousness, and there is always the risk of background noise.

Make sure you keep in touch with the local media and their staff and feed stories to them, which builds up your skills and good will. Watching them at work with politicians indicates their style and favorite issues. Preparation and experience is rewarded with growing confidence.

CAREER PLANNING

Career planning today relies on being flexible and open-minded. A range of factors can influence career directions—a future that is less easy to predict, changes in the workplace, and changes in the family.

One of the factors—that of the family—needs careful thought and discussion. It affects people and relationships, especially since traditional roles have changed.

The demographics indicate that in many countries the birthrate is falling. Raising a family involves decisions about when or whether to have a child, and there is evidence that women have been delaying pregnancy in order to establish their careers. In an established career, a higher income helps to pay for childcare and other costs. But delaying the decision to have a family can mean that women do not achieve motherhood, as Hewlett (2002) has described.

Dig DEEPER

Hewlett, Sylvia Ann. 2002. "Executive Women and the Myth of Having It All." *Harvard Business Review* 80 (4): 66-73

Professional women who had their children in the '70s and '80s and took a break in their careers may now face the problem of caring for elderly relatives and perhaps needing to take another career break. Even with current societal changes, it is still generally the woman who takes greater responsibility for the home and caring for the family.

Decisions about career moves become harder to make when it involves the careers of two partners, and even more complicated when schooling has to be taken into consideration. Moving houses is also a cause of stress. Of course families can be mobile and women can raise a family and return to a career after a short or longer break, but anyone in a relationship who is conducting a career change should consider his or her partner.

Thinking About the Next Move?—Test the Water

One way of "testing the water" for a new direction is to examine the range of flexible working practices discussed in chapter 9. Since many services operate over extended hours, flexibility is often easier to organize than in many other organizations.

Part-time posts may be available. Job shares can be organized, in which two people covering one post have a degree of autonomy within which they can arrange their responsibilities. A job share is one way of using acquired professional expertise while moving into a new field.

Flexible hours and annualized hours can be arranged in larger services. These arrangements can bring benefits to the employer by retaining the services of a valued staff member for some hours, rather than losing them altogether.

Working from home on a freelance basis can be effective in some fields of professional practice. Indexers and abstractors have worked in this way for many years, and it now extends to information brokers, consultants, and editors. The range of work is expanding as more services are outsourced. Working in this way requires good organization and communication skills, close attention to customer care and the client, and probably the upgrade of ICT facilities. Professional associations offer advice on the professional indemnity insurance that is needed when working independently in the information field.

Another option is to take a temporary or contract post. Changes in the labor market have resulted in a greater number of people being employed on limited term contracts. Contract working provides an opportunity to experience work with a range of employers or in a variety of specialist posts. There are an increasing number of employment agencies that can help an individual manage a career based on contract posts, particularly in the private sector.

A number of writers in the management field have suggested that we will develop portfolio careers in the future involving greater flexibility and we will experience more switches between jobs. But there is one precaution to take if stepping back from a permanent or full-time post: consider the vital pension plan and health and other insurance. This may not seem important to a person in their twenties or thirties, but it can have an impact later in life. Take advice from a financial counselor.

The Next Major Move

OK, so you've been there, done that, and you really want to move on. Think carefully and remember that you are of the generation that job-hops more frequently today. If your boss is of a different generation, they may not understand this.

Why do you want to move on? Understanding your reasons will help to identify the next major move.

- Are you getting stale?
- Have you met the goals you set for yourself in your current role?
- Are you not feeling motivated enough?
- Do you want to gain new skills?
- Do you want to work in a different sector, and are your skills transferable?
- Do you have a hankering to move to a different part of the country?

- Do you want a better work/life balance?

If you are working in a small organization, then gaining promotion will almost certainly involve moving to a different organization. Anecdotal evidence appears to indicate that moving between organizations helps to move up the career ladder.

Frequent job moves at the early stages of a career may increase visibility and help to build bigger networks that, in turn, can facilitate job changes. But moving further up the career ladder tends to reduce the opportunities for movement. Ask yourself some questions.

- Do you have time available to put in the job search? The more effort you put into it, the less time it takes to get a new post.
- Are you considering a move for the right reasons—positive rather than negative?
- Have you talked with your mentor?
- Do you want to move within the organization, or to a different one?
- Are there any family factors to take into account?
- What is the state of the job market?
- What are you worth in terms of salary and benefits?
- Do you want to remain in the same area of the information profession?
- Would you prefer to work in a different part of the country, or even overseas?
- Do you have the funds for a geographic shift?
- Have you updated your résumé recently?
- Are there skills, knowledge, or expertise to brush up before you can apply for a new post?

Take a long, hard look at the answers to these questions. The answers will help you consider the realistic possibilities that are open to you. Jumping in and answering an advertisement that looks attractive might not be the wisest action; you must carefully choose a position that will be critical.

Writing a job application at the next level is even more of an art than at your current level, so get some advice from a human resource professional.

Tailor your basic résumé to each job application, and create a customized cover letter.

You'll need to look closely at references to choose the most appropriate ones for the application. Talk with your immediate boss, who will want to understand why you feel you should move on. Seek permission from all referees and send them a copy of your résumé and the job application. Give them time to think and draft a reference—they will do a better job.

Never, never, never fail to contact a referee. The writer knows the problems of trying to prepare an adequate reference with limited or outdated information at hand. It is not a time for creative writing. You need to keep in touch with the movements of the referees—they change jobs too. And always let them know the outcome of each application—after all, they must be interested in you, otherwise they would not have agreed to be a referee.

Submit an application when you are sure you have enough basic information to know that you have the attributes for the post and know why you feel it would be a good move.

If you are offered an interview, prepare well:

- Gather information about the organization.
- Ask about the format and length of the interview or selection process.
- Get someone you can trust to do a practice interview.
- Demonstrate you know about the organization, the sector, and the challenges it faces.
- Be ready to discuss your achievements.
- Prepare questions for the interviewers and be ready to ask the human resources staff about salaries, benefits, and transfer and housing assistance. They will welcome a businesslike approach.

Tip

Write down five or six sentences that demonstrate your strengths, using past experience, competencies, and transferable skills.

Keep in mind what you know about the post, the service, and the parent organization so that you can stress to the selection panel how valuable you will be.

Don't try to learn it by heart, but take a keyword for each sentence that will help you recall your strengths. Keywords will be easy to recall during the interview and help to overcome any nerves.

Take the list with you, read it on the way, and review it while waiting to be called.

At the level you are aiming for, you may find that the selection panel uses approaches designed to put you under pressure. Those with the best practice avoid these tactics, but they are often encountered in the corporate sector. The tactics that are may be used include:

- asking awkward questions
- showing aggression through questioning or body language
- posing embarrassing or offensive questions
- employing a prolonged silence
- asking unlawful questions

It is a difficult situation, and one for which you may not be prepared. It is especially disconcerting if you are really interested in the job. But don't get into an argument or lose your cool. Remember, you can choose not to work for an organization that puts prospective employees in a hostile or difficult situation; such tactics may be an indication of the organizational culture.

On the other hand, managers expect to come under pressure—from users, senior managers, or members of their team—and this may be one way to test how you handle stress. Your response should be assertive without returning the aggression. Stay calm and buy time by asking questions to clarify what you have been asked.

If it gets really uncomfortable, you can always leave the room, or even end the interview. No job is worth the cost of working in an extremely stressful environment.

Handle discriminatory questions in the same way. The writer recalls being told by the chair of a selection panel that he hadn't worked with any woman in a senior management post in his university and didn't think he could handle it. One point to highlight is the dilemma about whether to make a formal complaint in such a situation. Networks in some sectors such as universities are small—you have to use your judgment and take advice.

Ensure you have an adequate visit to the organization and meet members of the team. You will probably have to make a presentation, but you should also have questions that will help you to assess the strengths and weaknesses of the team and how well they perform.

Taking a critical look at the potential boss and senior management team may help you to assess whether the chemistry will be right. It will also help in determining the nature of the organizational culture, climate, and values. There needs to be a reasonable match with your preferred managerial style.

QUITTING THE CURRENT POST

There has been little focus on how to quit a job. It is important to do it well—for your own pride, for what it might add to your boss's view of you, for the organization, and above all, for your team. Some points and action shouldn't be overlooked in a rush to the new job.

1. Consider carefully the date you will leave. Try to make it convenient for the organization you are leaving, the one you are joining, and for yourself. Recall the advice in chapter 2—have time to prepare for the new post.

2. Work out your entitlements to leave, superannuation, and other benefits—some negotiation may be needed.

3. Carefully draft your letter of resignation, even if you are frustrated in the current job or don't have a good relationship with your boss. You may need the boss for a reference at sometime in the future.

4. Check over files, both paper and electronic, to make sure that they are in good order, and ask for help if needed. Consult the records manager. Weed out personal messages and correspondence, but otherwise do not remove or change material.

5. Start preparing a checklist for the person who will take over— the job description, tasks that may not be listed, and useful contacts both within and external to the organization. Prepare

a list of committees and critical dates to provide a framework, but don't offer advice on how to handle them—just provide the information.

6. Meet with individual members of the team and the boss to thank them for their support.

7. Be gracious and think about what you will say when the team organizes a farewell.

8. Empty your desk over a period of time; don't rush and risk losing or forgetting items.

9. Send a notice of the move to your professional associations for their journals and records.

10. Don't look too happy at the thought of a move; this can cause resentment in staff who are remaining in the organization.

11. If you are moving any distance, arrange a comfortable place to stay before you leave and allow time to settle in the new neighborhood before starting the new post.

12. Remember how busy you were in the first days of the current job…and that you will be even busier now that you are moving up the ladder once again.

CRITICAL SUCCESS FACTORS FOR A REWARDING CAREER

Here is a list of factors that we feel contribute to success in whatever direction a career takes.

- Recognize that your greatest asset is yourself—develop it.
- Know yourself—your strengths and the weaknesses.
- Stay fit and healthy and have lots of energy.
- Keep a good self-image—be comfortable with who you are.
- Have high standards—both personal and professional—and demonstrate them in your daily work.
- Demonstrate commitment to whatever job you have—including an emotional commitment.
- Be reliable and truthful.
- Cultivate clear thinking—maintain an objective viewpoint.
- Develop good communication and negotiation skills.
- Understand the way that others think.
- Never lose your sense of humor—cultivate it.
- Show a concern for others in your professional and personal life.
- Extend your managerial knowledge and know what is best practice in management thinking.
- Stay on the cutting edge of change.
- See what's coming down the track.
- Ensure that you are working effectively as a member of a team.

- Acquire and hone political and analytical skills.
- Know how to make decisions, and to change them if the situation demands.
- Remember the importance of delegation, and use it whenever possible.
- Maintain control over your own time.
- Recognize mistakes that you have made—and learn from them.
- Believe in yourself—tell yourself "you can do it."
- Enjoy the job you are doing—and if not, find another.

Words of Experience...

Joanne Euster (1996), university librarian at the University of California, Irvine, has written:

> ...On one particularly memorable occasion, only very recently (and with woefully little preparation) and unexpectedly appointed director of the small college library, I said wistfully to a senior colleague that things seemed to be going well, but I was feeling much discomfort with the sense of just, as I put it, "faking it"—making seat-of-the-pants decisions, not really knowing enough to feel in charge. Somehow, I thought, this long-time director at a larger and older college would be able to make it all clear to me. Instead, his reply was, "Oh, you'll get used to feeling like that," which is still memorable more than 20 years later. The lesson? You are not really ever going to feel that you know enough to be fully in charge, so get on with it.

AFTER READING THIS CHAPTER YOU SHOULD BE AWARE:

- of ways to extend leadership skills
- of the value of mentoring
- that you have many options for continuing professional development and extending managerial skills
- that careers can be more flexible today
- of the steps to take when you quit a post
- that many factors contribute to success

REFERENCES

Bennis, Warren. 2002. "Will the Legacy Live On?" *Harvard Business Review* 80 (2): 95-99.

Bennis, Warren, and Burt Nanus. 1985. *Leaders*. New York: Harper & Row.

Blake-Beard, Stacy D. 2001. "Taking a Hard Look at Formal Mentoring Programs: A Consideration of the Challenges Facing Women." *Journal of Management Development* 20 (4): 331-345.

Bruch, Heike, and Sumantra Ghosal. 2002. "Beware the Busy Manager." *Harvard Business Review* 80 (2): 62-69.

Chowdhury, Subir, ed. 2000. *Management 21C: Someday We'll All Manage This Way*. London, Financial Times: Prentice-Hall

Clark, Charles. 1999. *How to Give Effective Business Briefings*. London: Kogan Page.

Conger, Jay A., and Beth Benjamin. 1999. *Building Leaders: How Successful Companies Develop the Next Generation*. San Francisco: Jossey-Bass.

Drucker, Peter. 2002. "They're Not Employees, They're People." *Harvard Business Review* 80 (2): 70-77.

Eglin, Roger. 2001. "Inspired Leaders Can Revamp a Company." *The Times* (London), 8 July, sec. 7, p. 14.

Euster, Joanne R. 1996. "Maturity, Leadership and Generational Change in Libraries." *Library Management* 17 (1): 5-10.

Greenleaf, Robert. 1977. *The Power of Servant-Leadership: A Journey Into the Nature of Legitimate Power*. New York: Paulist Press.

Hewlett, Sylvia Ann. 2002. "Executive Women and the Myth of Having It All." *Harvard Business Review* 80 (4): 66-73

Kets de Vries, Manfred. 2001. *The Leadership Mystique*. London: Financial Times: Prentice-Hall.

Ritchie, Ann, and Paul Genoni. 2002. "Group Mentoring and Professionalism: A Programme Evaluation." *Library Management* 23 (1/2): 68-78.

Sorcher, Melvin, and James Brant. 2002. "Are You Picking the Right Leader?" *Harvard Business Review* 80 (2): 78-85.

Walker, Carol. 2002. "Saving Your Rookie Manager." *Harvard Business Review* 80 (4): 97-102.

Launching Pad

Bennis, Warren.1998. *Managing People Is Like Herding Cats*. London: Kogan Page.

Bolles, Richard Nelson. 2002. *What Color Is Your Parachute? A Practical Manual for Job-Hunters and Career-Changers*. Berkeley, Calif.: Ten Speed Press.

Collingwood, Harris, and Diane Coutu. 2002. "Jack on Jack: The HBR Interview." *Harvard Business Review* 80 (2): 88-94.

Corwin, Vivien, Thomas B. Lawrence, and Peter J. Frost. 2001. "Five Strategies of Successful Part-Time Work." *Harvard Business Review* 79 (7): 121-127.

Hare, Catherine. 2002. "Lifelong Learning to Be a Records Manager." *Records Management Bulletin* 108: 13-15, 17, 20, 22.

Ibarra, Herminia. 2002. "How to Stay Stuck in the Wrong Career." *Harvard Business Review* 80 (12): 40-47.

Lore, Nicholas. 1998. *The Pathfinder: How to Choose or Change Your Career for a Lifetime of Satisfaction and Success.* New York: Fireside Press.

Nichols, Nancy A., ed. 1994. *Women and the Changing Facts of Worklife.* Boston: Harvard Business School Press.

Phelan, Daniel F., and Richard Malinski, eds. 2002. "Midlife Career Decisions of Librarians." *Library Trends* 50 (4): 575-758.

Di Vecchio, Jerry. 1998. "Transforming an Oral Presentation for Publication." *Library Administration and Management* 12 (3): 138-141 .

Winston, Mark D., and Lisa Dunkley. 2002 "Leadership Competencies for Academic Librarians: the Importance of Development and Fund-raising." *College and Research Libraries* 63 (2): 171-182.

AUTHOR INDEX

SUBJECT INDEX